WE WON'T PAY! WE WON'T PAY!

AND OTHER PLAYS

WE WON'T PAY! WE WON'T PAY!

AND OTHER PLAYS

THE COLLECTED PLAYS OF DARIO FO

VOLUME ONE

EDITED BY **FRANCA RAME**

TRANSLATED BY **RON JENKINS**

THEATRE COMMUNICATIONS GROUP NEW YORK

We Won't Pay! We Won't Pay! And Other Plays: The Collected Plays of Dario Fo, Volume One is published by Theatre Communications Group, Inc., 355 Lexington Ave., New York, NY 10017–6603.

This edition is published by arrangement of Giulio Einaudi Editore, Via Umberto Biancamano 2, 10121 Torino, Italy,.

This publication is made possible in part with public funds from the New York State Council on the Arts, a State Agency.

TCG books are exclusively distributed to the book trade by Consortium Book Sales and Distribution, 1045 Westgate Dr., St. Paul, MN 55114.

LIBRARY OF CONGRESS CATALOGING-IN-PUBLICATION DATA

Fo, Dario.
[Plays, English]
We won't pay! We won't pay! and other plays: the collected plays of Dario Fo / by Dario Fo ; translated by Ron Jenkins.—1st ed.
p. cm.
ISBN 1-55936-183-2 (alk. paper) — ISBN 1-55936-182-4 (pbk. : alk. paper)
1. Fo, Dario—Translations into English. I. Jenkins, Ronald Scott. II. Title.
PQ4866.O2 A24 2000
852'.914—dc21 00-037754

Cover photo of Dario Fo is by Massimo Menghini and is reprinted from *Dario Fo & Franca Rame: Artful Laughter* by Ron Jenkins (Aperture, New York, 2001).
Cover design, and text design and composition by Lisa Govan

First Edition, September 2001

CONTENTS

TRANSLATOR'S ACKNOWLEDGMENTS

It is humbling to consider how many people have helped me in my ongoing efforts to understand the work of Dario Fo and Franca Rame. First, of course, I owe a tremendous debt to Dario and Franca themselves for welcoming me into their home, trusting me to translate their texts, granting me endless interviews (Franca insists that by now I must know everything about her except the year she started menopause), and making fun of me whenever I take my work (and theirs) too seriously. I am also indebted to my friend Joel Schechter, who first suggested that I might find Fo's plays intriguing without realizing the lengths to which I would go in proving him right. Harvard University made the initial phases of my research possible by awarding me a Sheldon Traveling Fellowship to spend a year with Fo and Rame in Italy in 1985. Walter Valeri helped me to locate them. Anna Maria Lisi, Cristina Nutrizio, Lino Avolio and Piero Sciotto, members of the Fo/Rame company, befriended me during my first months in Italy when I needed all the help I could get, and have continued to be generous in their support ever since. Marina de Juli, Deborah de Flammineis, Eliel Ferreira De Souza, Chiara Bonfatti, Mario Pirovano, Sylvia Varale and Marco Scordo have gone beyond expectations in facilitating my research at the Fo/Rame archives in Milan, as well as providing invaluable assistance while the company was touring throughout Italy. Jacopo Fo, Fulvio Fo and Bianca Fo Garambois have also been helpful in providing valuable perspective on their family's accomplishments.

Bob Brustein of the American Repertory Theatre, the first artistic director brave enough to present Fo and Rame in the United States, gave me the opportunity to serve as the onstage translator for their American premiere, and later produced two of my translations of their plays. Thomas Derrah proved that it was possible for an American actor to play Fo's roles with wit and distinction when I directed him in Fo's monologue, *The Tiger Story*. He then tackled the text of *We Won't Pay! We Won't Pay!* in collaboration with Ken Cheeseman, Caroline Hall, Will Lebow, Karen MacDonald and Marisa Tomei to prove that an ensemble of American actors could bring Fo's plays to life with a collective virtuosity, which delighted audiences night after night. Tomei used her superb comic timing and intelligence to introduce Rame's monologue on orgasms to America, an effort that was continued admirably by Deborah Wise. My sister Tamara Jenkins graciously agreed to lend her considerable comedic talents to acting in the American premiere of Fo's play, *Eve's Diary*, before embarking on her glorious career as a filmmaker. My brother Robert Jenkins impressed Fo in person with his Harvard student production of *Accidental Death of an Anarchist* before embarking on his glorious career as a political scientist. Leora Rivlin brought new dimensions to Fo's words when I directed her in *Eve's Diary* in Israel, as did Kathleen Donohue, who equally played the role with playful passion. Arvidas Dapsys brought political bite to *The Tiger Story* when I directed him in the play during the Soviet occupation of Lithuania. Sally Schwager made countless contributions, on stage and off, to my translation of *Archangels Don't Play Pinball*. Lloyd Richards assembled a talented cast to produce my translation of Fo's *Elizabeth* at the Yale Repertory Theatre. I would never have fully understood the multiple dimensions of the plays of Fo and Rame without the impressive artistry shown by all these actors and directors in bringing these works to the stage.

Despina Mouzaki provided cinematic insights into the American tour of Fo and Rame by making the first documentary of their work to be broadcast on American television. Marina Kotzamani helped me to understand Aristophanes' connection to Fo and Rame during their visit to Delphi, Greece. Gloria Pastorino provided me with new perspectives on Fo when she introduced me to *Ho Visto un Re* and assisted me in revising the translation of *Archangels*. Stefania Taviano deepened my understanding of Fo's language during our collaborative translation work on *Johan Padan*, as did Cristina Nutrizio during our translation work on *Eve's Diary*. Marisa Pizza shared her enormous knowledge of the working process of Fo and Rame. Jules Frawley donated her audio equipment. Kathy Wilson generously offered her observations on the visual nuances of Fo's paintings. Howard Gardner proved to be a valuable critic and mentor in more ways than he imagines. Eugenio Barba and the staff of the International School of Theater Anthropology (ISTA) have been constant sources of information and inspiration, especially Professors Claudio Meldolesi, Nando Taviani, Nicola Savarese, Cristina Valenti, Kirsten Hastrup, Franco Ruffino, Mirella Schino, Marco de Marinis, Ian Watson, Janne Risum, Jean-Marie Pradier, Eugenia Casini Ropa, Jonah Salz, Mark Oshima, Clelia Falletti, Giovanni Azzaroni, Tom Leabhart, and the Odin Teatret company members Kai Bredholt, Julia Valery, Iben Nagel Rasmussen, Torgeir Wethel, Frans Winther, Jan Ferslev, Roberta Carreri, Patricia Alves and Rina Skeel.

Special thanks should be given to the dedicated community of international scholars and translators whose writings have become fundamental to understanding the reception of the work of Fo and Rame around the world. These include Joel Schechter, author of *Durov's Pig* and *Satiric Impersonations*; Joe Farrell, translator of *Tricks of the Trade* and author of a forthcoming Fo/Rame biography; Antonio Scuderi, author of *Dario Fo and Popular Performance*, and editor with Farrell of *Dario Fo: Stage, Text, and Tradition*; Walter Valeri, editor of *Franca Rame: A Woman on Stage*; Claudio Meldolesi, author of *Su un Comico in Rivolta*; Christopher Cairns, author of *Dario Fo e la Pittura Scenica*; Tony Mitchell, author of *Dario Fo: People's Court Jester*; Tom Behan, author of *Dario Fo: Revolutionary Theatre*; Marisa Pizza, author of *Il Gesto, La Parola, L'azione*; Ed Emerly, translator of many Fo plays in Great Britain; Peter Chotjewitz, translator of Fo's plays in Germany; Bent Holm, translator of Fo's plays in Denmark; and Carlo Barsotti, translator of Fo's plays in Sweden.

I also want to express my deep gratitude to the John Simon Guggenheim Memorial Foundation for providing me with the fellowship that made it possible for me to devote a year to my work with Fo and Rame, and to my colleagues at Wesleyan University for providing me with the time to do so. I am particularly grateful to President Doug Bennet, former Vice President Richard Boyd, and to Professor Jack Carr, who graciously took over the responsibility of chairing the theatre department during my absence. Finally I give my heartfelt thanks to Hanne Mogensen, who supported me lovingly through everything.

—Ron Jenkins

TRANSLATING PARADOX INTO ACTION

By Ron Jenkins

I'm interested in discovering the basic contradictions in a situation through the use of paradox, absurdity and inversion. This enables me to transform one reality into another reality, not as a trick, but so people will understand that reality is not flat, but that it is full of contradictions and reversals, and that often absurdity is a reality that is closer to the truth than those things which seem to be sacred and absolute, but are almost always false.

—Dario Fo

Like all tricksters, Dario Fo envisions the world in a state of flux. He sees paradox, absurdity and inversion as tools of transformation that underscore the contradictions of everyday life. Resurrecting the traditions of Aristophanes, Harlequin and Molière, Fo uses these tools to probe beneath the placid surface of a situation and turn it into a kinetic comic event. Fo's comedy is kinetic in the sense that it pulses with physical actions that complement its verbal complexity. He is an artist who thrives on action. "I always walk to get ideas," says Fo. "Movement stimulates my thoughts."[1] When Fo takes a walk, the results are usually eventful. He has an unassuming but charismatic presence that draws people toward him. In Italy, where he is an instantly recognizable celebrity, Fo is regularly approached for autographs and graciously engages his fans in conversation. But even when he goes abroad, and walks in relative anonymity, Fo often talks to local residents about the architecture of their town, gossips with shopkeepers or invents ironic stories about the history of whatever region he happens to be visiting. Fo's antennae are always out, scanning his environment for new ideas. The restless landscape of his comic imagination manifests itself in texts, drawings and physical performances that explode with action. The swirling figures he draws on paper propel him to write language that is charged with physicality. His vibrant syntax in turn inspires stage performances of acrobatic virtuosity, in which the actor's body nimbly twists, bends and contradicts itself as it aspires to the muscular truth of slapstick.

Working as their translator since 1986 has convinced me that the plays of Fo and Rame cannot be fully appreciated without acknowledging the visual images and physical actions that are encoded in the language of their texts. I came to understand this through translating their plays, sometimes onstage as their simultaneous interpreter. From this privileged vantage point I watched them sculpt language into a form that achieves an extraordinary equilibrium between spoken words, graphic design and bodies in motion.

Unlike other forms of theatre, comedy provides the translator with an immediate measure of failure or success. Having performed their material around the world for decades, Fo and Rame know they are funny. When the audience doesn't laugh, there is no one to blame but the translator. This harsh test compelled me to grasp the essence of their art as quickly as possible. After three months working as the onstage interpreter for their 1986 American tour, I learned that Fo and Rame build their comedy out of action, and that maintaining the rhythmic momentum of that action is crucial to the successful translation of their texts. I gradually began shaping the words of the translation to fit the gestures they used in performance. As the years passed and I began translating their texts for productions with other actors, I found myself referring more and more not only to those remembered gestures but to the drawings that Fo sketched while writing his plays. These sketches captured the choreography of the performance in a primal blueprint, a score for movement that somehow had to be incorporated into the translation.

When Fo introduces me to people he often says, "This is my American translator. He makes very creative mistakes. Sometimes his mistakes are so interesting, I translate them into Italian and put them into the original." Fo's joke reverses our roles and mocks the concept of translation, just as he did during his 1986 American tour of *Mistero Buffo*, when I stood next to him onstage and struggled to translate his live and often improvised performances. Defying the skeptics who said that this awkward arrangement would kill the humor of his plays, Fo found unorthodox ways to use the presence of a translator to his advantage, and ended up playing to rave reviews and full houses in New York, New Haven, Baltimore, Cambridge and Washington, D.C.

Inevitably there were times when I would falter and interrupt the relentless flow of Fo's comic cadences. Initially these moments terrified me, but eventually I came to look forward to them. Whenever Fo sensed me hesitate or alter the timing of our closely synchronized deliveries, he always found a way to turn the mishap into a source of laughter. If I shortened a long list of commedia dell'arte characters, Fo joked that "synthesis is the principal talent of the average American." If I used an inverted word instead of a literal translation, Fo noticed the onomatopoeic quality of the sound and repeated it several times in English like a child playing with a new toy. "Pope mobile" was one of his favorites. If I asked him to repeat a phrase, he teased me by telling the audience how he stayed up all night looking in the dictionary for arcane words to stump the translator.

By calling attention to our relationship Fo made the act of translation a part of the performance, strengthening his sense of complicity with the audience by inviting them to participate in what was happening onstage. Wanting to remind the public that words are not flat and lifeless but malleable and full of contradictions, Fo implicitly urged them to step out of their role as passive listeners and become active participants in a game of bilingual ping-pong. The reliability of words is usually taken for granted in the theatre, but Fo transforms language into an elusive living entity, teeming with paradoxes and absurdities that leap out at you with the unpredictability of a time bomb. "Some of you will laugh when I speak in Italian," Fo tells his audience. "Some of you will laugh when you hear the translation, and some of you won't get the jokes at all until you leave the theatre, but then you'll laugh all the way home."[2]

Franca Rame is equally adept at turning translation into an active element of her art. When I was the onstage interpreter for her 1995 Toronto performance of a play she wrote with Fo called *Sex? Don't Mind if I Do!*, Rame played with the fact that her jokes about the male sex were being translated by a man. At the beginning of the show she apologized to the audience on my behalf: "You'll have to forgive Ron if he makes any mistakes," she announced, "We've been rehearsing for two days straight and talking about nothing but sex. By the time we're through he's going to need a psychiatrist."[3] In 1986, when we first worked together, on a production of Rame's play *It's All About Bed, Home, and Church* at the Kennedy Center, a *Washington Post* reviewer noted that Rame often made her translator blush. "You see," Rame told me, "the audience likes that. You have to blush all the time."[4] When I told her I was not accomplished enough as an actor to blush without actually being embarrassed, Rame took it as a personal challenge to find a new way to embarrass me onstage every night, and to the delight of the audience she always succeeded.

The ease with which Fo and Rame exploit the comic potential of mistakes is rooted in the improvised medieval and Renaissance traditions that inspire their work. Their finely honed improvisational skills allow them to assimilate the potentially troublesome presence of an onstage translator into the fabric of their performance as smoothly as if it had been written into the script. Traveling players in the Middle Ages and commedia dell'arte actors of the Renaissance relied on a similar style of improvisation that incorporated random events into a performance. For example, a dog wandering onto a commedia dell'arte stage would not be seen as an interruption, but as an opportunity for Harlequin to invent new jokes and interact with the audience. Fo explains the nature of this technique in an anecdote about the seventeenth-century actor/playwright Molière, who was deeply influenced by the improvisational style of his era's traveling commedia troupes. When a commedia actor asked Molière's performers what they would do if the roof of the theatre began to crumble, they said that they would stop the show. "That's the difference between our theatre of improvisation and a theatre that relies entirely on a written script," replied the commedia actor, as paraphrased by Fo. "You drop the curtains and close down in the face of the unexpected . . . For you an accident is problematic. For us it is an advantage. We perform the accident. The collapse of the theatre frightens you. For us it would be a stimulus to create something new."[5]

Fo and Rame adhere to the same principle of readiness. They thrive on the unexpected occurrences that make live theatre unique. Fo often begins his performances by ushering spectators to their seats and inviting some of them to sit onstage with him to get a better view. He also makes a show of asking the technicians to change the microphone levels, even if there is nothing wrong with them. These actions help to create a rapport of intimacy with the audience, establishing the performance as something that is being spontaneously created with the public's participation.

Fo attributes his success in improvisation to what he has learned from working onstage with Rame, who was born into a family of traveling players that had performed in the commedia tradition for generations. "My work in the theatre would not be possible without Franca," says Fo, "because Franca was born in the theatre. But she was not born in the theatre seventy years ago, which is her age. She was born in the theatre four hundred years ago. This woman has at least four hundred years of life in the theatre, maybe five hundred. In her DNA is the memory of all her ancestors, grandparents and great-grandparents who worked in the theatre. Her family has the entire history of European theatre in their collective memory: the itinerant theatre, puppets, melodrama, Shakespeare, the commedia dell'arte, circus, epic theatre, pantomime theatre. When I have an idea and write it down and read it to her, this is the most delicate moment for me. It is as if it were Molière who was judging me, together with about thirty actors from the commedia dell'arte. If Franca tells me that it doesn't work or that the situation lacks comedy, I cry and go into my room. Sometimes I get mad and say, 'No. It's good.' But she is always right."[6]

Fo's explanation of his relationship to Rame is typical of his epic approach to comedy: it is full of absurdities that clarify the truth of the situation by putting it in a wider context. He blurs time frames, conflates history and invokes biology to create an image of his wife's DNA as a container for caravans of circus acrobats, Shakespearean actors, puppeteers and pantomime clowns; he pictures himself trembling before a tribunal of seventeenth-century commedia dell'arte actors overseen by Molière; he even throws in the sound effects of comic wailing, asking his listener to imagine him weeping inconsolably in his room at the harsh judgment passed down by his five-hundred-year-old wife. In a few short sentences Fo conjures up the verbal equivalent of an epic film with period costumes and science-fiction special effects. For all its absurdity, this slapstick summary captures the essence of his respect for Rame's talent with crystalline precision. His images are outrageous, but they succeed in converting complex ideas into visually exuberant arguments that are vivid, memorable and persuasive.

One reason Fo adapts so easily to the rhythms of translation is that he is a master translator in his own right. In performance he frequently shifts back and forth between Italian and a variety of local dialects, but besides his fluency in linguistic translation, he has a gift for transforming the mundane world around him into the visual language of comic paradox. In Copenhagen, Fo mesmerizes an international gathering of anthropologists by translating the cadences of an obscure Italian folk song into the rowing gestures of the medieval boatmen who first sang it, linking the breathing pauses in their gestures to the rhythmic structure of the melody.[7] In Milan's most prestigious business school he gives lessons in communications to executives from all over the world, translating the body language of sixteenth-century aristocrats into practical advice for modern businessmen. "Relax and never raise your voice," counsels Fo with a grin. "People with real power never exert themselves."[8] At the site of the Delphic Oracle he translates classical Greek poetry into an onomatopoeic simulation of ancient Greek so convincing that classics scholars claim to understand what he is saying.[9] Fo is obsessed with transformation. He is always translating past history into current events, ancient dialects into modern vernacular, and obscene anecdotes into epic fables.

At the core of Fo's transformative imagination is his ability to visualize the world in drawings and gestures. He trained as a painter and architect at Milan's Brera Academy of the Arts, and he has continued throughout his career to use drawing to visualize his thoughts, rendering the basic characters and situations of his plays into sketches that capture the absurdity of their predicaments. The people in Fo's drawings fly through the air, hang upside-down, and sprout the body parts of exotic animals. Like his stories, Fo's drawings are capable of capturing multiple time frames in a single epic collage, suggesting a narrative sequence that has been stopped in mid-action. The figures in Fo's artwork seem swept up in a whirlwind of motion, and Fo often animates his characters onstage with the same swirling gestures that appear in his designs. The pictographic language Fo uses is inextricably linked to both the drawings that inspire his stories and the physical gestures of the actors who bring them to life through movement.

The relationship between Fo's drawings, texts and gestures is fundamental to his comic vision. The dynamic interaction among these elements is most apparent when he is in the early stages of creating his work. At Fo's home in Milan I've watched him paint for hours as he prepared shows on Leonardo da Vinci and Saint Francis of Assisi. The walls of his apartment are covered with artwork. Masks from Africa, Asia and Europe hang over the passageway from the living room to his study. An eighteenth-century statue of the Madonna cradling Christ sits on a table next to the bust of a medieval jester. Planted in the middle of these treasures is a wide-screen television with a remote control that Fo uses to switch channels incessantly back and forth between news stations, sporting events and old movies, creating the same kind of dizzying montage on his home screen that he does in the theatre. When Fo asks why I never get tired of watching him draw, I tell him that it is like watching him rehearse a new play. He agrees, and continues drawing. Fo rarely rehearses his solo performances, preferring instead to try them out directly on an audience, so that drawing becomes a subliminal rehearsal process in which he acts out his scenarios on paper as a prelude to translating them to the stage.

Sometimes the images in Fo's performances come from visual sources other than his drawings. He has borrowed scenes from Bosch, Goya and Giotto, among others, and just as frequently he turns to newspaper photographs and television news broadcasts for images that link the past to the present. During his 1986 American tour of *Mistero Buffo*, Fo immersed himself in the imagery of the United States, incorporating observations on late-breaking current events into the improvised prologues to his medieval stories. Ronald Reagan was a recurring subject. In the early 1980s, Fo and Rame had been denied entry into the United States by Reagan's State Department, which invoked the McLaren Act to declare the couple a threat to national security. Finally granted a visa to perform, Fo toured with *Mistero Buffo*, and commented ironically on the controversy and the media coverage it had generated: "President Reagan offered us all that free publicity as a professional courtesy," quipped Fo. "It was the least he could do for a fellow actor."[10]

Fascinated by Reagan's blatant use of theatrical rhetoric, Fo watched the president regularly on the television news in his hotel. The image that remained with him most strongly, however, was a giant cardboard cutout photograph of Reagan that he saw on the streets of Washington, D.C. An urban entrepreneur was charging tourists a fee to have their picture taken next to Reagan's likeness. Near the cardboard president, homeless people were eating out of garbage cans. That night in his performance Fo translated the scenario into a commentary on hunger in America. Having read Reagan's opinion that the only thing hungry people needed was information about where to find government food programs, Fo decided to include it in his introduction to a piece about hunger in Renaissance Italy: he put a variation of Reagan's declaration into the mouth of the fifteenth-century doge of Venice, who had ruled over one of his era's richest empires and had denied that there was hunger in his realm. "It's only a question of information," says Fo's doge, echoing Reagan. "The poor people don't know where the garbage cans are located." Fo also mocked Reagan's dependence on his wife by imagining a summit meeting with Gorbachev in which Nancy Reagan hid under the table to give the president advice. "Nancy pulled on his left pant's leg when she wanted him to say yes," claimed Fo. "She pulled on his right pant's leg when she wanted him to say no. And when she wasn't sure, she pulled in the middle. This was the origin of Reagan's well-known prostate problem."

The musical rhythms of Fo's delivery are crucial elements in his comedic architecture, and I soon discovered the necessity of translating them as faithfully as I translated his language. Often the tempo of his language is linked to the visual pictures he paints with words and gestures. During the 1986 American tour, in a passage describing the arrival of Pope John Paul II at the Madrid airport, Fo compared the once athletic pontiff to a hero of American popular culture: "There he was in all his magnificence," said Fo. "Blue eyes. Big smile. Neck of a bull. Pectoral muscles bulging. Abdominal muscles well defined. And above all, a red cloak that fell down to his knees. Superman!"[11] The staccato beat of each physical detail built a momentum that climaxed in the punch line: "Superman!" which Fo delivered in English. Then his description soared into a spiral of lyrical absurdity that ended with the assembled crowd imagining the pope taking off into the air without a plane: "They could already see him in their imaginations. His cloak billowing in the wind. Skywriting streaming out from under his gowns. In yellow-and-white smoke that read: 'God is with us . . . and he's Polish.'" The passage was accompanied by vivid movements that shifted from crisp hand gestures during the staccato delivery of "Superman" to full, flowing body movements that suggested the pope's airborne trajectory. These gestures had to be taken into account in the word choice and timing of the translation's delivery. Some gestures were intertwined in the words that inspired them; others required a beat of silence to achieve their intended comic effect. I often stepped to the back of the stage, when I sensed that Fo needed room to execute a particularly large movement sequence like the flight of the pope. Following Fo's imagination from the fifteenth-century doge of Milan to the modern American welfare system to Ronald Reagan's prostate gland, my job was to remain as invisible as possible while standing in plain view.

Working onstage with Fo was like entering the landscape of one of the paintings he would frequently sketch in his dressing room before a performance. His drawing technique is similar to his writing style: starting with an image that is real and concrete, he gradually transforms it into something fantastical and absurd, but slyly believable. The pope really did appear at the airport in Madrid wearing splendid cloaks and robes. His love of athletics is well known, and his followers do attribute all kinds of supernatural powers to him. The idea of their imagining him as Superman in flight was built on a foundation of fact, with Fo's fantastical details added on one at a time, so that the absurdity seemed a natural consequence of the truth. It is a process Fo uses regularly in his paintings, adding colors and details that heighten the intensity of a scene until it bursts into something surreal, like colored kites that metamorphose into flying horses and angels.

In performance Fo's flying-pope scene employed a similar kind of transformation. The realistic descriptions of the pope's "blue eyes" and "big smile" were part of a list that inched into absurdity with the "neck of a bull" and well-defined abdominal muscles, so that by the time Fo got to the long red cloak, the image of Superman in flight became almost inevitable. In staging the pope's flight, Fo's words and gestures coalesced into the theatrical equivalent of an epic documentary film, a zany montage of images that juxtaposed fact and fantasy with a seamless flow of close-ups, long shots and dissolves. And as Fo zoomed in on the pope's smile, panned to a long shot of the crowd watching the pontiff fly, and dissolved into skywriting that proclaimed the Polish origins of God, it was my responsibility to provide spoken subtitles for it all, a job that reminded me of the film *Sherlock Junior*, in which Buster Keaton steps into a movie screen and has to learn to survive the jump cuts that keep pulling the scenery out from under him. Like Keaton's bumbling protagonist, I was forced to anticipate and adapt to the ever-shifting viewpoints of a visual imagination that leapt from scene to scene with childlike comic abandon.

The performances of Fo and Rame are epic in both the standard and the theatrical usage of the word. They are bigger than life in that they present stories of individuals in the context of larger issues and events, but they are also epic in the sense of the word as it was used by Bertolt Brecht, who championed a nonnaturalistic theatre that actively engaged the audience's attention by presenting familiar events in a surprising manner (*Verfremdungseffekt*). Fo and Rame often refer to Brecht's ideas, but they understand that epic performances existed long before Brecht's time, and their plays are more directly inspired by the traditions of ancient Greek comedy, medieval theatre and the commedia dell'arte than by theoretical discussions of epic comedy.

Like the traditional comic actors they emulate in their performances, Fo and Rame make the familiar seem strange by highlighting the comic contradictions inherent in the stories they tell. This technique of epic comedy is designed to provoke audiences to thoughtful laughter, laughter that awakens outrage at injustice and indignation over the abuse of power. Fo and Rame unleash the epic dimension of their stories by presenting them from multiple points of view: the tyrant, the victim, the anonymous onlooker and others. These changing perspectives ask spectators to perform a mental double take, reexamining events that they had accepted unquestioningly, but that are actually riddled with paradox. Is the pope Superman? Is God Polish? What are the limits of the power of the Catholic Church? Fo and Rame examine events from historical perspectives, political perspectives, religious perspectives, social perspectives, moral perspectives and ironic perspectives. Their work superimposes all these frames on one another in an epic montage of paradoxical action that sometimes seems anarchic but is in fact the product of an artful comic vision rooted in the deft teamwork of a clown trained in architecture and an actress who was born on the stage.

•

This essay is excerpted from the book *Dario Fo & Franca Rame: Artful Laughter* by Ron Jenkins (Aperture, New York, 2001).

NOTES

1. Dario Fo, interview with the author, Delphi, Greece, July 2, 2000. The epigraph to this chapter comes from the same interview. Unless otherwise noted, this quotation and all others in the book are translated from the Italian by Jenkins.
2. Fo, performing the prologue of *Mistero Buffo* in New York, June 4, 1986.
3. Franca Rame, performing the prologue to *Sex? Don't Mind if I Do!* in Toronto, June 6, 1995.
4. Rame, in conversation with Jenkins, Washington, D.C., June 12, 1986.
5. Fo, *Fabulazzo*, Lorenzo Ruggiero and Walter Valeri, eds. (Milan: Kaos, 1992), 95.
6. Fo, interview with Jenkins, Delphi, Greece, July 2, 2000.
7. Fo, lecture/demonstration at a meeting of the International School of Theater Anthropology, Copenhagen, May 10, 1996.
8. Fo, lecture/demonstration at an international management symposium hosted by Milan's graduate school of business, Milan, November 8, 1989.
9. Fo, lecture/demonstration at the international theatre symposium: "From Aristophanes to Dario Fo," Delphi, Greece, July 2, 2000.
10. Fo, prologue to *Mistero Buffo*, Kennedy Center, Washington, D.C., June 12, 1986. This and the following quotations about Ronald Reagan are taken from tapes of this performance.
11. Fo, prologue to *Mistero Buffo*, Joyce Theater, New York, June 4, 1986. This and the following quotations about Pope John Paul II are taken from tapes of this performance.

WE WON'T PAY!
WE WON'T PAY!

BY **DARIO FO**

EDITED BY **FRANCA RAME**

TRANSLATED BY **RON JENKINS**

THE COMEDY OF HUNGER

Hunger is a recurring theme in the comedies of Dario Fo. His characters are not just hungry for food. They are hungry for dignity, hungry for justice, hungry for love. The protagonists of *We Won't Pay! We Won't Pay!* are driven by their collective hungers to break free from the constraints in which their poverty has confined them. Their initial challenge to the laws of the "free market" propels them into a comic defiance of the laws of human reproduction. Men get pregnant, women give birth to cabbages, and amniotic fluid becomes the source of a gourmet meal. Slapstick confusion begets new understanding as the mechanisms of farce become metaphors for liberation.

Although they inhabit a world of spiraling absurdity, Fo's characters are as real as their hunger. A few months after the play's 1974 premiere in Italy, several women were arrested for "liberating" food from supermarkets in much the same manner as depicted in *We Won't Pay! We Won't Pay!* The prosecuting attorneys tried to draw Fo into the trial as an accessory for inciting the crime, but the judge overruled the suggestion, apparently agreeing with the author, who claims that his plays are nothing more than "documentary reflections of a world in which reality has become its own satire."

We Won't Pay! We Won't Pay! has been staged in more than thirty countries around the world. "It's a mistake," says Fo, "to dismiss these people as crazy Italian caricatures who speak in phony accents, sing corny love songs and eat pasta on red-and-white checkered tablecloths. The stereotypes that foreigners have of Italians are full of clichés that keep us at a distance and prevent a genuine understanding of the problems we all share in common." Like Chaplin's tramp reduced to eating his shoe in *The Gold Rush,* Fo's clowns suffer from hungers with which everyone can identify. Samuel Beckett wrote that "Nothing is funnier than unhappiness." In the comedies of Dario Fo, the same might be said of starvation.

—Ron Jenkins

TRANSLATOR'S ACKNOWLEDGMENTS

Special thanks are due to the following individuals and organizations for their assistance in the evolution of this translation:

Franca Rame, for her tireless and essential work in editing the text and providing insights into its production history in Italy;

Sasha Perugina, for bringing the Italian text to life in an informal reading in the spring of 1998;

Tom Lee, Myra Mayman and the Harvard Office for the Arts, for sponsoring the first public reading of this translation in Harvard's Learning from Performer's series in September 1998;

Violet Brown and Haverford College for sponsoring the second public reading of this translation as part of the Paul Desjardins Memorial Symposium in March 1999;

Robert Brustein, Robert Orchard, Jan Geidt and the staff of the American Repertory Theatre for their support during the American premiere of this translation;

Ken Cheeseman, Thomas Derrah, Caroline Hall, Randall Jaynes, Will LeBow, Karen MacDonald and Marisa Tomei for enriching the text with their superb acting instincts during readings, rehearsals and performances.

PRODUCTION HISTORY

This translation was prepared in consultation with Dario Fo and Franca Rame in 1999 for its premiere at the American Repertory Theatre in Cambridge, Massachusetts. Andrei Belgrader was the director. Set design was by Anita Stewart, costume design was by Evin Sanna Olsen and sound design was by Christopher Walker. The cast was as follows:

ANTONIA	Marisa Tomei
GIOVANNI	Thomas Derrah
MARGHERITA	Caroline Hall
LUIGI	Ken Cheeseman
STATE TROOPER, POLICE SERGEANT, GRAVEDIGGER, GRANDFATHER	Will Lebow

FIVE CHARACTERS

ANTONIA
GIOVANNI
MARGHERITA
LUIGI
STATE TROOPER

POLICE SERGEANT
GRAVEDIGGER
GRANDFATHER
SEVERAL TROOPERS AND POLICEMEN

NOTE: The role of the State Trooper, the Police Sergeant, the Gravedigger and the Grandfather are played by the same actor.

ACT ONE

Antonia's apartment: a modest working-class home. On the right side of the stage is a dresser and a bed. On the left side is a hat rack and a wardrobe. Center stage is a table. Upstage is a set of glass-doored shelves for dishes. There is a refrigerator, a gas stove and two gas tanks hooked together for welding.

The lights go up on the entrance to the apartment. Antonia and her younger friend, Margherita, enter. They are loaded down with numerous plastic bags overflowing with merchandise. They set the bags down on the table.

ANTONIA: It's a good thing I ran into you, or I don't know how I ever could have carried all this stuff.

MARGHERITA: Can I ask where you found the money to pay for it all.

ANTONIA: I won it . . . in a lottery . . . the church was raffling off scratch tickets . . . mine had a portrait of the pope, in silhouette, in the pope mobile.

MARGHERITA: The pope mobile . . . come on!

ANTONIA: Why, you don't believe it?

MARGHERITA: No!

ANTONIA: Okay, then I'll tell you the truth.

MARGHERITA *(Sitting)*: Go on. Tell me.

ANTONIA: This morning I had to go grocery shopping, but I didn't know how I could buy anything, because I didn't have any money. So I walked into the supermarket, and I see a crowd of women. They're all raising hell because the prices are higher than they were just the day before.

(She looks into the sacks and goes back and forth putting things into the kitchen shelves) The manager's trying to calm them down. "Well, there's nothing I can do about it," he said. "The distributors set the prices, and they've decided to raise them." "They decided? With whose permission?" "With nobody's permission. It's the free market. Free competition." "Free competition against who? Against us? And we're supposed to give in? . . . While they fire our husbands . . . and keep raising prices . . ." So I yelled, "You're the thieves!" . . . And then I hid, because I was really scared.

MARGHERITA: Good for you!

ANTONIA: Then one of the women said, "We've had enough! This time, we're setting the prices. We'll pay what we paid last month. And if you don't like it, we won't pay nothing. Understand?" You should have seen the manager. He turned white as a sheet. "You're out of your minds. I'm calling the police." He runs for the telephone behind the cash register, but the phone doesn't work. Somebody cut the line. "Excuse me. I've got to get to my office. Excuse me . . ." But he can't get through . . . not with all the women around him . . . so he pushes them . . . they push him . . . and while we were pushing, a woman pretended he'd punched her in the belly, and fell down on the ground as if she'd fainted.

MARGHERITA: Ah . . . nice move!

ANTONIA: You should have seen what an artist she was! Just like the real thing . . . And there was a fat old woman there, she was huge, waving her finger like it was a machine gun . . . she pointed it at the manager and said, "Coward! Picking a fight with a defenseless woman, and she's pregnant. And now if she loses her baby, what's going to happen to you! They'll throw you in jail. Murderer." And then we all started chanting together: "BABY KILLER! BABY KILLER! BABY KILLER!" *(Bursts out laughing)* It was great.

MARGHERITA: And then . . . what happened?

ANTONIA: Well, that prick of a manager was so scared he caved in completely . . . we paid whatever we wanted to pay.

MARGHERITA *(Laughing)*: Ah! Ah!

ANTONIA: "The cops are coming," someone shouts. We all start running. We're dropping our bags on the ground. We're crying with fear. It's a false alarm. Some truckers came to help when they heard us shouting: "Hey. Calm down. What's there to be afraid of. Don't get your panties in a wad worrying about the police. You're within your rights to pay a fair price. Let 'em have it!" So this is the payback for all the money they've stolen from us in all years we've been shopping there. And then a woman yelled, "We won't pay anything! We won't pay. We won't pay. We won't pay. We won't pay!" We went back and started shopping all over again. We shopped and we shopped and we shopped. You don't know how good it feels to shop without spending money.

MARGHERITA: Ah, how beautiful! What a shame I wasn't there!

ANTONIA: But in the meantime, the police actually did show up, for real . . . in riot gear . . . I can't tell you how scared I was! I was shaking, we were all shaking, our bags were shaking . . . the noise from the plastic was deafening! But this time, none of the women ran away. We walked calmly out of the supermarket with decisive faces . . . so firm, so honest . . . we looked like Hillary Clinton defending her man . . . and we said to the cops, "Oh, thank God you're here. Finally! Go in there and arrest those thieves!"

MARGHERITA: How beautiful!

ANTONIA: It was thrilling! It was a shopping spree to end all shopping sprees! Not because we didn't pay for the stuff, but because suddenly we were all there together with the courage to stand up for ourselves. And we caught the bastards off balance. Now they're the ones who are afraid. Soon supermarkets will have to put those plastic theft protection devices on every onion.

MARGHERITA: But what are you going to tell your husband? You're not going to try to sell him the story about the pope mobile.

ANTONIA: Why, you don't think he'll buy it?

MARGHERITA: Not a chance.

ANTONIA: Yeah . . . maybe it's a bit much. The problem is, he's a man. You know how men are. They can't see the big picture. He's a law-and-order freak. Who knows what kind of tantrum he'll throw! "How could you do such a thing?" he'll say. "My father built a good life for his children by following the rules. I follow the rules. We're poor, but we're honest!" He doesn't know that I've spent everything, that there's nothing left to pay the gas, the electric or the rent . . . I don't even know how many months behind we are . . .

MARGHERITA: I haven't paid the rent for five months! And I didn't manage to get in on the shopping spree like you did . . .

ANTONIA: There's enough stuff here to feed a day-care center. Take some home.

MARGHERITA: No, no, please. Thanks, but I don't have any money to pay for it.

ANTONIA *(Serious)*: Well, if you can't pay for it . . . *(Changes tone)* Are you crazy! I donated this stuff to myself . . . Go on, take it home. Take it!

MARGHERITA: Sure, and then what am I going to tell my husband? He'd murder me!

ANTONIA *(Taking cans out of the bag)*: Mine would just lock himself in the closet.

MARGHERITA *(Astonished)*: In the closet?

ANTONIA *(Points at wardrobe)*: Yeah! For ten years . . . every time we have an argument . . . he locks himself in that wardrobe. He's very organized about it! He has his little flashlight, his little chair. And he reads Dante's *Inferno*. He's trying to memorize it. *(Looks at can in her hand)* What's this? *(Reads)* "Meat compost for cats and dogs"?

MARGHERITA *(Reads)*: "Homogenized for the beefy flavor your pet can't resist"! But why did you take this?

ANTONIA: In the confusion . . . I just grabbed what was there . . . *(Takes another can)* Look at this one!!

MARGHERITA *(Reads)*: "Bird seed for canaries"!!

ANTONIA: Well, it's a good thing I didn't pay for this stuff, or I'd be eating . . . *(Reads)* "Frozen rabbit heads"!

MARGHERITA: Frozen heads?

ANTONIA: That's what it says: "To enrich the meals of your chickens . . . five rabbit heads for twenty cents." At least it's cheap. *(Disappointed)* But I can't return this stuff . . . they'll just arrest me.

MARGHERITA *(Laughing)*: And you wanted me to bring this junk home to my Luigi?

ANTONIA: Oh, no! I'm much too attached to my rabbit heads . . . You take home the bad stuff: the oil, the pasta . . . go on, get moving. Your husband's on the night shift, so you'll have time to hide it all.

MARGHERITA: Yeah . . . and what if the police start searching house to house?

ANTONIA: Don't be silly! The whole neighborhood was at the supermarket . . . you think the police are going to come and search every house . . . *(Opens a window)* Oh dammit, my husband! He's coming up. Quick, get this stuff out of here . . .

MARGHERITA *(Frightened)*: Where should I put it?

ANTONIA: Under your coat! *(Margherita stuffs some of the bags under her coat)* Help me get it under the bed . . . *(Takes all the bags on the table and stuffs them under the bed. She puts the animal food on the counter behind her)* If Giovanni finds out, he'll call the police. "Officer, arrest my wife. She's an enemy of the people!" Come on, run . . . and keep it quiet! Tell him some fairy tale.

(Margherita goes to the door and bumps into Antonia's husband, Giovanni, entering the house.)

MARGHERITA *(In a hurry, very embarrassed)*: Good morning, Giovanni.

GIOVANNI: Oh, good morning, Margherita . . . how are you?

MARGHERITA: Fine, thank you . . . 'Bye, Antonia, see you later . . . *(She leaves)*

(Giovanni remains perplexed and looks at Margherita's belly as she leaves.)

ANTONIA: So, Giovanni, why are you standing there? It's about time you came home. Where have you been?

(Antonia prepares the table for dinner, plastic plates, napkins, etc.)

GIOVANNI: What's up with Margherita?

ANTONIA: Why, what should be up?

GIOVANNI: Well . . . she's all fat up front: there's a belly!

ANTONIA: So? Is that the first time you ever saw a married woman with a belly?

GIOVANNI: You mean she's pregnant?

ANTONIA: Well, it's one of those things that can happen when you make love.

GIOVANNI: But, how many months is it? I just saw her last Sunday and it didn't seem like . . .

ANTONIA: What do you know about these things? It's already been a week since last Sunday . . . and in a week, who knows what could happen!

GIOVANNI: Listen, I'm not that stupid . . . Luigi works next to me on the assembly line. He tells me everything . . . and he never said anything about having a baby . . .

ANTONIA: Well . . . there are some things . . . people don't bother to talk about.

GIOVANNI: What are you talking about? Is it too embarrassing? "Oh, God, I made my wife pregnant!"

ANTONIA *(Searching)*: Maybe . . . he hasn't said anything . . . because he doesn't know yet. *(Giovanni looks at her dumbfounded. She continues unperturbed)* And if he doesn't know, how could he tell you?

GIOVANNI: What do you mean he doesn't know?

ANTONIA: Eh, yes. It's obvious. She doesn't want to tell him.

GIOVANNI: What do you mean she doesn't want to tell him?

ANTONIA: Eh, yes, because she . . . that girl . . . is very shy. And he, Luigi . . . is always saying it's too soon, it's not the right time, they have to get organized first . . . and if she gets pregnant the company where she works will fire her. He's so worried about it that he makes her take the pill.

GIOVANNI: And if he makes her take the pill, how come she's pregnant?

ANTONIA: Well, obviously, it had no effect. It happens, you know!

GIOVANNI: And if it happens, then why does she have to hide it from her husband. It's not her fault, is it?

ANTONIA: Well, maybe the pill had no effect, because of the fact . . . that she didn't take it . . . if you don't take the pill

. . . *(Doesn't know what to say)* . . . it can happen that the pill . . . has no effect.

GIOVANNI: But what are you saying?!

ANTONIA: Eh . . . yes . . . she's very Catholic. And since the pope has declared the pill to be a mortal sin . . .

GIOVANNI: You're crazy! The pope! Her with a nine-month belly and her husband hasn't noticed?

ANTONIA *(Getting in deeper difficulty)*: Maybe Luigi hasn't noticed . . . because Margherita . . . binds herself up!

GIOVANNI: Binds herself up!?

ANTONIA: Yes, yes. She ties it all in tight . . . very tight . . . so no one can see! It got to the point where today I just had to say, "You're crazy. Do you want to lose the baby? Unbind yourself immediately, and who cares if they fire you! The baby's more important!" Was I right?

GIOVANNI: Of course you were right. You were right, yes!

ANTONIA: Did I do the right thing?

GIOVANNI: Yes, yes . . . the right thing.

ANTONIA: And so she . . . Margherita . . . decided to unbind herself and: ploff!!! A big belly!! You should have seen it, Giovanni!

GIOVANNI: I saw it!

ANTONIA: And I also said, "If your husband gives you any trouble, tell him to come to my house, and my Giovanni will teach him a thing or two." Was I right?

GIOVANNI: Of course you were right?

ANTONIA: Did I do the right thing?

GIOVANNI: Yes, yes . . .

ANTONIA: Listen to you: "Yes, yes . . ." Is that any way to answer? Are you holding something against me? Tell me, what have I done now? *(Takes a broom and starts sweeping the house)*

GIOVANNI: No, I'm not holding anything against you. If I'm upset it's because of what happened at work today.

ANTONIA: Why, what happened?

GIOVANNI: There's all this tension in the air . . . All this talk about downsizing . . . yesterday the company fired four dead men . . . Yes, four dead men! Died two months ago . . . four welders . . . and they fired them . . . for absenteeism.

There's so much mistrust floating around that you can never relax. And then today in the cafeteria some guys . . . five of them, started raising hell about the food: "It's disgusting. Pig slop. Right out of the dumpster!"

ANTONIA: When it was really fine cuisine cooked with farm fresh ingredients?

GIOVANNI: No, no . . . it was absolutely disgusting . . . but that's no reason to whip everyone up into a mass frenzy.

ANTONIA: A mass frenzy? You said there were only five of them.

GIOVANNI: At first! But then everyone got into it . . . they all ate and left without paying!

ANTONIA: Them, too?

GIOVANNI: What do you mean, "Them, too?"

ANTONIA: I mean, not only those five, but all the others, too . . .

GIOVANNI: Yes, everybody got into the act.

ANTONIA *(Feigning indignation)*: How shocking!

GIOVANNI: But that's not all: I passed by a bunch of women at the supermarket, the one near work . . . and they were all shouting . . . maybe three hundred of them . . . loaded down with bags of stuff. So I asked what was going on . . . and they told me that they had only paid what they decided they wanted to pay!

ANTONIA *(Still more indignant)*: Oh, what a thing to do!

GIOVANNI: And what's worse, they stormed the checkout counter, and most of them left without paying anything at all.

ANTONIA: Them, too?!

GIOVANNI: What do you mean, "Them, too?!"

ANTONIA: Eh, I mean . . . like those bums from your factory who didn't pay for their lunches.

GIOVANNI: Eh, yes, them, too!

ANTONIA: Oh, what a thing to do! Look at me, I'm standing here in shock.

GIOVANNI: I don't know what kind of husbands those women have, but if my wife ever did anything like that I'd make her eat every tin can she stole . . . and the can opener too! And I hope you don't get it into your head to pull a stunt like that, because if I find out you've been ripping off supermarkets, or even paying one penny less than what is marked on those little stickers, I'll . . . I'll . . .

ANTONIA: I know . . . you'll make me eat every tin can I stole and the can opener too.

GIOVANNI: No, worse! . . . I'd pack my bags and you'd never see me again. And what's more, I'd murder you first, and divorce you later!

ANTONIA *(Furious)*: Listen, with that attitude you can leave now . . . without a divorce. How dare you even insinuate that I . . . ? Look, before I'd bring home anything that was not bought at a legal price, I'd . . . I'd . . . I'd let you starve to death!

GIOVANNI: That's more like it. And speaking of starving, what's for dinner? *(Sits at the table)*

ANTONIA: This! *(Angrily, she throws on the table a can of meat for cats and dogs)*

GIOVANNI: What's this?

ANTONIA: Can't you read? It's meat compost for cats and dogs.

GIOVANNI: Meat compost for cats and dogs?

ANTONIA: It's delicious!

GIOVANNI: Delicious for dogs maybe!

ANTONIA: That's all I could afford. Besides, it's cheap, and nutritious . . . and full of protein . . . estrogen-free . . . so it won't make you fat! It's exquisite! Look, it says so right here!

GIOVANNI: Are you kidding?

ANTONIA: Who's kidding? You don't know what it's like to go grocery shopping without any money.

GIOVANNI: Come on, I'm not a dog. You eat it!

ANTONIA: Oh, yes. I'll eat it, yes! *(Starts barking)*

GIOVANNI: Isn't there anything else?

ANTONIA: Yes, I can make you a little soup.

GIOVANNI: What kind?

ANTONIA *(Pulling out the package from the shelf)*: Bird seed for canaries.

GIOVANNI: Bird seed!

ANTONIA: Yes, it's delicious . . . and you know it helps fight diabetes!

GIOVANNI: But I don't have diabetes!

ANTONIA: Well, it's not my fault you don't have it yet . . . and besides, it's half the price of rice.

GIOVANNI: Listen, you've got to make up your mind. Am I a dog or a canary?

ANTONIA: Oh, don't be silly . . . Angela next door makes it every morning for her husband . . . and he loves it . . .

GIOVANNI: Yeah, I noticed he's been growing a few feathers lately! And this morning when we were waiting for the bus his foot started going like this. *(Makes chicken movement)* Then his neck went like this. *(Mimes chicken walk)* And when the bus came he . . . *(Imitates rooster)* "Cockadoodledoo" *(Mimes a rooster flapping wings)* "I think I'll be getting to work on my own today."

ANTONIA: Stop joking around. This bird seed is a blessing! The secret is in the broth . . . see, I also got some frozen rabbit heads. *(Puts the package with the rabbit heads under his nose)*

GIOVANNI: Rabbit heads?

ANTONIA: Sure! Bird seed soup is always made with rabbit! Only the heads, though . . . frozen.

GIOVANNI *(Puts on his jacket and goes toward the door)*: Okay, okay . . . I get it . . . see you later!

ANTONIA: Where are you going?

GIOVANNI: Where do you want me to go? I'm going out for dinner.

ANTONIA: And what are you going to do for money?

GIOVANNI: Right, give me some money.

ANTONIA: From where?

GIOVANNI: What do you mean, from where? Don't tell me there's none left . . .

ANTONIA: No, but maybe you forgot that tomorrow we have to pay the gas, electricity and rent. Or do you want them to evict us, and cut off the gas and lights.

GIOVANNI: Dammit! We'll starve to death, but at least we'll be illuminated.

(Antonia puts on her coat)

Where are you going?

ANTONIA: To Margherita's. She did a lot of shopping today, and I'm going to borrow a few things. I'll be right back.

GIOVANNI: Don't come back with any rabbit heads.

ANTONIA: No, I'll just bring the feet. *(She leaves)*

GIOVANNI: Yeah, very funny . . . while I'm here hungry as a . . . I could even eat a . . . *(Takes a can in his hand, turning it as he reads the label)* "A gourmet treat for your dogs and cats! Homogenized, tasty . . ." Well, maybe I'll just see what it smells like. How do you open it? Look at that. Typical. They forget to give you the key. Oh, look, it's self-opening. For dogs and cats who are self-starters. *(Opens the can and sniffs it)* Ah, doesn't smell too bad . . . kind of like ground kidney with pickled marmalade and a dash of cod-liver oil. *(Puts the can next to his ear and laughs)* You can hear the ocean! *(Laughs in disgust; changes tone)* Who knows, maybe I'll try just a taste! *(From outside there are the sounds of police sirens, shouting crowds and military orders)* What's going on out there? *(Goes to an imaginary window in the middle of the proscenium and makes signs to a neighbor across the street)* Aldo! Hey, Aldo! What's happening? Yes, I can see it's the police . . . but what do they want? Oh, stolen merchandise! From where? What, the supermarket? Which supermarket? Oh, here too? The one in the neighborhood? But when did it happen? Today? Who did it? What do you mean, everyone? Stop exaggerating! A thousand women! No, my wife wasn't there, I'm sure. She's so set against that kind of stuff that she'd rather eat frozen rabbit heads! No, just the heads . . . you throw the rest away. They're delicious. You crack them in half with a few drops of lemon and . . . *(Mimes eating one)* . . . like an oyster! No, no. No way . . . My wife didn't even leave the house today. She had to unbind her best friend's belly. No, no, it doesn't hurt . . . she just took off the wrapping that she tied herself up with so her husband, Luigi, wouldn't know she was pregnant . . . because he was making her take the pill . . . but she had orders from the pope, so the pill had no effect, and it only took a week for her belly to blow up like a beach ball . . . what!! What do you mean, you don't understand? *(Looks down on the street, hears the shouts and orders)* What's that? A house to house search? Well if they try to come in here, I'll teach them a thing or two! Because that's an out and out provocation!

(There's a knock at the door.)

VOICE FROM OUTSIDE: Can I come in?

GIOVANNI: Who is it?

VOICE FROM OUTSIDE: Open up. Police!

GIOVANNI *(Opening the door)*: Police? What do you want?

(A Police Sergeant enters. A local cop on the beat.)

SERGEANT: This is a search. Here's the warrant. We're searching the whole building.

GIOVANNI: For what?

SERGEANT: There was an assault on the supermarket today. A thousand women, and men too, removed a large quantity of merchandise at reduced prices . . . and some of them didn't pay anything at all. We're looking for the stolen goods or, if you prefer, the merchandise acquired at deep discount.

GIOVANNI: So you come looking for it at my house. That's like calling me a thief, a looter, a hooligan!

SERGEANT: Listen. This is not my choice. I get my orders and I have to carry them out.

GIOVANNI: Just following orders, eh . . . but I'm warning you . . . this is a provocation . . . You come here insulting people dying of hunger . . . Look at what we're reduced to eating: homogenized meat compost for cats and dogs! *(Thrusts the can toward the officer)*

SERGEANT: What?!

GIOVANNI: Yeah! We can't afford decent food . . . We've got to be creative. Use our heads . . . rabbit heads! *(Puts the bag of frozen rabbit heads under the officer's nose)*

SERGEANT: You really eat this stuff?

GIOVANNI: It's not bad, you know! Do you want to try some? No kidding . . . a few drops of lemon and it goes down like cat shit! Taste it. It's good for the nerves.

SERGEANT: No thanks . . . I never vomit before dinner.

GIOVANNI: I understand . . . Maybe you'd prefer me to fix you a nice soup made from bird seed for canaries?

SERGEANT: Bird seed?

GIOVANNI: Yeah! Look it's right here: costs only ten cents a pound . . . eat a little bit . . . and before you know it . . . a few feathers . . . and then . . . then your wings start to flutter . . . *(Imitates a rooster)* and you become a chicken. Or maybe you'd prefer another barnyard animal. A pig perhaps. *(He snorts)* After all you are a cop. *(Snorts again)*

SERGEANT: I can see you've been reduced to hard times here. And to tell you the truth, on a policeman's salary, my family's not doing much better. My wife has to perform miracles in the kitchen too! Listen, I understand what you're going through . . . and, I shouldn't say this, but I understand why the neighborhood women had to do what they did today. Personally I sympathize with them completely: the only defense against thieves is confiscation.

GIOVANNI *(Astonished, looks at the officer incredulously)*: You mean, you mean . . . you think they were right.

SERGEANT: Sure they were . . . they couldn't put up with all this for much longer. You might not believe me, but sometimes it disgusts me to be a policeman . . . to have to rob people of their dignity. And for who . . . for the politicians and slumlords who steal them blind and leave them homeless and hungry . . . Those bastards are the real thieves. *(Takes off his hat)*

GIOVANNI: Are you really a cop?

SERGEANT: Yes, I'm a cop.

GIOVANNI: You've got some pretty strange ideas for a policeman.

SERGEANT: I'm just a guy who thinks things out, and gets pissed off about them! You've got to stop looking at us policemen as a bunch of idiots who salivate when we hear a whistle and follow orders—jump, bark, bite—like a bunch of guard dogs! As if we didn't have minds of our own.

GIOVANNI: If that's how you feel, may I ask why you chose to join the police force?

SERGEANT: Did you choose to eat that dog food or those rabbit heads?

GIOVANNI: No! It was my nutritionist's idea. *(Becomes serious)* No, of course not.

SERGEANT: See. I didn't make this choice on my own either. It was sign up or die hungry. And *inter nos*, I've got a college degree, dear sir.

GIOVANNI: Oh, college? Is that where you learned to say *"inter nos"*?

MALE VOICE *(From outside)*: Sergeant . . . we've finished out here . . . what should we do . . . keep looking?

SERGEANT *(Toward the door, to the man outside)*: Don't stand around busting my balls . . . Search the other goddamn floors you scumbag. *(Continues his discussion with Giovanni)* Anyway, I was saying that I've got a degree. My father tightened his belt for years so I could go to college . . . and in the end what did it get me? Nothing: I had no choice . . . dear sir! "Join the police force and see the world." I've seen the world. It's a world of bastards, thieves and con men!

GIOVANNI: But not all policemen think like you. Some of them like being police.

SERGEANT: Sure, some guys buy into it. They get off on giving orders. They need to oppress somebody else to feel good about themselves.

GIOVANNI: This is amazing! Excuse me, but are you really a cop? Because now I feel it's my turn to defend the police. We need police, don't we? Without them, we'd have chaos . . . someone has to lay down the law!

SERGEANT: And what if the law is wrong? What if it's just a cover-up for robbery?

GIOVANNI: Well, uh, then there's the political parties . . . the democratic system . . . laws can be reformed.

SERGEANT: But who's going to do the reforming? Where are the reforms? What is reform! Lies, that's what reforms are! They've been promising us reforms for umpteen years, but has that gotten us better health care, or less homeless people on the streets. Believe me, the only real reform will come when people start thinking for themselves and reforming things on their own. Because until the day that people have faith in each other, with trust, patience, a sense of responsibility, and self-discipline . . . and move on . . . nothing is going to change! And now, if you'll excuse me, I have to do my job. *(Puts his hat on and goes toward the door)*

GIOVANNI *(Snickering)*: I was waiting for that. The utopian subversive puts his hat back on and turns into a policeman again.

SERGEANT: You're right. I'm all words . . . I vent and I'm gone.

GIOVANNI: Without even conducting a little search? Come on! You're insulting me! Do a little snooping just to humor me . . . anywhere, under the bed, in the cupboard . . .

SERGEANT: Thanks, but I'll pass. Good-bye and good eating! *(He leaves)*

GIOVANNI: That guy was an undercover agent. He was trying to trick me into talking, and if I had agreed with him he'd be: "Stop right there! You're under arrest."

(Antonia comes in out of breath.)

ANTONIA: Have they been here too?

GIOVANNI: Who?

ANTONIA: They're searching the neighborhood, house to house.

GIOVANNI: Yes, I know.

ANTONIA: They've already arrested the Mambettis and the Fossanis . . . they've found groceries in lots of houses, and confiscated everything!

GIOVANNI: It serves them right. That's what they get for breaking the law.

ANTONIA: But they've also taken away things people paid for legitimately.

GIOVANNI: Of course, it always happens that way. When looters go wild, people who have nothing to do with it always end up suffering. For example when they came here—

ANTONIA: They came here?

GIOVANNI: Of course.

ANTONIA: And what did they find?

GIOVANNI *(Surprised)*: Why, what should they find?

ANTONIA *(Trying to divert him, changes tone)*: Nothing. No, I was just saying . . . you never know . . . sometimes you're convinced that you don't have anything in the house, and then out of nowhere . . .

GIOVANNI: And then out of nowhere?

ANTONIA: And then out of nowhere the police plant stuff in your house . . . to trap you! It wouldn't be the first time . . .

GIOVANNI: You mean you think they'd actually put bags of pasta and sugar under the bed? I'd better take a look.

ANTONIA *(Grabs him from behind, stopping him with a violent jerk)*: No!

GIOVANNI: What are you doing? Are you crazy? You displaced a vertebra!

ANTONIA: I forbid you to touch my bedcover! I just washed it . . . I'll give a look myself . . . meanwhile, you go and let in Margherita.

GIOVANNI: Margherita? Where is she?

ANTONIA: She's there, behind the door. *(Pretends to look under the bed)* No, there's nothing's there.

GIOVANNI *(Goes to the door)*: Are you losing your mind, letting a poor pregnant woman stand out in the hall?

Oh, my God, Margherita, what are you doing there. Come inside, come in. *(Margherita enters trying to stop herself from laughing)* What's wrong. Why are you crying?

ANTONIA *(Goes to Margherita and sits her down on the bed)*: Come here, Margherita . . . *(To her husband)* Oh, the poor girl was home all alone . . . and with all those police sniffing around, she was terrified! Can you believe that one of the officers wanted to squeeze her belly?

GIOVANNI: What for?

ANTONIA: Because he got it in his head that instead of a baby, she had bags of pasta and fine herbs in there.

GIOVANNI: The son of a bitch!

ANTONIA: Yeah, you said it . . . And so I told her to come over here to our house. Did I do the right thing?

GIOVANNI: Of course you did the right thing! *(Approaches Margherita and tries to help her take off her coat)* Stay here and relax, Margherita . . . take off your coat . . .

MARGHERITA *(Frightened)*: No!

GIOVANNI: Make yourself comfortable . . .

MARGHERITA: No!

(Antonia intercepts Giovanni and grabs him by the shoulder.)

GIOVANNI *(Lets out a scream, then turns toward Antonia, furiously)*: If you keep smacking around my vertebra every five minutes, I'm going to go into the wardrobe and never come out again.

ANTONIA: She told you she'd rather keep her coat on! She's cold!

GIOVANNI: But it's hot in here!

ANTONIA: It's hot for you, but pregnant women are always cold! Maybe she's got a fever!

GIOVANNI: A fever! Is she sick!

ANTONIA: She's in labor!

GIOVANNI: Already?

ANTONIA: What do you mean, "Already?" What do you know about it? A half hour ago you didn't even know she was pregnant and now you're amazed that she's in labor!

GIOVANNI: Well, it seems to me, you might say . . . maybe it's a little premature!

ANTONIA: You think you know better than her?

GIOVANNI: But if she's in labor, maybe we should call the doctor, or an ambulance.

(Antonia goes to the cupboard and takes out two pillows. She places them on the bed so that Margherita can lie down comfortably.)

ANTONIA: Oh sure, an ambulance. There's not a chance in hell we'd find a vacant bed! You have no idea what it's like in those hospitals. You have to make reservations a month in advance!

GIOVANNI: So why didn't she reserve a place?

ANTONIA: That's right, we run the errands, we make the babies, and you want us to make the reservations too! And why didn't her husband do it?

GIOVANNI: But her husband didn't know about it. How could he think of it?

ANTONIA: Very convenient! Just give us the paychecks and then it's, "Pay the bills!" You make us pregnant and then, "Take care of it yourself! Take the pill." And who cares if the poor wife, who's a strict Catholic, dreams all night of the pope saying, "It's a sin, you must procreate!"

GIOVANNI: Apart from the pope . . . how long has Margherita been pregnant?

ANTONIA: What do you care?

GIOVANNI: No, I was just saying . . . because she hasn't even been married five months yet . . .

ANTONIA: So what? Isn't it possible that they might have made love before they got married . . . or are you turning moralistic on us . . . you're worse than the pope!

GIOVANNI: Luigi told me that they only made love after they were married.

MARGHERITA: My Luigi talks to you about those things?!!

GIOVANNI *(Embarrassed)*: We were playing pool . . .

ANTONIA: Jesus, Mary and Joseph!!! What a bum! Margherita, that's grounds for divorce!

GIOVANNI: Let's not get carried away . . .

ANTONIA: What do you mean? Going around talking about private, personal moments . . . to just anyone out on the street.

GIOVANNI *(Insulted)*: I'm not "just anyone out on the street." I'm his friend! His best friend! He tells me everything. He asks my advice . . . because I'm older, and I've got more experience!

ANTONIA *(Shoots him a look full of irony)*: Oh, oh, he's got more experience! *(Giovanni is about to respond, but there is a knock at the door)* Who's there?

VOICE FROM OUTSIDE: Police. Open up!

GIOVANNI: Again?

MARGHERITA: Oh, God!

(Giovanni opens the door. The same actor who played the Police Sergeant is now wearing the uniform of a State Trooper and has a mustache. Two other troopers enter behind him.)

GIOVANNI: Well, hello . . . you again?

TROOPER: What do you mean, "you again?"

GIOVANNI: Sorry, I thought you were the one from before.

TROOPER: Which one from before?

GIOVANNI: The police sergeant.

TROOPER: But I'm a state trooper.

GIOVANNI: I see. And you've got a mustache too. So you must be someone else. What can I do for you?

TROOPER: We have to conduct a search.

GIOVANNI: Your colleague from the police force just did that a little while ago.

TROOPER: That doesn't matter. We'll do it again ourselves.

GIOVANNI: So you don't trust them . . . You've come to make sure they haven't botched things up! Then I guess the National Guard will come to check up on you. Next it'll be the CIA . . . and then frogmen from the Marines will show up in our bathtub . . . *(Mimes a grotesque frogman)*

TROOPER *(Angry)*: Listen, cut the comedy. Just show us around and let us do our job.

ANTONIA *(Bursts out)*: Sure, your job is to make sure we comply with orders. *(Troopers open the wardrobe and cupboards)* Why don't you ever check to make sure that management is honoring our contracts, that the air in our workplaces is breathable, that they're not downsizing our jobs so that they can exploit child workers in third world countries, that they're not evicting us from our homes, and starving us to death! *(Giovanni tries to calm his wife)*

GIOVANNI: No, no. You shouldn't talk like that, because they're disgusted by all those things themselves. Isn't that true, officer, that you're fed up with robbing people in the name of authority. Tell my wife how you police officers are sick and tired of salivating when the whistle blows: "Follow orders! Jump. Bark! Bite like a bunch of guard dogs . . ." *(Howls like a guard dog on a chain)*

TROOPER: Could you say that again, please? *(Giovanni barks)* No, the part about the guard dogs?

GIOVANNI: Yes, I was just saying that you're just bought and sold by the politicians to help them get reelected!

TROOPER: Is that right?

GIOVANNI: Yes, I was just . . .

TROOPER *(Turns to the two Troopers)*: Cuff him!

(The two Troopers move to put handcuffs on Giovanni.)

GIOVANNI: Handcuffs? Excuse me, but why?

TROOPER: For insulting a public official.

GIOVANNI: What insult? I'm just saying what your colleague, the police sergeant, told me a few minutes ago . . . he's the one who told me that you feel like servants of the politicians, slaves of the system.

TROOPER: Who's "you"? . . . us state troopers?

GIOVANNI: No, he was talking about them . . . the city cops on the street.

TROOPER: Oh, the city cops. *(Laughs derisively at the insult to city cops)* Okay, take off the handcuffs. But watch what you say about us state troopers.

GIOVANNI: Okay, okay, I'm watching, I'm watching.

(The Troopers continue their search. One of them begins searching near the bed.)

ANTONIA *(To Margherita)*: Moan, go on, cry!

MARGHERITA: Aihoooaooo!

ANTONIA: Louder.

MARGHERITA *(Agonizing cries)*: Ahiouua! Ahiaaooioo!

TROOPER: What is it? What's wrong with her?

ANTONIA: Pain, a lot of pain . . . she's in labor.

GIOVANNI: She's five months premature!

ANTONIA: She was traumatized a little while ago . . . the police tried to squeeze her belly . . .

TROOPER: Squeeze her belly?

GIOVANNI: Yeah, to see if, maybe, instead of a baby, she had rice or pasta in there. Go on, why don't you help yourselves while you're here: squeeze her to make sure! Go ahead, squeeze away!

(Margherita continues screaming hysterically.)

TROOPER: Have you called an ambulance?

ANTONIA: An ambulance? Why?

TROOPER: Do you want her to die right here? Besides, if she's premature like you say, she might lose the baby.

GIOVANNI: He's right! I told you we should have called an ambulance.

ANTONIA: And I told you already that without a reservation, the hospital won't admit her. They'll send her driving around to every hospital in town. She'll die in the car!

(From outside there is the sound of a siren.)

TROOPER *(Looking out the window)* Look, it's the ambulance that we called for the sick woman downstairs. *(Turns to the two Troopers)* Come on, give me a hand. We can take her too.

ANTONIA *(Stopping them)*: No, for God's sake . . . don't disturb her.

MARGHERITA *(Crying in fear)*: No, I don't want to go to the hospital.

ANTONIA: See, she doesn't want to go.

MARGHERITA: I want my husband, my husband . . . Ahio! Ahiuaaoo!

ANTONIA: Hear that? She wants her husband . . . and he's not around because he works the night shift. I'm sorry, but without her husband's consent, we can't take this responsibility.

GIOVANNI: Eh, no, we can't take it.

TROOPER: Oh, you can't take it, can you. You'd rather take responsibility for having her die right here?

ANTONIA: What difference does it make?

TROOPER: In the hospital they might be able to save her, and maybe the baby too!

GIOVANNI: But it's premature. I already told you!

ANTONIA: Yes, it's premature! And with all those potholes in the road, the baby will pop out right in the car. How could a five-month baby survive that?

TROOPER: Obviously, you have no idea of the progress that modern medicine has made in our times. Haven't you ever heard about test-tube babies?

ANTONIA: Yes, I've heard about them, but what's this got to do with test tubes? The baby's five months old. You can't stuff it in a test tube . . . you can't even put it in an oxygen tent.

GIOVANNI: Of course not, such a little baby under a tent . . . what's he going to do, go camping?

TROOPER: You people are completely ignorant! Haven't you ever seen the hospital equipment they're using these days . . . at the gynecological centers? I worked a shift there five months ago, and I actually saw the doctors perform a transplant.

GIOVANNI AND ANTONIA: What kind of transplant?

TROOPER: A premature baby transplant. They took a four-and-a-half-month-old fetus from a woman who couldn't hold it any longer and put it in the belly of another woman.

GIOVANNI: In her belly?!

TROOPER: Yes, a cesarean. They put it in there with the placenta and everything . . . and four months later . . . just last month, it was born again, healthy as a fish!

GIOVANNI *(Incredulous)*: A fish? . . .

TROOPER: Yes!

GIOVANNI: I think it was some kind of a trick.

TROOPER: What do you mean trick? I saw it myself. Sure it's hard to believe: a baby that's born twice . . . a baby with two mothers!

MARGHERITA: I don't want to do it. I don't want to do it. I won't give my consent.

ANTONIA: See . . . she won't give her consent . . . so we can't make her go.

TROOPER: I'll give the consent. I'll take responsibility.

ANTONIA: That is complete and utter arrogance! You come into our home, you search everywhere, put us in handcuffs . . . and now you want to drag us into an ambulance! We know you won't leave us alone to live our lives, but at least you can let us die in peace wherever we want to.

TROOPER: No, you can't die in peace wherever you want to.

GIOVANNI: Of course not, we have to die according to the law! *(Goes toward the wardrobe)*

TROOPER: And you, enough with the jokes. I already told you once . . . Where's he going?

GIOVANNI *(Opens the wardrobe door, enters, and sticks his head out)*: I'll be in my office . . .

ANTONIA: Come out. Stop it! Now's not the time. Come on, let's bring her downstairs.

TROOPER: Should we get a stretcher?

ANTONIA: No, she'll go down on her own . . . You can walk, can't you?

MARGHERITA: Yes, yes . . . (*She gets up. She suddenly puts her hands on her belly to arrange the stolen goods)* Oh, no, no, it's slipping out! . . .

ANTONIA: Dammit! Could you please step outside a moment . . .

TROOPER: Why?

ANTONIA: It's a woman's thing! *(The men leave. To Margherita, angrily)* Idiot! *(Imitates her)* "It's slipping out! . . ." *(Changes tone)* This trooper's going to hang us!

MARGHERITA: If it's slipping out, it's slipping out!

ANTONIA: Oh, shut up! And another thing, is that any way to walk? Haven't you ever seen the way pregnant women walk? Do they walk like this? *(Grotesquely imitates Margherita)* Who are you kidding! When a pregnant woman walks . . . think of the Virgin Mary! *(Advances majestically)*

MARGHERITA: I knew it would end up like this! What's going to happen at the hospital when they realize I'm pregnant with rice and tin cans?

ANTONIA: Nothing's going to happen, because we're never going to get to the hospital.

MARGHERITA: Sure, because they're going to arrest us first.

ANTONIA: Stop whining! As soon as we get into the ambulance, we'll tell the driver where things stand . . . I'm sure he'll help us.

MARGHERITA: What if he turns us in instead?

ANTONIA: Stop it, he's not going to turn us in! And pull up your belly! *(She helps her)*

MARGHERITA: Another bag's slipping out. I'm falling apart!

ANTONIA: Hold onto it! Oh what a mess!

MARGHERITA: No, don't press there . . . Oh, my God, you ripped the packet of olives in pickle juice. Ahhhhhh!!!!

(Giovanni and the Troopers return, alarmed by her shouting.)

GIOVANNI: Now what happened?

MARGHERITA: It's coming out! It's all coming out!

GIOVANNI: The baby's coming out! The baby's coming out! Quick, officers, help me grab her arms!

(They follow his lead.)

TROOPER *(Supporting Margherita's back with his arm)*: She's all wet! What is it?

ANTONIA: She's breaking her water!

GIOVANNI: Ohhh! Look at that water! . . . *(Mimes being in a swamp)* Quick, or she'll have the baby right here!

MARGHERITA: It's coming out! It's coming out!

(Margherita is carried offstage. Giovanni returns immediately.)

GIOVANNI: Wait for me. I'll get my jacket and be right there.

ANTONIA: Where are you going?

GIOVANNI: To see the premature baby get born . . .

ANTONIA: No, you stay home! This is a woman's thing. I'll go! *(Puts on her coat)* Get a rag and clean all that water off the floor. *(She leaves)*

GIOVANNI: I see, okay . . . I'll get a rag and start cleaning . . . because that's a man's thing! *(Grabs a rag and leans against the window)* What a mess! Who knows how Luigi will take it when he comes home tomorrow and all of a sudden finds out he's a father . . . he'll have a stroke! And then what if he finds his kid transplanted into the belly of another woman . . . he'll have a double stroke . . . and drop dead on the spot! I've got to talk to him first. Prepare him for it, little by little . . . give him the big picture . . . yeah, that's it . . . I'll start with the pope . . . *(Down on his hands and knees wiping up the floor)* Ohhh!! All that water! But what a funny odor . . . it smells like vinegar . . . *(Sniffs the rag)* It's pickle juice. *(Taken aback)* Pickle juice? I never knew! Before we're born, we spend nine months floating in pickle juice? *(Continues to wash the pavement)* Oh, look at that . . . what's that? An olive? We float in pickle juice with olives? Oh, that's how it . . . No! No! Olives have nothing to do with it. *(Hears another siren and gets up to go to the window)* Well, they're on their way. I hope it all turns out okay. But where did this olive come from? Oh, look, another one! Two olives? If I wasn't so unsure about where they came from I'd eat 'em . . . I'm starving! *(Puts the two olives on a plate on the table)* Maybe I'll try cooking up a little of that bird seed soup. At least it's organic. The water's already boiling. I'll put in a bouillon cube, some onion . . . *(Opens the refrigerator)* Look at that. I knew it . . . there's no bouillon . . . not even an onion . . . All I've got to put in is this rabbit head!

Goddammit! *(Without thinking he leans against the welding canister)* How many times do I have to tell that dopey Antonia that this is a welding gun, not a lighter for the gas stove. It's dangerous! One day it'll blow up the house!

(Luigi, Margherita's husband, opens the door.)

LUIGI: Can I come in? Anybody home?

GIOVANNI: Oh, Luigi! But what are you doing here at this hour? You don't get off work until tomorrow morning.

LUIGI: Something happened. I'll explain later . . . but what I want to know is, where's my wife? I went home and the doors were open, but nobody was there.

GIOVANNI: Oh yeah, your wife was just here a few minutes ago. She went out with Antonia.

LUIGI: Where'd she go? What for?

GIOVANNI: Well, you know, it's a woman's thing.

LUIGI: And what would that be, that woman's thing.

GIOVANNI: It would be a thing that we wouldn't be interested in. We should only be interested in men's things.

LUIGI: What do you mean I shouldn't be interested? I'm very interested!

GIOVANNI: Ah, now you're interested, are you? And how come you weren't interested last month when you were supposed to reserve a bed like everyone else does?

LUIGI: A bed? For what?

GIOVANNI: Oh sure, that's woman's work, huh? It's the same old story! We give them our paychecks, and then we say, "Pay the bills." We make love to 'em and say, "Take the pill." We make them pregnant and it's, "You take care of it." They're the ones who nurse the babies.

LUIGI: What are you saying?

GIOVANNI: I'm saying that they're right. We're just a bunch of good-for-nothing loafers.

LUIGI: But what does all this have to do with the fact that my Margherita went off with the doors open and didn't even leave me a note, just disappeared like . . .

GIOVANNI: And why should she leave you a note? Weren't you supposed to be working the night shift? Which reminds me, how come you're home so early?

LUIGI: Work stoppage.

GIOVANNI: What do you mean?

LUIGI: We were protesting because they wanted to raise the price of our commuter passes thirty percent!

GIOVANNI: Christ! With all the tension there already, why would you want to screw things up even more?

LUIGI: Sure, sure, I agree it was a screwed-up thing to do. I even told the other guys, "Guys! It's useless trying to get them to bring down the price of our commuter passes."

GIOVANNI: Good for you!

LUIGI: "We should get our commuter passes for free!"

GIOVANNI: Are you out of your mind? We shouldn't pay anything?

LUIGI: Sure, the company should pay for our commute. And they should also pay us for the time we're on the train. Because we lose those hours, and believe you me, it ain't no vacation . . .

GIOVANNI: Who put this stuff in your head? Have you been talking to that police sergeant without the mustache who looks like the state trooper with the mustache?

LUIGI *(Tastes the contents of the open can)*: Hey, this pâté is great . . . what kind is it?

GIOVANNI: Did you eat the stuff in that can?

LUIGI: Yeah, it's not bad. Sorry, I was hungry.

GIOVANNI: Without any lemon?

LUIGI: Why? Are you supposed to eat it with lemon?

GIOVANNI: Uh . . . I don't know . . . but are you sure it tastes all right?

LUIGI: Yeah, it's delicious.

GIOVANNI: Let me taste. Oh, that's not bad! Go open that other can on the sink.

(They feast on the pet food at the table, making appreciative sounds of satisfaction.)

LUIGI: Hey, what is this stuff?

GIOVANNI: It's a kind of pâté . . . for rich cats and dogs.

LUIGI: Pâté for cats and dogs? Come on, are you crazy?

GIOVANNI: No, I'm a gourmet! And while you're at it, taste this. *(Pours him some of the soup)* Taste it. Taste it!

LUIGI: Hey, this isn't bad! What's in it?

GIOVANNI: It's one of my specialties: bird seed soup . . . with broth from frozen rabbit heads!

(Shocked, Luigi spits soup in Giovanni's face.)

LUIGI: Bird seed soup with rabbit heads?

GIOVANNI: Yeah, it's a Chinese delicacy. Over there they call it "consommé du Won Ton Dim Sum Hang Yan Lo." When Nixon went to China, he was nuts about it. "I'll never go back to America. I'm gonna stay here and eat this soup forever." It's in the tapes.

LUIGI: But the bird seed's a little crunchy . . .

GIOVANNI: That's because it's bird seed pilaf . . . you've got to serve it *al dente*. The bird seed is always *al dente* and the rabbit heads are medium rare . . . *(Alarmed)* Did you eat those olives?

LUIGI: Yeah. Why. Shouldn't I have?

GIOVANNI *(Almost hysterical)*: Eh, no, no, you shouldn't have! They were your wife's olives, you boob! You'd even stoop to eating fetus!

LUIGI: My wife's olives . . . fetus? . . .

GIOVANNI: Yeah. Don't you know that when a baby's born . . . the woman loses her pickle juice? First there's the slipping part . . . well, we'll leave that out for now . . . then there's the problem of the pill that has no effect . . . and that's because the pope never stays put . . . he's always running all over the place . . . he doesn't even know what day it is anymore . . . night . . . day . . . now he's in Africa . . . then he's in Brazil . . . next stop India . . . kisses the ground . . . then a little dip in the papal pool, filled with holy water! Some skiing! Always the steep slopes . . . SCVUM! SCVUM! And that's without the ski poles . . . so his arms are free to bless people on the way down. *(Mimes ski-borne benedictions)* Dominus Pacem. Dominus Pacem. Dominus Pacem. *(Mimes high-speed blessings)*

LUIGI: Giovanni, what kind of talk is that? The pope . . . olives . . . fetus?

GIOVANNI: Yeah, you're the voice of reason, aren't you? The company should pay our train fare and give us wages for commuting time. Next you'll want them to pay a bonus to our wives when they make love with us . . . because sex regenerates us, and makes us more productive!

LUIGI: That's right. You said it! We need some relief from this life of shit we're forced to live.

GIOVANNI: Well, let's not get carried away. It's not exactly a life of shit, is it . . . we're better off than we used to be. We've got a house, maybe a little run-down, but it has what we need . . . of course some of us have to work overtime . . .

LUIGI: So what if I've got a stove and a refrigerator, if I'm disgusted by my life . . . goddammit . . . with a job that could be done by a trained monkey *(Mimes the assembly line)* Weld! Hammer! Drill! Weld! Hammer! One piece finished, here comes the next. Weld! *(Mechanically, Giovanni joins the movement without thinking)* Hammer! Faster! Weld . . .

GIOVANNI: Hammer, drill, weld . . . weld *(Stops himself suddenly)* For God's sake, what have you got me doing. You're making me crazy, too!

LUIGI: No, I'm not the one making you crazy. It's the way we live. Everything's going down the drain . . . look at all the factories closing, toxic dumping, ethnic cleansing all over the world. Earthquakes. Hurricanes. The pope.

GIOVANNI: Yeah, scaring all the women in the world to make sure they get pregnant!

LUIGI: What were you saying about the pope getting pregnant? *(Laughs)*

GIOVANNI: No, he's not pregnant. I was talking about your wife.

LUIGI: What's my wife got to do with the pope?

GIOVANNI: Ah, you're pretending you don't know about it?

LUIGI: No. It's just that I don't know! What's this story about the pope?

GIOVANNI: Look, if you spent less time stirring up trouble at work and paid more attention to your wife, you'd know what she was dreaming about at night when the pope comes to her and says, "Don't take the pill for Christ's sake!"

LUIGI: Actually . . . Margherita doesn't take the pill.

GIOVANNI: Oh, so you know. Who told you?

LUIGI: Who do you think told me? She doesn't have to take the pill because she can't have babies. She's got a malformation down there in the whattayacallit . . .

GIOVANNI: You're the one with the malformation! In your head! Your wife is very healthy, and has no problem with having babies . . . in fact she's having one.

LUIGI: Having a baby? When?

GIOVANNI: Now. In fact she could be giving birth this minute: five months premature!

LUIGI: Don't be silly. Five months. She doesn't even have a belly.

GIOVANNI: She doesn't have one because she tied it up . . . and then Antonia untied it and . . . PLAFF . . . a belly big enough to be nine months . . . maybe even eleven!

LUIGI: Come on, are you kidding me?

GIOVANNI: My wife, if you must know, took her in an ambulance to the hospital . . . because she just about gave birth to the kid here on the floor.

LUIGI: Here on the floor?

GIOVANNI: She broke her water here . . . I cleaned it up myself!

LUIGI: You cleaned up her water?

GIOVANNI: Well, it wasn't exactly water . . . pickle juice . . . with a few olives. The ones you just ate.

LUIGI: Listen, stop joking around. Where's my wife?

GIOVANNI: I told you. At the hospital.

LUIGI: Which hospital?

GIOVANNI: Who knows. If you'd have reserved a room a month ago like you're supposed to, we'd know. But no . . . now the baby's going to be born in the car . . . poor kid, in the middle of all those olives!

LUIGI: Come on, stop this nonsense! Tell me what hospital she's in or I'll punch you out.

GIOVANNI: Hey, calm down. I already told you that I don't know . . . No, wait, maybe they went to that Gyne . . . Gyneco . . . that Gynecological Place.

LUIGI: The Gynecological Place?

GIOVANNI: Yeah, the place where they do the premature baby transplants.

LUIGI: The premature baby transplants?

GIOVANNI: Where have you been living? At the Gynecological Place there's a machine with a tent full of oxygen . . . they take the woman with the baby that's premature by four-and-a-half, or even five months . . . then they take another woman to be the second mother . . . they do a cesarean . . . put the baby in the new belly, stuff in the placenta and everything . . . and then four months later . . . *(Pause)* . . . a fish!

LUIGI: Cut it out. I don't give a damn about your transplant machines, and cesareans . . . I want to know where the hell is this Gynecological Place. Get the telephone book and we can look it up.

GIOVANNI: I don't have a phone. What would I do with a phone book: read up on who lives in the neighborhood?

LUIGI: Come on, we can go to the bar downstairs. They've got a phone?

GIOVANNI: I just remembered. It's next to the new mall.

LUIGI: The new mall? Why would they go so far away?

GIOVANNI: I told you! It's the only place where they do the transplants! They'd find another woman. A healthy woman who happens to be near by. *(Stops; he has an idea)* Another woman? *(He screams)* Antonia! *(Luigi screams)* She's going to be right there . . . She'll be the first one they ask . . . and she's crazy enough to do it! She's going to have a transplant, and come home pregnant. Quick! Let's go!

(They exit, running.)

ACT TWO

Antonia and Margherita return. Margherita still has a big belly; she is sniffling.

ANTONIA *(Calling)*: Giovanni. Giovanni! He's not here. He went to work. What time is it? *(Looks at the alarm clock on the shelves)* Five-thirty. Can you believe it? We've been out playing this charade for more than four hours. *(Peeks into the other room)*

MARGHERITA: I should never have listened to you! Look at the mess we're in now!

ANTONIA: You're such a complainer. It all worked out, didn't it? All we had to say to the ambulance team was, "Careful, this girl's not pregnant . . . but she's got a gut full of stolen goods," and they couldn't wait to give us a hand. They wanted to throw a party for us! And you were so worried . . . for nothing . . . you have to have faith in people! Me, I have faith in people! *(Looks into the refrigerator)* Where's the butter. Who stole my butter? Ah, no, there it is. Now I'll make you some soup. Ah, the rice. Give me a packet of rice. *(Margherita pulls a packet of rice out from the bag hidden under her coat. Antonia goes to the stove. She sees the pot)* But what's this stuff? The bird seed? Don't tell me that dopey Giovanni really cooked up a bird seed soup with rabbit heads! All you have to do is feed him a story and he swallows the whole thing. Let's see what I can whip up for you.

MARGHERITA: If you're making the soup just for me, don't bother. I'm not hungry. My stomach's all blocked up.

ANTONIA *(Margherita unpacks her "belly")*: What are you doing?

MARGHERITA: Did you think I was going to carry this stuff around the rest of my life?

ANTONIA: I don't want any stolen goods in my house! Is that clear? And while you're at it, could you help me get rid of the stuff under the bed. I'll make myself a little belly, too. *(Takes some pillowcases from a drawer)*

MARGHERITA: And where will we put it all?

ANTONIA: We'll carry it out to my father-in-law's little shed behind the railroad tracks. He grows vegetables there. It will be a great hiding place.

MARGHERITA: That's enough, I can't take this anymore . . . I've had it to here with your harebrained schemes. I'm going home.

ANTONIA: You're a loser.

MARGHERITA: Well, if you're so smart, tell me what I say to my husband when he sees me without a belly . . . or a baby?

ANTONIA: Oh, I thought of that already. We'll tell him that you had a hysterical pregnancy.

MARGHERITA: Hysterical?

ANTONIA: Yes, it happens all the time . . . a woman thinks she's pregnant, her belly blows up, and then, when she's ready to give birth, all that comes out is air. Just air!

MARGHERITA: And how would I have gotten this hysterical pregnancy?

ANTONIA: From the pope. He kept coming to you in your dreams and saying, "Make a baby! Make a baby!" So you obeyed him: you made a baby . . . of air. Just the soul of a baby!

MARGHERITA: Now we drag the pope into the story.

ANTONIA: Look at all the times he's dragged us into his stories. *(Margherita has removed her bundles, while Antonia has re-stuffed her coat)* I'll be back in ten minutes . . .

MARGHERITA: But why don't you just get a cart and carry it all over there at once, instead of playing this pregnant mother game?

ANTONIA: Because we'd be caught right away. See those police wagons down there. They're waiting to catch you in the act! *(Brings the welding tanks to the stove)*

MARGHERITA: What are you doing? Won't you ruin it?

ANTONIA: No. It's Giovanni's welding canister. It's made of iron . . . it's special stuff called animonio . . . it can heat up to two thousand degrees without even turning red . . . *(Lights the gas stove with it)*

MARGHERITA *(Standing by the window, peeking out)*: Look, it's Maria from the third floor. She's pregnant, too.

ANTONIA: Stealing all my ideas. Before you know it there'll be pregnant dogs walking by . . . pregnant men . . .

MARGHERITA: Listen, I thought it over. I'm coming with you. *(Starts reinserting the bags in her "belly" under her coat)*

ANTONIA: Brava! I knew you'd change your mind. Let's go. Today is the day of the mammas!

(Scene change. A half-curtain runs the length of the proscenium. Giovanni and Luigi enter as if walking on the street. Luigi pulls out a beret and puts it on his head. Giovanni does the same.)

LUIGI: Listen. I want to tell you something.

GIOVANNI: What.

LUIGI *(Can't bring himself to say it)*: Look, it's raining. Like the saying goes, "When it rains, the government is stealing something."

GIOVANNI: Well, that's just to remind you that when it's sunny, the government is murdering somebody.

LUIGI: Goddammit, do you still have the energy to make jokes and keep laughing?

GIOVANNI: Me, no! But my feet, yes. They're dying for a good laugh! You and your bright idea of checking every hospital in town on foot. I've had enough. I'm going back to the station and get a train to work. I'll already be docked an hour's pay as it is.

(Two stagehands walk by as the sound effect of a truck plays on the loudspeaker. The stagehands/truck drop several sacks in front of Luigi and Giovanni as they pass by, then exit.)

Look! Those sacks must have fallen off that . . . truck. They're filled with coffee.

LUIGI: Yeah. Ethiopian. Kenyan. French vanilla. Let's take some home.

GIOVANNI: Are you crazy? Do you want to lower yourself to the level of thieves and looters? I don't take stuff that's not mine. I work for what I have.

LUIGI: Listen. What I was trying to tell you before is . . . starting tomorrow we're all being downsized.

GIOVANNI: Downsized?

LUIGI: Yeah. I heard it on the train. Six thousand out of twenty-six thousand employees are being downsized now. And the rest of the plant closes in the next few months.

GIOVANNI: They're closing the plant?

LUIGI: Not only that. We won't get paid for our last two weeks.

GIOVANNI: Come on. Help me load up this stuff. Let's take it all.

(As they leave the State Trooper enters.)

TROOPER: Drop those sacks or I'll shoot.

LUIGI: Look. He's got a gun.

TROOPER: Stop or I'll shoot.

GIOVANNI: Go ahead and shoot.

TROOPER *(Chases them offstage)*: Those bastards.

(Change of scene. The curtain stays down; only the lights change to indicate another street. It's dark. From stage left, Giovanni and Luigi reenter with their sacks.)

GIOVANNI: You can do it. We're almost there. Wait. There's a police van . . . in front of my house . . .

LUIGI: Look at those two women crossing the street. Aren't they our wives?

GIOVANNI: No, it can't be them.

LUIGI: Sure, they're standing there in front of the building you live in. And one of them's pregnant.

GIOVANNI: No, take a better look . . . they're both pregnant.

LUIGI: Oh, I guess it's not them.

GIOVANNI *(Grabbing his shoulder)*: Goddammit, we're trapped. Look across the street. It's the state trooper who was chasing us!

LUIGI: Why not? He knows where you live . . . he'll head straight to your house to find us!

GIOVANNI: So we'll go to your house!

LUIGI: Right. Keep moving. Let's go this way and shake him off. *(They exit through the curtain)*

(The Trooper crosses the entire stage and exits to the left. He returns again, still looking for Luigi and Giovanni.)

TROOPER: You can't get away . . . I know where you live! I know the streets! . . . I know how to read too!

(In the dark the curtain rises and we find ourselves again in the house of Giovanni and Antonia. The two women are entering with big bellies. They are overwhelmed and exhausted.)

ANTONIA: I want to die . . . I want to die . . .

MARGHERITA: Load, unload, I feel like I'm turning into a truck!

ANTONIA *(Goes to sit on the bed)*: I want to die . . . Oh, God, the exhaustion of pregnancy.

MARGHERITA *(Loosens her coat and removes some lettuce leaves and a few cabbages)*: Look, look at all the vegetables we have here from your father's farm. There's enough to make salads for a year!

ANTONIA: At this rate we'll never get the stuff out of here . . . With the cops down there we can't go out with big bellies, and come home with no bellies . . . and go out again with big bellies . . . no bellies . . . big bellies . . . no bellies. The soup! *(Runs to the oven)* I forgot about the soup . . . it'll be all burned up! My God, the hunger's gone to my brain . . . *(Lifts pot cover)* That's a relief. It didn't even boil . . . but why? It's been on four hours? The gas! Those bastards cut off the gas! Disgusting creeps, murderers, thieves . . . just because I didn't pay the gas bill. And they cut off the electricity too . . .

MARGHERITA: They cut off the gas?

ANTONIA: Yes. The man was here yesterday to check up on it . . . *(There's a knock at the door)* Who is it?

VOICE *(From outside)*: Friends.

ANTONIA: What friends?

VOICE: I'm a friend of your husband's from work. He asked me to come and tell you something.

ANTONIA: Oh, my God! What could it be? *(Goes to open the door)*

MARGHERITA: Wait a second. Let me hide the lettuce. *(Puts it under her coat)*

ANTONIA: Just a moment please . . . I'm not dressed. *(Opens the door and sees the State Trooper)* You again? What kind of joke is this?

TROOPER: Stop right there, where you are! This time I've got you! Look at that. Now you're both pregnant! My how those bellies grow! I knew all along it was a trick!

ANTONIA: What kind of trick are you talking about?

MARGHERITA *(Letting herself flop on the bed in exhaustion)*: Now we're in for it. I knew it. I knew it.

TROOPER *(To Margherita)*: Glad to see you haven't lost your little bundle of joy. And you, madam . . . congratulations! In five hours you've made love, become a mommy, and arrived at your ninth month!

ANTONIA: Look, officer, you're making a mistake . . .

TROOPER: No, I made a mistake last time . . . when I fell for your little act with the labor pains and premature birth! But I'm not going to fall for it again. Out with the stolen goods!

ANTONIA: But what stolen goods are you talking about?

TROOPER: Let's stop playing games. Your scam's an open book: the husbands go out to commit the robberies, pass the bags to the wives, and all day long I see nothing but pregnant women! Now why is it that all the women in this neighborhood got buns in their ovens at the same time! Mature women, teenagers, little girls . . . Today I even saw an eighty-year-old woman who was pregnant . . . with twins!

ANTONIA: That's because . . . because of the Festival . . . the Festival of the Patron Saint . . . Santa Eulalia.

TROOPER: The Patron Saint?

ANTONIA: You don't know about her? What a saint! The holiest of saints! A good woman . . . who . . . who wanted to have children . . . she was obsessed . . . she wanted to get pregnant . . . but she couldn't do it . . . she just couldn't do it! Poor saint. Hard as she tried, she never succeeded . . . up to the point where the Heavenly Father Above took pity on her and: pscium! She was pregnant! . . . at sixty years old! A miracle!

TROOPER: Sixty years old?

ANTONIA: Yes, you can imagine, and her husband was over eighty!

TROOPER: But . . .

ANTONIA: The power of faith! They say, though, that the husband died immediately. Anyway, in memory of this miracle all the women in the neighborhood go around for three days with false bellies.

TROOPER: Oh, what a wonderful tradition. And is that why they empty out the supermarkets, to put stuff in their bellies? Come on! Enough with the fairy tales! Let me see what you have under there, or I'll lose my patience!

ANTONIA: And do what? Rip off our clothes? I warn you, that if you lay even a finger on us . . . a . . . a . . . a curse . . . will befall you!

TROOPER: Don't make me laugh. What curse?

ANTONIA: The same thing that happened to the incredulous husband of Santa Eulalia! The old man was a skeptic and he didn't believe her: "Santa Eulalia, come here right away. Open your blouse and let me see what you have in your belly, and I warn you, if you really are pregnant, I'll strangle you, because that baby's not mine." And then she, Santa Eulalia, opened her blouse, and a second miracle: out of her stomach . . . out of her stomach . . . came roses . . . roses . . . a cascade of roses.

TROOPER: Roses?

ANTONIA: Yes, but that's not all . . . all of a sudden the old man's eyes went black: "I can't see anymore. I can't see anymore," he shouted. "I'm blind! God has punished me!" "Oh, skeptic, now you believe," said Santa Eulalia. "Yes, I believe!" And then, third miracle: out of the roses sprang a ten-month-old baby boy who could already speak, and he said, "Papa, Papa, the Lord forgives you. Now you can die in peace." The baby put his little hand on the old man's head, and he dropped dead just like that.

TROOPER: Okay, story time's over. Now show me the roses . . . I mean . . . the goods. Hurry up!

ANTONIA: So you don't believe in the miracle?

TROOPER: Not at all.

ANTONIA: You're not afraid of the curse?

TROOPER: No, I said so already!

ANTONIA: Okay. Have it your way! Don't say I didn't warn you. *(To Margherita)* Come on. Get up and we'll show him together:

Santa Eulalia of the big belly
On whomever does not believe in the miracle
Let fall the curse
To whomever does not believe the oracle
Let come the evil black bastard
To darken his sight
Santa Eulalia, Santa Pia,
Unleash your curse
And so be it!!!!!

(The two women open their coats.)

TROOPER: What's all that stuff in there?

ANTONIA: What stuff? *(The two women make sounds of amazement)* Oh, look at that! It's a salad!

TROOPER: Salad?

ANTONIA: Yes, an apparition of a salad: chicory, endive, fennel and even a cabbage!

MARGHERITA: Me too, me too—I have a cabbage!

TROOPER: What's going on here? Why are you hiding all these vegetables in your stomach?

ANTONIA: But we didn't hide anything. Can't you see? It's a miracle!?

TROOPER: Yeah, the miracle of Our Lady of the Cabbage!

ANTONIA: Well, these days you make a miracle with whatever vegetable you can get your hands on. But whether you believe or not, there's nothing wrong with it, is there? Is there some law that says a citizen is not allowed to carry chicory, endive, fennel and cabbage in her belly? Is it prohibited?

TROOPER: No.

ANTONIA: Is there a law against it?

TROOPER: No.

ANTONIA: Then good-bye! *(Begins to usher him out)*

TROOPER: What do you mean, "good-bye!" *(Grabs the cabbage and presses the nozzle of his gun against it, as if holding it hostage)* All right! That's it! Tell me why you put all this stuff under your clothes . . . or else!

ANTONIA: I told you already. To make a belly in honor of the miracle of Santa Eulalia! And anyone who doesn't believe in it is cursed!

(The lights dim slowly.)

ANTONIA AND MARGHERITA:

Santa Eulalia of the big belly
On whomever does not believe in the miracle
Let fall the curse . . .

(The women repeat the "prayer to Santa Eulalia." They notice with anxiety the dimming of the lights.)

TROOPER: What's happening now? The lights are going out.

ANTONIA *(Very calmly)*: What are you talking about, officer?

TROOPER: Can't you see . . . *(Worried)* It's getting dark . . .

ANTONIA: No, you must be mistaken . . . I can see just fine. *(To Margherita)* Can you see?

MARGHERITA *(Antonia kicks her)*: Yes, yes . . . I can see . . .

ANTONIA: We can see. Maybe your eyesight is fading.

MARGHERITA *(Moves close to Antonia and whispers)*: They cut off the electricity.

ANTONIA: Quiet!

TROOPER: Come on, stop kidding around. The light switch. Where's the light switch?

ANTONIA *(Moving comfortably, in spite of the darkness)*: It's right here. Can't you see it? Wait, I'll try it . . . *(Clicks the switch audibly)* There, you see. Now it's off. Now it's on. There's an awful lot of light in my house! Don't you see it?

TROOPER: No, I can't see.

ANTONIA: Oh, my God. He's gone blind! It's the curse!

TROOPER: Cut it out! Open the window . . . I want to see outside!

ANTONIA: But the window is open!

MARGHERITA: Yes, the window's open. Can't you see?

ANTONIA: Come on, come and look. *(Leads him to a chair)* Look, over here. Watch out for the chair!

TROOPER *(Bumps into the chair)*: Ahhiaa . . . Owww. That hurt!

ANTONIA: Pay attention when you walk!

TROOPER: How can I, if I can't see?

ANTONIA: Oh, I forgot, you're blind.

TROOPER *(Scared and angry)*: Blind!!!!!!!!!!

ANTONIA: Come on . . . there's the window. *(Takes him to the shelves and opens the two glass cabinet doors on top)* Careful now . . . look, we're opening the window . . . feel the glass? *(The Trooper touches the glass tentatively)* Look out there . . . what a panorama! Sometimes I forget myself how beautiful it is. Let's hope the landlord doesn't realize what a great view this is, or he'll raise the rent!

TROOPER *(Desperate)*: No I don't see it. I can't see anything. Dammit, what happened to me? A match . . . Light a match!

ANTONIA *(Worried)*: A match? . . . I have something better than a match *(Goes and gets the welding tank)* Stay there. Don't move. You don't know the house, and you might hurt yourself . . . I'll bring it over . . . it's a welding torch . . . *(She lights it)* Look, look . . . what a beautiful red flame!

TROOPER: I don't see any flame . . . let me touch it.

ANTONIA: No, no, can't you see it's red hot . . .

TROOPER *(Arrogant)*: I said let me touch it. That's an order! *(Antonia obeys)* Ah, ahiiaaoohoooo! My hand! I burned my hand! Oh God, that hurts! What a burn!

ANTONIA: I tried to warn you.

TROOPER *(Cries desperately)*: I'm blind!

ANTONIA: Don't cry . . . it's going to be all right . . . come on . . . at the end of the day what happened . . . it's nothing . . . so you've gone a little blind . . .

TROOPER: I want to get out of here . . . I've got to get out! *(Becoming more desperate)* I want to get out of this house . . . to my superiors . . .

ANTONIA: Wait, wait, I'll help you to the door . . . Here it is . . . there's the door . . . *(Opens door to wardrobe)*

(The State Trooper rushes into it like a madman, smashes his head on the interior, falls back staggering, and collapses on the floor.)

MARGHERITA: He hit his head!

TROOPER: Ahhii! Who punched me?

ANTONIA *(Searching)*: The baby . . . It's Santa Eulalia's baby. He's touched your forehead with his little hand!

TROOPER: That's some little hand! *(Collapses on the floor)*

ANTONIA: Officer . . . Officer! Dammit, he fainted. *(She gets down on her knees by the Trooper)*

MARGHERITA: Maybe he's dead!

ANTONIA: Always the optimist! What do you mean, dead . . . get a pillow . . . *(Margherita obeys)* No, he's not dead. He's just having some faintness . . . a slight case of faintness . . . he's fine . . . he's breathing . . .

MARGHERITA: He's dead, he's dead . . . he's not breathing anymore!

ANTONIA: He's breathing . . . he's breathing . . . no . . . he's not breathing! And his heart's not beating either!

MARGHERITA: Oh God! We killed a cop!

ANTONIA: Oh, yeah! Maybe I got a little carried away. What do we do now?

MARGHERITA: Ah, you're asking me? What do I have to do with it? It was all your idea . . . I'm sorry but I'm going home . . . The keys! Where did I put the keys to my house?

ANTONIA: Some friend you are. Walking out on me just like that.

MARGHERITA *(Finds keys on the shelf)*: Ah, here they are! But I have another pair in my pocket. Two sets of keys! These are my husband's! So he was here . . . he came looking for me . . . and he forgot them!

ANTONIA: What do I care about that! I'm here with a dead cop and you're talking to me about keys!

MARGHERITA: That means that Luigi met Giovanni and he must have told him that I was pregnant, and now what am I supposed to say? You've got to think up something to get me out of this mess . . .

ANTONIA: I'm desperate. *(Crying, she speaks to the unconscious Trooper)* Officer . . . don't be that way . . . let's make up . . .

It was just a little bump on the head . . . officer . . . wake up *(Lifts the officer's arm and lets it go. The arm falls heavily without life)* He's dead! He's really dead!

MARGHERITA: See what happens when you make fun of miracles?

ANTONIA: No, he was the one making fun of them . . . I even warned him: watch out for the curse, because Santa Eulalia is an awesome saint! *(She grabs him by the shoulders, lifts him up and drops him)*

MARGHERITA: And now what are you doing?

ANTONIA: Artificial respiration.

MARGHERITA: No. You have to use mouth-to-mouth resuscitation like they do when people drown.

ANTONIA: Now you want me to kiss a cop! With my political background! No . . . you kiss him . . .

MARGHERITA: No. I can't do it! Maybe we should get him an oxygen tank.

ANTONIA *(Thinks a moment)*: I've got one. It's with Giovanni's welding equipment. One valve's for hydrogen, and the other's for oxygen. Come here and help me . . . close the hydrogen valve . . . like that . . . and open the one for oxygen. Stay calm . . . you'll see. As soon as he gets the oxygen, he'll come around! He'll even feel better than before! Like he spent a month in the mountains!

MARGHERITA: Are you sure it's going to work?

ANTONIA: No problem. You'll see . . . *(Puts the welding canister tube into the officer's mouth)* The oxygen's going to his stomach . . . you see, his chest is rising . . . and then it falls . . . look . . . he's waking up . . . he's breathing . . . see how nicely that chest rises . . . and how it falls.

MARGHERITA: It looks to me like it's only rising . . . and his stomach too . . . stop . . . you're going to blow him up.

(The two women frantically try to turn off the infernal machine.)

ANTONIA *(Lifts the tube up to the officer's mouth)*: Oh, no. I gave him hydrogen instead of oxygen . . . Oh God, what a belly . . . what a belly! I made a policeman pregnant!

(Blackout. Curtain falls.

Giovanni and Luigi enter. The area in front of the curtain is understood to be the street outside Luigi's apartment. Giovanni and Luigi stand outside.)

GIOVANNI: Well, we can't keep on sitting outside your place like a couple of bums. I'm going to see if I can break down the door with my shoulder.

LUIGI: No, you saw what happened when I tried. I couldn't get past the two locks.

GIOVANNI: Why do you have all that hardware?

LUIGI: My wife made me install it. She's terrified of thieves.

GIOVANNI: We're screwed.

LUIGI: Son of a bitch! Now I remember where I left the keys. At your house . . . yeah . . . on the table.

GIOVANNI: Are you sure?

LUIGI: Absolutely. Come on. Give me the keys to your house and I'll go get them.

GIOVANNI: Yeah, with that state trooper waiting outside my place! TRAC . . . You're under arrest!

LUIGI: No, after all this time, he must be gone.

GIOVANNI: Don't kid yourself. That guy's a bloodhound. We can't even think of going back there.

(They hear noises.)

Dammit, someone's coming . . .

LUIGI: Calm down, it's probably just a neighbor.

GIOVANNI: What do you mean, neighbor. It's that cop . . . *(Tries to hide the bags)*

VOICE *(Offstage)*: Excuse me, I need some information.

GIOVANNI: Dammit, we're screwed.

(Gravedigger enters. It is the same actor who plays the Trooper.)

LUIGI: No, it's not him. It looks like him, but it's not him.

GIOVANNI: You're right. It's not him.

GRAVEDIGGER: What were you saying? Who do I look like?

GIOVANNI: Damn, he looks just like him. Ah, I'm sorry for laughing, but you are the spitting image of the sergeant without the mustache who looks like the state trooper with the mustache. I feel like I'm in a play that I saw when I was a kid . . . you know, one of those theatre companies where they can't afford to pay more than a few actors, so one of them has to play the parts of all the cops.

GRAVEDIGGER: But, really, I'm not a policeman.

GIOVANNI: Ah no, and what do you do?

GRAVEDIGGER: I'm an undertaker.

GIOVANNI AND LUIGI: Oh, Mother of God! *(With rapid gestures, the two of them touch their testicles)*

GIOVANNI *(Explains to the audience)*: This is an Italian gesture expressing the fear of death. *(Demonstrates the gesture again and then turns to the Gravedigger)* Sorry, it was just an instinct.

GRAVEDIGGER: Oh, don't worry . . . I understand . . . everyone does that when they meet me . . . I do it myself whenever I look in the mirror.

GIOVANNI: How nice.

GRAVEDIGGER: Can you tell me if a certain Sergio Prampolini lives around here.

LUIGI: Sure, he's upstairs on the third floor. But I'm sure he's not home. He's in the hospital. The poor guy is always sick! . . .

GRAVEDIGGER: He's dead. But do you know if anyone in his family is coming home today? I've got to get someone to sign for the casket I've got out there.

GIOVANNI: Oh well, just leave it in the hall . . . with a little note on it . . . and when the son comes home: "Oh, it's Dad!" *(Mimes the action of carrying the casket on his shoulder)*

GRAVEDIGGER: A casket in the hallway? Abandoned? . . . With all the people passing by . . . little kids jumping in to play Indians paddling their canoe? No, I can't do that. I have to have the papers signed by someone who's responsible. You live here, don't you?

LUIGI: Yes, I live right there.

GRAVEDIGGER: Good, then it's all set. I'll leave the casket with you, you keep it in your house . . . and this evening when the son of the deceased . . .

GIOVANNI *(Shocked)*: A dead man's coffin in my house?

GRAVEDIGGER: It doesn't take up much space, you know . . . and if you overlook its macabre function, it's actually quite decorative.

GIOVANNI: Sure, put a little doily on top, and it's a portable bar!

GRAVEDIGGER: Be serious.

GIOVANNI: I'm dead serious.

LUIGI: The fact is, you see . . . we locked ourselves out.

GRAVEDIGGER: Oh, what a shame! Then, I'll have to return it to the warehouse.

GIOVANNI: No . . . maybe we can take it to my house. I live just down the street . . . I'll take care of everything. But you'd have to let us load these sacks into the casket . . . so our stuff won't get wet in the rain. The casket has a lid I hope?

GRAVEDIGGER: Yes, yes, it's a regulation casket. It's cheap, but even so we never make them without the lid.

GIOVANNI: What a great country we live in! Every coffin has a lid!

GRAVEDIGGER: OK. I'll leave the casket with you. *(He leaves)*

(Giovanni and Luigi gather the bags.)

GIOVANNI: I'd like to see a cop who's got the guts to stick his nose into a dead man's casket. I'll be the corpse, and you can be the undertaker making a delivery to the house. Come on. Let's get the sacks and go. *(They leave)*

(Blackout. The curtain rises on the women in the house. The Trooper is still stretched out on the floor. Antonia is filling up a bag with the food from under the bed. Margherita is furious.)

MARGHERITA: You're crazy. We're here with a dead man in the house and you're still worried about smuggling out rice and pasta.

ANTONIA: Well, it's the last trip. And besides, if he's dead, he's dead. Just come over here and help me lift the guy up . . . so we can get rid of him.

MARGHERITA: Where are we going to put him?

ANTONIA: In the wardrobe.

MARGHERITA: In the wardrobe?

ANTONIA: Where else? Haven't you ever seen a detective movie? They always put the body in the wardrobe.

(They lift the officer to his feet. Antonia lifts him over her shoulders.)

MARGHERITA *(Struggling)*: He's heavy.

ANTONIA: What do you expect? He's a cop! *(Manipulates him as if he were a puppet and stows him away in the wardrobe)* There, he's in. Now let's put a coat hanger under his jacket so we can suspend him from this hook . . . *(They do it)* Perfect! Dammit, the door won't close. Let's push . . . come on. *(They push hard)* There! Look how nicely he fits in now! Just like Baby Jesus in the manger! *(Closes wardrobe door)*

MARGHERITA: Well, that's that. *(Mimes opening the window)* The rain's coming down by the bucketful.

ANTONIA: I'll be right back . . . I'm going in there for a minute . . . load up your belly . . . just one more trip and we're done . . . so exhausting! *(Goes out to the bathroom)*

(The door opens. Luigi is there. He's wearing the cap of the Gravedigger.)

LUIGI *(Barely peeking in, whispers)*: Hey, is anybody home?

MARGHERITA: Who's there? . . . *(Frightened)* Luigi, is that you? What are you doing dressed up like that?

LUIGI: Margherita, my sweetie pie, finally . . . How are you? . . . Let me look at you! But don't you have a belly? The baby? Where's the baby? Did you lose it?

MARGHERITA: No, no . . . don't worry . . . everything's fine . . .

LUIGI: Really, everything's fine? And you're okay? Tell me . . .

MARGHERITA: Later, later . . . it's better if Antonia tells you . . .

LUIGI: Why Antonia?

GRAVEDIGGER *(From outside the door)*: Hey this casket's heavy, are we coming in or not?

LUIGI: Yes, yes, come on in . . .

(At that moment the door of the wardrobe opens so that the Trooper can be seen hanging inside. Margherita closes it quickly and runs into the other room.)

Come on, Giovanni, get out of the casket . . .

GIOVANNI *(From outside the door)*: Too bad, I was just getting comfortable in here . . .

(The wardrobe door opens again. Without seeing what's inside, Giovanni closes the door. They put the coffin on the table.)

MARGHERITA *(From the other room)*: Antonia, Antonia, come here . . . hurry.

ANTONIA: *(From offstage)*: What is it . . . can't I even pee in peace?

GIOVANNI: They're both back?

LUIGI: Yes, yes, and everything's fine . . . they're all doing fine.

GIOVANNI: That's good . . . Close it, close the lid . . . *(To the Gravedigger)* Thank you. Thanks for everything.

GRAVEDIGGER: Don't mention it. *(He leaves)*

LUIGI: Listen, I have an idea. Let's close the door and lock ourselves in here until we unload everything. Then we can hide the stuff under the bed, and stand up the casket in the closet.

GIOVANNI: All right, go lock the door. *(Luigi does. They take the bags out of the casket and put them under the bed)*

MARGHERITA *(From the other room)*: Hurry up, Antonia. I have to tell you something.

ANTONIA: I'm coming. I'm fixing my clothes. Everything's falling out.

GIOVANNI: There, it's done . . . the bags are all out of sight. Push, push them further under.

LUIGI: Look at that! We push the bags in on one side and they come out on the other . . . (*Bends over to look under the bed)* It didn't seem like that much in the casket! It looks like twice as much!

GIOVANNI: Of course it does, if you look at it with your head upside down . . . everything seems exaggerated that way . . . they call it the yoga effect . . . Come on, help me lift up the casket . . . No, wait, first let's take off the lid so it won't be too thick.

(Giovanni and Luigi lift the casket and insert it into the wardrobe, after resting the lid up against the wall.)

LUIGI: You're right . . . But what was that yoga effect you were talking about?

GIOVANNI: Oh, that was discovered in India . . . people there are so poor that when their hunger gets too much to bear . . . they stand on their heads . . . and while they're upside down they imagine whatever they want . . . all kinds of things to eat and drink . . .

LUIGI: And that makes the hunger go away?

GIOVANNI: No, but it keeps people off the streets. Come on, we've almost got it in—push.

(They manage to squeeze in the coffin so that the Trooper fits within it. They close the door without seeing the Trooper.)

LUIGI: Ah, so the illusion is enough to satisfy them . . . is that it?

GIOVANNI: Yeah, that's it . . . *(Tries to close the door of the wardrobe)*

LUIGI: You know I had an illusion, too.

GIOVANNI: Yeah, you told me.

LUIGI: No, no, another one . . . I thought I saw the state trooper in the closet.

GIOVANNI: State trooper? *(Opens the wardrobe door)* Good thing it was an illusion . . . Don't let me catch you standing on your head again, okay . . . Dammit, it won't close. *(Pushes, but door stays open)*

MARGHERITA *(From the other room)*: Listen, Antonia, I'm getting tired of this . . . I'll just wait in there . . .

GIOVANNI: Go open the door. I can't move . . .

(Luigi runs to open the door. Margherita enters and sees Giovanni leaning against the wardrobe door.)

MARGHERITA: Oh, thanks, that's better . . . *(Sees Giovanni)* Oh, Giovanni, hello.

GIOVANNI: Hello. Your husband told me that everything went well . . . So did you have the baby or not?

ANTONIA *(Enters suddenly; to Margherita)*: So what did you have to tell me that was so urgent?

(Antonia tries to hide her belly as much as possible, and slowly, bent over double, she goes toward the front door.)

GIOVANNI *(Blocks her with a shout)*: Antonia! Your belly! You had the transplant?!

LUIGI: The transplant?!

ANTONIA: Well . . .

GIOVANNI *(Starts to walk into the wardrobe, but turns suddenly to block her)*: Did you get the cesarean?

ANTONIA: A little.

GIOVANNI: What do you mean, a little?

ANTONIA: Well, in the end . . . it was the right thing.

LUIGI *(To Margherita)*: Did you have a cesarean, too?

MARGHERITA: Uh, yes, well, I don't know . . . Antonia, did I have one?

LUIGI: Why are you asking her . . . don't you know?

ANTONIA: Uh, no, poor thing. They put her to sleep. And since she was asleep, how could she know?

GIOVANNI: You mean they operated on you while you were awake?

ANTONIA: What's with this interrogation? Why the third degree. I take the fifth. *(Almost out of sympathy, the cupboard's glass shelf doors and the front door of the house start opening, setting off an absurd merry-go-round of activity)* You could have asked how our health is, if we're living or dying. What do you care that we dragged ourselves out of bed like idiots against the doctors orders so that you wouldn't worry about us. And what do you think I should have done . . . she was going to lose her baby . . . I was in a position to save it . . . how could I say no . . . Aren't you always telling me that we have to help one another . . .

GIOVANNI: Yes, yes, you're right . . . I'm sorry . . . maybe you did the right thing . . . yes, of course you did.

LUIGI: Thank you, Antonia. Thank you, Antonia, for all you did. You are truly a remarkable woman.

GIOVANNI: Yes, truly a remarkable woman.

LUIGI *(To Margherita)*: You tell her, too. Come on.

MARGHERITA: Yes, Antonia. You are a remarkable woman.

GIOVANNI: Come . . . come here . . . you shouldn't be standing up . . . *(Sits her on the bed)* not with that cesarean, you know . . . maybe it would have been better for you to stay there at the hospital.

ANTONIA: Don't be silly . . . I'm fine . . . didn't even notice it!

GIOVANNI: Yes, you look absolutely great . . . And look at that great big belly! *(Caresses her stomach)* It's moving already!

LUIGI: It's moving? Excuse me, Antonia, can I touch it, too?

MARGHERITA: No, you're not touching a damn thing!

LUIGI: Eh, but it's my son, too, you know?

GIOVANNI: Yeah . . . we're all related now.

MARGHERITA: What about me. All this cheering for Antonia . . .

ANTONIA: Yeah. Do some cheering for Margherita. Go lift her up on your shoulders. I have to go. *(Gets up and rushes toward the door)*

GIOVANNI *(Blocking her way)*: Go? Are you crazy? You're not going anywhere . . . except to bed . . . to stay warm . . . in fact we'll move the bed next to the heater. *(Begins to move the bed)*

LUIGI: Stop, what are you doing!?

(All look at him.)

GIOVANNI: You're right . . . it's too dangerous to move it, too dangerous . . . the gas tanks are there . . . *(Tries to put Antonia back on the bed)*

(Antonia stops him; she's seen the cover of the coffin inside the wardrobe.)

ANTONIA: Giovanni . . . what's that?

GIOVANNI *(Distracting her while he tries to come up with a plausible response)*: The gas tanks . . . are there . . . But you could at least have warned me . . . instead of letting me worry . . . all it would have taken was a phone call . . .

ANTONIA: Giovanni, what's that?

GIOVANNI: All it takes is a dime . . . a quarter . . . you could have asked a nurse . . . you could have said: "Look, call my house . . . no, call the bar downstairs from my house . . . and say . . . listen, tell my husband?"

ANTONIA *(Interrupting him)*: Excuse me, Giovanni, what is that thing . . .

GIOVANNI *(Desperate, doesn't know what to say)*: "Hello, could you tell my husband that everything's fine . . ."

ANTONIA: Giovanni, what is that brown wooden object?!

GIOVANNI: Don't change the subject! How come, instead of calling me . . . about the baby . . . you keep talking to me about that disgusting piece of wood . . . I'll burn it . . . I don't know why I ever bought the thing . . . it's . . . it's . . .

ANTONIA *(Exasperated)*: Giovanni, what is it?

GIOVANNI: You still don't get it do you? Don't you ever watch TV? A child . . . would understand right away, even a child . . . watching TV . . . the commercials . . . especially when you see the foam . . . the waves . . .

ANTONIA: But what is it, Giovanni?

GIOVANNI: It's a surf board! They sell them at the factory . . . in front of the gate . . .

LUIGI: The gate.

GIOVANNI: Yeah. We're going to be laid off until January . . . so what are we going to do in December? Surf the Atlantic. I know, I know . . . you don't believe it . . . in fact it's something else entirely . . .

ANTONIA: What is it? . . .

GIOVANNI: You have such a limited imagination! It's a cradle! When I said to Luigi, "Look, Luigi, your wife's expecting a baby," right away he said, "A cradle, a cradle!"

LUIGI: A cradle.

GIOVANNI: So I went into the first cradle store I could find. And got the most modern cradle on the market. From Japan. It's a Toyota. *(Luigi and Giovanni grab the cover and rock it)* You see, it's got four holes here, two on each side . . . so you can suspend it from the ceiling with two steel cables . . . you put the baby in . . . you barely have to touch it and look how the cradle swings for hours . . . then, when the baby cries, just give it a slap and—ZAC! The spin of death! And the baby *(Mimes baby's terror)* frozen stiff. Doesn't make a peep for a week!

ANTONIA *(Noticing the size of the lid)*: It looks a little big to me . . .

GIOVANNI: But babies are always growing!

(Antonia stretches out on the bed, unconvinced. An Old Man comes to the door. It's the same actor who played the Sergeant, etc., with a white wig, his face covered in a cobweb of wrinkles.)

OLD MAN: Excuse me. Am I disturbing you?

GIOVANNI: Oh, Papa, what a pleasure. Come in. Come in.

ANTONIA: Hi, Papa!

GIOVANNI: Do you know my friends? This is my father.

OLD MAN: My pleasure.

LUIGI: Giovanni, have you noticed that your father . . . looks a lot like the state trooper and the police sergeant?

GIOVANNI: Don't tell him, because he's already getting a little senile . . .

OLD MAN: I am not senile . . . *(Turns to Margherita)* How is my Antonia . . . oh, how beautiful you look . . . you're getting so much younger all the time.

GIOVANNI: No, Papa, she's not Antonia. That's Antonia.

OLD MAN: Is that so?

ANTONIA: Yes, Papa, it's me.

OLD MAN: What are you doing in bed? Are you sick?

GIOVANNI: No, she's expecting a baby.

OLD MAN: Oh, is that so? And where has he gone? Don't worry . . . you'll see, he'll come back. *(Looks at Luigi and confuses him for his grandson)* Oh, look, he's come back already. And he's all grown-up . . . You shouldn't keep your mamma waiting like that . . .

GIOVANNI: Dad, this is a friend.

OLD MAN: That's good! You should always be friends with your children. But I came here to tell you that they're throwing you out of your house.

GIOVANNI: Who?

OLD MAN: Your landlord. He sent the eviction letter to my house by mistake. Look here. It says that you haven't paid the rent for four months.

GIOVANNI: Don't be silly. It must be a mistake. Let me see that. Antonia always pays the rent on time, isn't that true Antonia?

ANTONIA: Yes, of course.

OLD MAN: In any case, they're going to clear out the whole building, because for months hardly anybody has been paying—

GIOVANNI: Who told you that?

OLD MAN: The sheriff . . . who's clearing people out apartment by apartment . . . a nice man!

(Almost imperceptibly, voices shouting orders are heard outside.)

LUIGI *(Goes to the window)*: Take a look out there on the street. There's a whole squadron of police cars . . .

GIOVANNI: Yeah . . . look at that formation. It's like a war out there. And look at all those trucks.

OLD MAN: Sure, to carry away the furniture and everything else. All for free.

(The noise outside increases: voices of women and children mixed with the shouting of orders.)

VOICE OF A POLICEMAN *(From outside)*: Come on . . . keep it moving . . . carry that stuff out . . . don't leave anything behind!

GIOVANNI: So I guess this eviction letter really is for us. Antonia, for God's sake! How did this happen?

ANTONIA: Don't shout. You'll scare the baby!

GIOVANNI: Okay, I'll speak softly. Antonia, is this true? Answer me.

ANTONIA: Okay: yes, it's true. I haven't paid the rent for four months, and I haven't paid the gas or electricity either . . . that's why they cut our service.

GIOVANNI: They cut off our gas and electric? Because you didn't pay the bill?

ANTONIA: Because with everything we earn between the two of us, there's barely enough to eat.

MARGHERITA: Luigi, I have something to tell you: I haven't paid the rent either.

LUIGI: No!

ANTONIA: See, see, we all have the same problem . . . everyone else who lives in our building, and the people across the street, too . . . and over there . . . everybody.

GIOVANNI: For God's sake, why didn't you tell me that you were short of money?

ANTONIA: But what could you have done . . . go out and commit a robbery?

GIOVANNI: Ah, no, of course not . . . but in the end . . .

ANTONIA: In the end, you would have had a fit and cursed the day you married me. *(Sniffles)*

LUIGI *(To Margherita)*: And you, did you at least pay the gas and electricity?

MARGHERITA: Yes, yes, the gas and the electric, yes!

LUIGI: That's a relief.

GIOVANNI: Come on, don't cry. It's not good for the baby.

OLD MAN: That's right, that's right, everything will be all right. Oh, I just remembered. I came by to bring you something. Wait, I left it outside in the hall. *(Gets a bag and puts it on the table)* Sometimes I'm just not all here. There, look at this. I found this in my shed. It must be yours.

LUIGI *(Goes to the bag and looks inside)*: What's this? Butter, flour, tomatoes?

ANTONIA: I've got nothing to do with it.

GIOVANNI: No, Papa, this isn't our stuff.

OLD MAN: Sure it is. I saw Antonia come out of my shed this morning?

ANTONIA: All right, yes, its the stuff I bought yesterday at reduced prices.

GIOVANNI: At the supermarket?

ANTONIA: Yes, but I only paid for half of it, the rest I stole . . .

GIOVANNI: Stole? You've become a robber?

ANTONIA: Yes!

LUIGI *(To Margherita)*: You, too?

MARGHERITA: Yes, me, too . . .

ANTONIA: No, it's not true . . . she had nothing to do with it! She was just helping me out.

(The two policemen from earlier enter.)

POLICEMAN: Excuse me? The Bardi family . . . is that you?

GIOVANNI: Yes . . .

POLICEMAN: I've got an eviction notice here. You've got a half-hour to get ready. We'll be back in a few minutes to give you a hand . . . *(They leave)*

GIOVANNI: This is really unbelievable . . . I'm losing my mind!

LUIGI: Calm down, Giovanni . . . when it comes to talking about stealing, we should keep our mouths shut.

GIOVANNI: What do you mean "keep our mouths shut"! What's that got to do with it? We were in the middle of the street, don't you understand the difference . . . she's a disgrace, a dishonest criminal.

ANTONIA: Sure, you're right . . . I'm nothing but a criminal who throws mud on your poor but honorable name . . . and who also toys with your delicate sentiments of fatherhood . . . because you should know . . . *(Removes packages from belly)* all I've got in my belly is sugar, rice and pasta.

LUIGI: The baby, the transplant . . . *(To his wife)* Margherita?

GIOVANNI: I'm going to murder her . . . I'll murder her! *(Goes toward Antonia; Luigi blocks him)*

OLD MAN: Well, now that I've done what I came for . . . I'll bid you children good-bye. Have a nice day. *(He leaves)*

(The noises outside get louder: women and men yelling, people shouting orders, sirens.)

GIOVANNI: You dirty liar. How dare you joke about the story of our son! *(To Luigi)* Let me go.

ANTONIA: Let him kill me! Go ahead. I'm sick of this lousy life! And I'm fed up with your sermonizing . . . about law and order, and how you follow the rules, rules, rules . . . with such pride. Bullshit! You swallow your pride every day. And then when other people try to find a little dignity by breaking free of the rules you call them looters, bums, terrorists. Terrorism . . . Terrorism is being held hostage by a minimum-wage job. But you don't want to know how things really are.

GIOVANNI: I know how things are. And I can see. I'm mad as hell and I'm frustrated and I'm not the only one. Nobody can make ends meet. There's Aldo across the street whose wife left him when he lost his job. And how about our neighbors next door. They sleep four to a bed. People are hungry. And when they ask for help nobody listens. And the rage I feel isn't at you . . . it's at myself, and at the impotence I feel . . . when I'm being screwed over every day . . . because I don't see a way out. And it seems there's nobody out there who gives a shit about the people who end up on the street with no place to live. And you know what. I'm starting to take it personally. Because in just a few minutes the homeless are us.

ANTONIA: What happened, Giovanni, is that really you talking? Is your head screwed on straight?

GIOVANNI: I've felt like this for a long time . . . I just never had the courage to say it before. And there's something else you should know about me. I'm a thief too. Look under here. Luigi and I stole these: bags of coffee!

ANTONIA *(Truly astonished)*: You stole!

LUIGI *(Going to the rescue)*: Yes, but he only did it after he got mad about us getting laid off our jobs.

GIOVANNI: No, that was just the last straw . . . because for a long time I'd already been mad enough to scream . . . *(To Antonia)* And one more thing, Antonia . . . This is not a cradle. It's the lid to a dead man's coffin! *(Antonia reaches for her crotch, making the sign that expresses the fear of death)* Look in here. *(Goes to the wardrobe, Antonia and Margherita try to stop him)*

ANTONIA: No, stop, what are you doing?

GIOVANNI: I'm doing what I have to do . . . you should know everything . . .

(Luigi helps Giovanni pull out the casket. The State Trooper is revealed.)

STATE TROOPER: I can see! *(Comes out of wardrobe)* I can see! Santa Eulalia forgave me . . . she blessed me! *(Notices his belly)* I'm pregnant! God bless Santa Eulalia! . . . I'm a mother . . . I'm a mother! *(Exits running)* I'm a mother.

GIOVANNI: What day is it today? *(Hears shots and shouts from outside and runs to the window)* Look, the women are pulling their stuff off of the trucks. The police are shooting!

(The others go to the window.)

LUIGI: Yeah, and look at those kids on the rooftops . . . they're throwing things . . . tiles . . . bricks!

GIOVANNI: The police are shooting to kill. One kid's already down.

MARGHERITA: They're firing for keeps!

(The four of them shout insults out the window.)

ALL: Murderers . . . bastards . . . cowards . . .

LUIGI: They're running away . . . the police are running away!

ANTONIA: And over there, look! That woman has a hunting rifle. There in that window. She's shooting.

LUIGI: It's happening.

GIOVANNI: Of course it's happening. People have been putting up with things out of fear. But fear can turn into rage when you can't see any way out, and you watch your bills piling up and up and up, and you've got nothing in the bank. And you keep getting downsized and downsized and downsized until no one can even see you anymore.

MARGHERITA: There's a limit to what people can take.

ANTONIA: People are hungry. They're not just hungry for food. They're hungry for dignity. They're hungry for justice, for a chance.

GIOVANNI *(To the audience)*: Desperation's funny, isn't it? Especially when it's somebody else's. Then it's really funny. It's a scream. It's a riot. Remember the Los Angeles riots. Nobody expected them. You're smiling, aren't you? Sure, we all know that the poor people just burned down their own neighborhoods, and left themselves flat on their asses with nothing to show for all their rage. But just wait, because it might turn out that, little by little, they're going to get up off their asses onto their knees. And then they just might drag themselves up off the ground and onto their feet. And that's when we better start paying attention, because when people stand up for themselves, they can always find a way to make things happen.

(During this last speech, the lights dim until darkness is complete.

Blackout.)

THE END

ABOUT FACE

BY **DARIO FO**

EDITED BY **FRANCA RAME**

TRANSLATED BY **RON JENKINS**

COMEDY, MADNESS AND FREEDOM

In many of Fo's plays the factual foundation of the plot is based on the complex machinations of Italian politics. The infamous kidnapping of the former prime minister, Aldo Moro, is a case that Fo refers to indirectly in many of his plays. The government refused to negotiate with the kidnappers, who eventually murdered Moro, leading to speculation that he had been abandoned by his fellow politicians who disapproved of his efforts to bring left-wing parties into the government coalition. The Moro case is a landmark in Italian political history that has left the country with vivid and traumatic memories of their government's vulnerability. Fo toys with these memories in plays like *Elizabeth*, in which an elaborate kidnapping plot is part of a conspiracy to remove the Queen from her throne, but the parallels are even stronger in *About Face*, in which Gianni Agnelli, the chairman of Fiat, is abducted by political activists. Agnelli is a well-known figure in Italy and many details in the play are borrowed from the Moro case, but these real-life elements are only Fo's point of departure. He uses the premise to launch into a farcical plot in which Agnelli undergoes plastic surgery that makes him look like one of the workers on his Fiat assembly line. This leads to a continuing crisis of mistaken identities that culminates with a scene in which the worker's wife tries to feed him food that is funneled through a sausage grinder harnessed to his face. Agnelli, who looks like her husband, has told her that after his surgery the only way he can eat is to insert pureed foods through a tube directly into his trachea. When she tries this unusual feeding method on her actual husband he thinks she is trying to punish him for his extramarital affairs, and when the police enter the scene, they make plans to adopt the meat grinder device as an official interrogation method. There is real hunger and the shadow of a genuine national tragedy at the core of this absurd scenario, but Fo uses these elements of reality as a stepping stone for uninhibited lunacy.

Fo's method of mining laughter from actual events provokes his audience into seeing their world from fresh perspectives. In the Brechtian terms of epic theatre, Fo makes the familiar strange, presenting situations that everyone thinks they understand in a context that forces a reexamination of what was once taken for granted.

"Comedy is a form of madness," says Fo, "but it confirms the superiority of reason. If you think of the techniques of comedy . . . they are always directed toward confirming the victory of reason in every discourse, in every story. The authority figure tries to cancel out reason and its dialectic. He wants to substitute a rigid sense of order: 'That's the rule and you have to accept it as written . . . you can't ask for the reason behind it . . . you can't challenge it.' But in the comic's use of paradox there is always a slaughtering of the definitive rules of stability that allows you to watch the prince rolling around with his backside in the air. This changes your perspective on things so that you can see the contradictions and are given the possibility to shout: 'Hey, the figures don't add up; the rules of the game are different; let's think the whole thing out again from the top.'"[1]

Rejecting the commonplace idea that comedy is a realm of irrationality, Fo argues that the disorder of comedy has a deeper purpose. "The irrationality of the comic is only in respect to the irrationality of the rules," says Fo. "In truth, the comic is 'rational.' Walter Benjamin said, 'If the Germans had had a better sense of humor, they would have realized how ridiculous they were and would never have accepted Nazism.' In the moment in which one forgets how to use laughter, reason dies of suffocation. Irony is a irreplaceable dimension of reason. I don't know if you remember another famous paraphrasing of Benjamin who toyed with a phrase of Goya's. Instead of 'the sleep of reason gives birth to monsters,' he said 'the sleep of irony gives birth to monsters . . . who teach in German schools.'"[2]

In Fo's vision of the world clowns are the opposite of dogmatic German school teachers. A clown uses the paradox of comic situations to re-imagine the world as it might be instead of accepting it blindly as it is. When the characters in plays like *About Face* unleash the spirit of carnival into the mundane landscapes they inhabit, there is a sense that justice is being restored. Inspired by the giullari of the Middle Ages, Fo's conception of comedy is similar to the Rabelasian principles articulated by Mikhail Bakhtin in which laughter possesses an "indissoluble and essential relation to freedom."[3]

—Ron Jenkins

This essay is excerpted from the book *Dario Fo & Franca Rame: Artful Laughter* by Ron Jenkins (Aperture, New York, 2001).

1. *Dialogo provocatorio sul comic, il tragico, la follia e la ragione* by Dario Fo with Luigi Allegri (Rome, 1990), 116.
2. Ibid., 116–117.
3. *Rabelais and His World* by Mikhail Bakhtin (University of Indiana Press, Bloomington, 1984), 88–89.

PRODUCTION HISTORY

This translation was first performed at the TOMI Theatre in New York in 1987. The cast was as follows:

ANTONIO BERARDI/GIANNI AGNELLI	Joe Bellan
LUCIA RISMONDI	Lisa Meryll
ROSA BERARDI	Sharon Lockwood
DOCTOR/SPY	Joseph Siravo
INSPECTOR	Victor Arnold
JUDGE/ORDERLY/SPY	Philip Abrams
POLICEMAN/ORDERLY/STAGEHAND	Brian Hargrove
GROUP LEADER/ORDERLY	Warren Keith
	Paul Kerry

CHARACTERS

ANTONIO BERARDI/GIANNI AGNELLI
LUCIA RISMONDI
ROSA BERARDI
DOCTOR/SPY
INSPECTOR
JUDGE/ORDERLY/SPY
POLICEMAN/ORDERLY/STAGEHAND
GROUP LEADER/ORDERLY
WASHING MACHINE MAN/INTERN

SETTING

Prologue

A junkyard

Act One

Scene 1: A hospital in Turin, Italy
Scene 2: The same, two months later

Act Two

Scene 1: Rosa Berardi's apartment
Scene 2: The same, one week later

PROLOGUE

Antonio appears in an automobile junkyard. He stands near the two front seats of the remains of a crashed car.

THE ACTOR PLAYING ANTONIO: Good evening, folks. Tonight I'll be playing the part of Antonio, but I wanted to talk to you first, just so you don't get the wrong idea about this play. Now some of you know that the guy who wrote this farce, Dario Fo, wasn't allowed into the U.S. for several years, because people thought he was trying to overthrow the government. So we want to make it clear right from the start that the incidents described in this play are not intended to be in any way satirical of American politics. Just because there are references to hostage deals that get mixed up with business deals, don't go thinking that this play has anything to do with Ollie North and the Iran-Contra affair. And just because the key figure in the story gets amnesia that allows him to conveniently forget unpleasant details, don't think for a minute that there is any allegorical relationship between this character and our charmingly forgetful former president, Ronald Reagan. Any lingering doubts should be cleared up when we remind you that our character is incapable of telling lies.

Which brings me to tonight's play, in which I play the part of Antonio Berardi, an auto worker for Fiat. The story really began last night about two in the morning when I parked my car in a secluded spot on the outskirts of Turin, just off the road that runs along the canal bank by Barriera di Milano. No, I wasn't alone. I was with a woman . . . and to be honest, it wasn't the woman I'm currently living with, Lucia, the one that Rosa calls "the bitch" . . . Now, don't get me wrong . . . it wasn't an erotic adventure. She was a colleague from work . . . our union delegate. We were talking about layoffs. She told me that the other day at Fiat they sacked two workers for absenteeism—and then they discovered they'd been dead for more than a month. Anyway, one thing led to another, and unexpectedly we made love. Afterwards, I told Lucia about it. Lucia, could you come in please. *(Lucia enters and sits)* When we met this morning at dawn her reaction was less than delicate . . .

LUCIA: So there you were, humping the slut in the middle of the night. Is that what you mean by closer relationships between union leadership and the rank and file?

ANTONIO: For God's sake, will you let me finish my sentence! You're worse than my wife. Don't you realize the trouble I'm in? This is a matter of life and death!

LUCIA: What? Life and death? I'm sorry, Antonio . . . go ahead, tell me. I promise, I won't say another word.

ANTONIO: Let's hope not. How did I ever get mixed up in all this? There I was . . . on the canal bank. . . hugging the union delegate . . . when all of a sudden I see two cars tearing along, neck and neck, trying to pass each other. I said, "Look at those reckless lunatics, racing around at this time of night, on this kind of road. They're liable to skid." I'd hardly finished speaking, when one of the cars skidded. A tremendous crash. The Fiat 132, I recognized it right away because it's the kind we make at the plant, the 132 ended up in a mangled heap just thirty feet away from us . . . The other one comes along, bounces off it, and ends up nose down in the ground. I said: "They've got to be dead."

LUCIA: I would think so. So, what did you do?

ANTONIO: What did I do? I jumped out of my Fiat 128, and ran to see what was happening, to see if I could save someone. The car doors were jammed. I kicked them open. Lots of smoke poured out . . . hell, my eyes were tearing . . . I was coughing . . . but I carried on, all the same: I dragged them out . . . one, two, three . . . they were asphyxiated. All of them, asphyxiated. I tried to pull out the fourth one. You should have seen the state of him. His face was all squashed up against the windshield. What a mess: all pushed-in. Flattened! He was a human pancake! So I dragged him out by the armpits. And just as I was stretching him out on the grass, the engine exploded. BOOM! The flames caught us right in the face, both of us.

LUCIA: Oh, Christ.

ANTONIO: No, not both of us, just him. Because as soon as I saw the flames, I instinctively lifted up the pancake man, and put him in front of me. You know how it is. Instinct. No time to think. So now he's on fire. I start pulling off his clothes: the jacket, the shirt, the pants . . . but he kept on burning all the same, so I took off my jacket and wrapped it around him to put out the last flames. I didn't know what I was getting myself into.

LUCIA: Speaking of getting yourself into things, what about your colleague, the union delegate . . . Did she delegate everything to you, or did she just sit there and watch?

ANTONIO: No. She ran away. As soon as she saw the flames, she grabbed her stuff and ran off with nothing on but her high heels . . . stark naked.

LUCIA: So, she was naked, eh? And you, too.

ANTONIO: No. I was wearing my jacket. No pants, but a jacket. A touch of class. And it was buttoned.

LUCIA: Just a minute, Antonio. Do you have any idea who it was that you pulled out of that burning car?

ANTONIO: No. I don't. Do you?

LUCIA: I have a suspicion. Well, has it occurred to you that it might not have been an ordinary road accident, but that it might have been . . . I don't know . . . an attempted kidnapping?

ANTONIO: I'm no dummy. Of course it occurred to me. But only afterwards. When they began shooting at me with guns.

LUCIA: Shooting at you? But who? When?

ANTONIO: For pity's sake—stop interrupting me.

LUCIA: I won't say another word.

ANTONIO: All right. So I took the pancake man out of the fire. I was dragging him away wrapped in my jacket, when all of a sudden the other three—the asphyxiated ones—start coughing and coming to. So I shouted, "Stop coughing, and come help me take your friend to the hospital. He's dying." But they ignored me. Just staggered around on all fours like constipated sheep. So I dragged the pancake into my car. Put on my pants. Started the engine. And just at that moment: bang, bang, bang. Who was it? The asphyxiated ones. They were coughing and shooting at me. Bastards. I save their lives and they use me for target practice.

LUCIA: What did you do?

ANTONIO: I blinded them with my headlights and tried to run them over. They leapt out of the way. Like frogs. I drove into town to the rotary where the Red Cross ambulances park, and called the stretcher-bearers to come and get the pancake out of my car. They come over with the stretcher and right away they start with the jokes: "Look at the state of this one. Is it homemade or factory fresh?" Suddenly I realized that they thought I was the one who had done it. "Look," I said, "let's just get him down to the hospital, the emergency ward. There'll be a policeman there. I can explain everything to him. The important thing is to get there in a hurry. OK?" "OK." So they put the pancake into the ambulance and told me to follow them in the car. As soon as we got to the first intersection, I cut out.

LUCIA: You're crazy. Why did you do a thing like that?

ANTONIO: Because I was afraid. The police would never believe me.

LUCIA: You're right. But, Antonio, do you know who you saved?

ANTONIO: No. Why? Do you?

LUCIA: Of course. It was Agnelli.

ANTONIO: Agnelli? The president of Fiat? Italy's answer to Lee Iacocca? Cut the crap! Agnelli?

LUCIA: What crap? They announced it this morning on television, in a news flash: "The kidnapping occurred about two o'clock this morning in Barriera di Milano." That's your pancake.

ANTONIO: Agnelli. I saved Agnelli? I took him in my arms. I wrapped him in my jacket . . . Me? If my co-workers at the plant hear about this, they'll come running to greet me with bulldozers. They'll put me against a wall and spit at me . . . and with all the bronchitis that's going around . . . But why didn't you tell me instead of letting me babble like an idiot . . .

LUCIA: I wanted to be sure. But what a mess. This will teach you to go out whoring with union delegates.

ANTONIO: It serves me right. "He who goes whoring with union delegates will be punished by God and forced to save Agnelli." Come on. What else did they say on television?

LUCIA: That Agnelli's been kidnapped. That the kidnappers used a bazooka to shoot poisonous gas into Agnelli's car, paralyzing him and his bodyguards. That the bodyguards came to just in time to see one of the terrorists' accomplices, who "had clearly been parked by the canal for some time."

ANTONIO: Accomplice, eh. So now I'm an accomplice. I'm finished. That's what I get for being a good samaritan. Those bastards!

LUCIA: Antonio. Calm down. You'll see. As soon as Agnelli regains consciousness in the hospital, he'll explain that he's Gianni Agnelli, and he'll tell how you saved his life, and everything will be fine and dandy.

ANTONIO: Sure. As soon as he wakes up he'll say: "Hello, I'm Gianni Agnelli . . . I demand to see immediately the metal mechanic without his pants who saved my life. I love him. I'll marry him. In white." Forget it. With the beating he took, it'll be a miracle if he even remembers his name when he wakes up. "Who are you? Mama!"

LUCIA: Is he really in such bad shape?

ANTONIO: No. I'm the one who's in bad shape. Do you realize that the stretcher-bearers saw my face from only three feet away? My portrait is going to be in all the papers today. A police sketch. And underneath there'll be a caption: "Head Terrorist."

LUCIA: You're exaggerating, as usual. First of all, there's no police sketch in the paper. *(Pulls a paper out of her bag and gives it to Antonio)*

ANTONIO: What paper is that?

LUCIA: Special edition. I bought it an hour ago.

ANTONIO: Christ, they're quick. *(Reads)* "Terrorists take car czar for a ride . . . Lee Iacocca might be next victim . . . Headless body found at topless bar . . . Pope offers himself as hostage in exchange for Agnelli . . . Along with thirteen cardinals, ten of whom are black."

LUCIA: There, you see? It's the usual crap. But not a word about you or Agnelli in the hospital. Listen, Antonio. Tomorrow you should go into work at Fiat, as if nothing had happened.

ANTONIO: You're crazy. Go down there and say, "Here I am . . ." Here I am!

LUCIA: Where?

ANTONIO: Here. I'm here at the bottom of the page: "Fried-Faced Factory Worker: Thirty-year-old, Antonio Berardi, skilled worker at the Mira Fiori Fiat plant, was admitted to the hospital by persons unknown, early this morning. His face was severely disfigured by burns. His wife, Rosa Berardi, has been traced thanks to documents which the victim had in his jacket." I left everything in my jacket. I left my driver's license. My union card. *(Stops. He laughs)* Ha. Ha. Ha.

LUCIA: What's so funny?

ANTONIO: Agnelli is a member of the union! If he dies now, they'll give him a funeral with red flags. Look at this! "Rosa Berardi has been invited to the hospital to identify her husband."

LUCIA: Hey, Antonio, Rosa's bound to identify Agnelli as you.

ANTONIO: Look, you're going to have to stop thinking of my wife as a mental incompetent. This is a trap and I'm not falling for it.

LUCIA: What kind of trap?

ANTONIO: They wrote it to trick me into going to the hospital like some kind of prick: "Hey, Rosa, don't identify him as me, because here I am, big as life. He's somebody else." BAM! Immediate arrest of half-wit terrorist. Why don't you go and check it out?

LUCIA: You're right. I'll go to the hospital and find out what's happening.

(Blackout.)

ACT ONE

SCENE 1

Curtain goes up on the intensive care unit of a hospital. Scaffolding descends from the ceiling full of lamps and gadgets that make it resemble the cockpit of a spaceship. Nurses scurry about in green shirts and pants, green caps and plastic gloves. They wear clownish antiseptic masks on their faces. With stylized movements they bring in electronic apparatuses and rolling chairs, all covered in plastic to indicate a scrupulously antiseptic atmosphere. A nurse rolls in a silver bust mounted on a metal base, also wrapped in plastic.

Enter Rosa, the Doctor and Orderlies.

DOCTOR: This way please, madam.

ROSA *(Almost bumping into the bust of Agnelli)*: Oh, God, who's that?

DOCTOR: It's a statue of Agnelli. The entire Recovery Ward was built with funds from the Agnelli Foundation.

ROSA: I thought it was a saint. *(Nurse offers Rosa a robe)* Do I have to put it on?

ORDERLY: Of course, madam.

DOCTOR: Madam, if you don't feel up to it, we could postpone it until later . . .

ROSA: No. No. I want to see him right away. I'm ready.

DOCTOR: I'm afraid he looks pretty awful, even to us. And we're used to it. He's completely disfigured, you know.

ROSA: Disfigured. *(Starts to cry)* Oh God. Poor Antonio . . . *(Nurse puts hospital overshoes on her feet)* What are you doing? Oh, it's for waxing the floor? Go right ahead. Thank you. Disfigured, eh? And to think, he had such a handsome face, so open and likeable . . . well, anyway, I liked it . . . You won't believe this, professor, but I still loved him, you know, even if he really didn't deserve it . . . the way he treated me . . .

DOCTOR: She's getting upset. Prepare me a solution with twenty drops of Asvanol Complex.

ROSA: Forget it, doc . . . I don't need it . . . I told you already . . . I don't have any emotions left . . . my husband was like a stranger to me.

DOCTOR: It's just a precaution. I don't want to risk provoking a trauma in you, but it's for identification purposes. Unfortunately the law requires it. Now come along, madam, and be strong.

(The Doctor gives a sign and a bed is rolled in. On it is a body, which is presumably Rosa's husband Antonio. Actually it is a puppet covered in bandages and casts from head to foot. The Nurses attach it to thin wires suspended from the ceiling scaffolding so that its limbs move when the wires are pulled, like a giant marionette. The puppet's arrival is accompanied by a musical flourish.)

ROSA: Oh, my God, Antonio. What have they done to you? *(She faints)*

DOCTOR: Come on. Come on. Be brave. Breathe deeply.

ROSA *(Waking up)*: His nose . . . he doesn't have a nose . . . It's mashed to a pulp . . . and he's already got a sinus condition. His chin too. It's gone. Let me get closer. Closer.

DOCTOR: No. Get her away.

ROSA: They erased him. There's nothing left . . . except for his ears. Antonio. Antonio. You see? He has two ears, but he doesn't listen to me.

DOCTOR: Of course not. He's in a deep coma.

ROSA: Oh, he's lost weight. It's that little bitch that ruined him, the one who stole him away from me. She has him out jogging. Imagine, a man of his age . . . You force him to go running in a red track suit with Penzoil written all over the back . . . a beret with Exxon stamped all over it, and Michelin track shoes . . . he looked like a Formula One Ferrari. And she's got him on a macrobiotic diet. He eats nothing but wheat germ.

DOCTOR: Hurry up with that solution and get me a syringe with Mecardizol.

ROSA: You can forget about the syringe, if it's for me. I'm allergic. It gives me an abscess on my butt. And they talk about crime and terrorism. What about this? What about those bastard managers at the Fiat plant, working for Agnelli. They must have sent him to repair some generator, hanging who knows how many feet up in the air without protection . . . and splat. A triple somersault without a net. Like a circus act . . .

DOCTOR: No, madam, the accident didn't happen at the circus . . . I mean at the Fiat factory.

ROSA: Oh no? And how can you be so sure. Were you there?

DOCTOR: No, but the hospital has already conducted an investigation. Yesterday, your husband was absent from work all afternoon.

ROSA: Then where did it happen?

DOCTOR: Maybe he was hit by a car. Hit and run. In fact the man who brought him to the Red Cross, disappeared immediately.

ROSA: Oh, Antonio. Dear Antonio. What a mess. If only you had stayed with me. I bet they ran you over while you were out jogging. It's all that bitch's fault . . . Don't get me wrong, doctor . . . she's a good-looking girl, but she's a dope. Any girl who's twenty-seven can make a guy fall for her. She makes me laugh. You should have seen me at that age. I don't want to brag, but when I walked down the street, store windows collapsed. What a crash!

DOCTOR: I believe it. After all, you're still a beautiful woman.

ROSA: I know.

DOCTOR: It's the truth . . . Now, if you don't mind, let's get back to your husband. Take a good look at his hands. Do you recognize them?

(Nurses pull the strings to move hands of puppet.)

ROSA: No, not now. They look like two pieces of boiled meat. But later, yes . . . when he's better . . . because he is going to get better, isn't he, doctor? . . . Swear to me that he'll get better!

DOCTOR: Yes, madam. I assure you, we're doing everything possible . . . your husband is a very strong man.

ROSA: Ah, yes. He's strong. Very strong. He was so healthy. So energetic. He never held himself back. For example, every year at the Unity Festival . . .

DOCTOR: So, you're communists, are you?

ROSA: Oh, we've been communists for generations . . . it's a family tradition . . . As I was saying, at the Unity Festival, he was in charge of everything: he used to put up the stalls, sell the books, and buy them too . . . In the political debates he would present all the arguments, and then he'd present all the counterarguments, and the self-criticism too, all by himself. It's not that he was a fanatic . . . No, far from it. He was always having discussions, especially with the Party leaders . . . Even after he had accepted the Third Road to socialism, he was always ready to try the shortcut to the Fourth Road, and the detour on the Fifth Road . . . because, as Karl Marx says, "The roads to socialism are infinite." Of course, she was always there behind him, the bitch, egging him on. Because she was an extremist. You know, she's one of those intellectuals who's always trying to tell working people what to think. The type who's crazy about the masses, but can't stand crowds. By the way, where is she now? Is she here?

(Inadvertantly Rosa grabs a cable which has the effect of raising up the entire bandaged body. The Nurses rush to the rescue.)

DOCTOR: No! Madam, what are you doing? Don't touch.

ROSA: Oh my God. What have I done? Did I break him? But it's your fault, too. Leaving your cords hanging out like that. Why don't you put up a sign: "Don't touch the cords"? Oh, what a scare. I'm going to cry. *(To an Orderly)* Excuse me, do you have a kleenex, so I can blow my nose.

ORDERLY: Here you are, madam.

ROSA: Poor Antonio. And how's he gonna blow his nose, now that he doesn't have one?

DOCTOR: Don't worry, madam. We'll make him another nose, and he'll be able to blow it as much as he wants.

(Three Nurses lift the Doctor so that he is suspended horizontally above the puppet. He inserts forceps into the puppet's face.)

ROSA: Do you always work in such an uncomfortable position, doctor? Another nose? You're going to transplant one from a dead man? But what if his body rejects it and his nose drops off in his handkerchief while he's blowing it. No, no nose. Give him back to me like this . . . streamlined.

DOCTOR: No, no transplant. You are very fortunate, madam. Our institution is at the forefront of plastic surgery techniques. Our chief surgeon is one of the best in the world.

ROSA: Doctor, he's looking at me. See, there. With the corner of his eye peeking out from the swelling. He sees me. He recognizes me. I'm sure of it. Antonio, Antonio, it's me, your Rosa. As soon as I heard what happened, I forgot everything . . . Here I am . . . no hard feelings . . . in fact, to tell you the truth, Antonio, I'm even happy that this terrible thing has happened . . . No, no. I don't mean that. What I mean is that I'm happy that you still need me. I forgive you . . . I still love you . . . I don't care about you jogging with her and eating wheat germ together. We'll forget everything, and make it all like it was before. We'll bury the past. *(The patient groans)* No, Antonio, I didn't say that we'd bury you. Oh, what a stupid thing to say. But his jawbone, it's all gone. There's just a big hole.

DOCTOR: The mandible is certainly in bad shape . . . unfortunately, we'll have to replace it with an entirely new prosthetic apparatus.

ROSA: An entirely new prosthetic apparatus?

DOCTOR: Exactly. We rebuild it entirely on the basis of the original bone structure. We remove the parts which are broken, and we replace them. Incidentally, you'll have to bring me some photographs. Do you have any recent ones?

ROSA: No, doctor. I'm sorry, but since my husband left me, I haven't been interested in having my photograph taken. I still work as a hairdresser, but I've let myself go a bit.

DOCTOR: No, you don't understand. Not photographs of you. Photographs of your husband.

ROSA: Ah, yes. How stupid of me. I have some that are stunning. It just so happens that I carry one with me all the time. It's recent. I'm sorry it's a little ripped up, but you see he was standing next to the bitch, and I didn't want to carry her around in my bag all day, so I cut her out and hung her on my wall . . . with two needles in her eyes for . . . People tell me that it really does work, you know. An Indian custom . . . You're a doctor. You wouldn't happen to know if that will make her go blind? *(Rosa shows him the photo)* Will that do? Look what a nice face he has.

DOCTOR: Yes, good. It's clear enough. We're lucky. It will help us a bit in the projections.

ROSA: Projections?

DOCTOR: Yes. First you project the image of the patient's face, from the photograph, and then you reconstruct it around a wax skull.

ROSA: A wax skull?

DOCTOR: Yes. First we reconstruct the bone structure, and then the whole thing is covered with skin.

ROSA: With skin? With artificial skin? Vinyl? What color will you make him for me?

DOCTOR: No. Not artificial. Real skin. His skin. We take it from here. From the gluteus.

ROSA: From his butt. You're going to take the skin off his ass and put it on his face. Oh, Antonio, Antonio. What a calamity.

(Rosa inadvertently leans on a lever that releases a lamp, which falls on the bandaged body.)

DOCTOR: No. Not the lever.

(Interlude: when the lamp falls the Inspector enters.)

INSPECTOR: Allow me . . . one moment . . . Are these photographs recent?

ROSA: Yes. Is he the head surgeon?

INSPECTOR: No. I'm a police inspector.

ROSA: Ah, police? Are you here to find out who messed up my husband?

INSPECTOR: Yes, of course . . .

ROSA: Well, there's no point in asking him. Go and ask those bastards at Fiat. Go and ask Agnelli.

INSPECTOR: Now, madam, there's no need to bring Mr. Agnelli into this. Who knows where the poor man is at the moment.

ROSA: Look, doctor, he woke up! When he heard Agnelli's name he opened his eyes. Antonio, Antonio, they kidnapped Agnelli. They don't know where he is, but, Antonio, I promise you that if they ever find him, I'll mash his face up just like yours.

DOCTOR: Madam, I've already told you he doesn't understand . . .

ROSA: He understands all right. There's a gleam in his eye. *(Enter Orderly with paper in his hand)*

ORDERLY: Excuse me, doctor, there's a woman outside. Claims to be a relative of the patient, Antonio Berardi. She's asking if it's possible to see him.

ROSA: Let me see that. Who is this relative?

ORDERLY: I don't know. Here're the details.

ROSA: Give that to me.

DOCTOR: No, madam, please. I am the doctor here, until proven otherwise, and I'm the one who decides who gets in. *(Reads)* Lucia Rismondi. Do you know her?

ROSA: It's the bitch. That bimbo! She's got the nerve to pass herself off as a relative, just because she was sleeping with my husband. The whore.

DOCTOR: Calm down, madam. Calm down.

ROSA: How dare she! Why should I calm down? I'm furious. Humiliating me like that. Here I am, heartbroken, with my streamlined husband, and she comes here just to spite me . . .

DOCTOR: Madam, stop it. I can't stand scenes. I warn you that if you don't start behaving more civilly, I'll have you thrown out and I won't let you come back to visit your husband for at least a month. Is that clear?

ROSA: Who do you think you're talking to? In that arrogant tone. Go use it on some patient in a coma. Not on me. I'm involved in politics. I've opened birth control clinics. I'm not some timid woman who lets herself be put down by the voice of authority. No, sir. I am the patient's wife. I can come whenever I want. That's the law. After all, my husband is in a coma. And if you try to stop me, I'll stage a sit-in right here in front of the hospital.

INSPECTOR: Madam, I'm conducting an investigation to find out what happened to your husband. This woman might be able to provide us with some clues.

ROSA: But she doesn't know anything, because she never saw anything. And anyway, she's about to go blind from the needles.

INSPECTOR: Get out. Get out.

ROSA: Oh God, I feel sick. Oh my head.

DOCTOR: Madam, don't start play-acting . . . Get me the smelling salts . . . come on. Come on. Breathe in deeply.

ROSA *(Coughing)*: I'm suffocating . . . Doctor . . . you're crazy. What kind of stench are you giving me to breathe . . . Now I really do feel sick.

DOCTOR: No, you're not sick. Be good and go over there.

ROSA: Wait a second. Let me catch my breath. I've got to do some self-criticism here.

DOCTOR: Oh my God.

ROSA: You're right. I've behaved really badly. I've been selfish. In the end, that poor girl has the right to see my husband, too. If she's in love, it's not her fault. She's so young and pretty too. She's educated. She's got a degree. A scholar. She could have taken up with a professor like yourself, or if she was really desperate, she could have taken up with an inspector, like you . . . But no . . . she decided to choose my husband . . . That's something a wife should be proud of, don't you think? I'm very happy. Please, inspector, don't send me away. I can't wait to meet her . . . the wonderful girl.

INSPECTOR: OK, OK. As long as you stay there and keep your mouth shut.

DOCTOR: All right, inspector. Shall we let her in?

INSPECTOR: Of course.

DOCTOR: Let the lady in.

(There is a moment of embarrassment when Lucia enters.)

LUCIA: Mrs. Berardi . . . excuse me for taking the liberty . . . perhaps I shouldn't have . . . I know . . .

ROSA: No, don't worry. You did right. He'll be glad to see you . . . maybe . . . even if he doesn't recognize you.

LUCIA: Hasn't he regained consciousness yet?

ROSA: Yes he has . . . and he recognized me. I don't know if he'll recognize you, since he's only known you for such a short time.

LUCIA: Are you sure it's really him?

INSPECTOR: One moment. Excuse me. Miss, would you mind coming over to the bed . . .

ROSA: Wait a moment, inspector.

LUCIA: Inspector?

ROSA: Yes, he's here for the investigation. Don't let him rush you. Now, come with me. I warn you, Antonio is in bad shape. You've got to be brave . . . He's got nothing left . . . except his ears.

LUCIA: Oh my God, it's terrible. It's him . . . it's him.

DOCTOR: Are you sure? How can you recognize him?

ROSA: It was his hands, wasn't it?

INSPECTOR: Don't prompt her.

ROSA: Who's prompting?

LUCIA: By his ears.

INSPECTOR: His ears?

LUCIA: Yes, I've studied every inch of those ears.

DOCTOR: You've studied his ears.

ROSA: She's studied his ears. What an intellectual.

LUCIA: Yes, you see . . . I practice acupuncture . . . I even went to China for a training course . . . and since Antonio had a sinus problem . . .

ROSA: Yes, yes, his sinuses. It's true. He suffered so much.

LUCIA: So in order to cure him, I put needles in his ears. That's how I recognize him now. As you know, professor, every ear has its own particular physiognomy . . . In fact, if you take a wax mold of the auditory pavilion, you get a shape which looks like a little fetus, which is none other than a miniature portrait of us as we were in our mothers' wombs.

INSPECTOR: Like seeing a snapshot of ourselves as a baby.

ROSA: A fetus in your ear. I'll have to tell them that at the birth control clinic.

DOCTOR: It's true. In Germany the police laboratories don't use fingerprints anymore, but take wax molds of the auditory chambers of their suspects.

INSPECTOR: Incredible. Every time they make an arrest. POW! A fistful of boiling wax in the ear. Incredible. Those Germans. Well, now there's no doubt about it. It's him. Antonio Berardi. Thank you, ma'am, for your cooperation.

LUCIA: Don't mention it.

ROSA: No, don't be modest. You were wonderful. Our Antonio made a good choice. He's so clever. Come, we'll let him see us both together. He'll like that . . . Antonio, here's your girlfriend. Are you happy? . . . Doctor, doctor, he's trying to say something.

(Rosa loses her balance and grabs some of the loose cords. The dummy flies up into the air. Chaos.
Blackout.)

SCENE 2

The same hospital, two months later. The bed is no longer there.

DOCTOR: Madam, this may seem immodest, but you're going to have to give us credit for the miraculous things that we've managed to achieve. You'll see: a masterpiece.

(The Double is rolled into the room in a wheelchair. His face is bandaged with a web of elastic bands, which are connected to rings on his chin, nose, cheeks and forehead. The Nurses hold strings connected to these rings.)

ROSA: I'm all choked up. It reminds me of a movie I saw when I was a girl: *The Living Mummy*, where they unbandaged someone just like this. There he is . . . Look . . . It's him . . . It's him . . . Frankenstein!

DOCTOR: What are you talking about, madam? He's perfect.

ROSA: Yes, yes. That's him exactly. You did a wonderful job, except for the stitches all over his face.

DOCTOR: Yes, that can't be helped . . . but they'll disappear in a few days. Some of them will dissolve . . . and with the rest you can just pull out the strings.

ROSA: But if I pull the thread out, everything will come undone and his face will fall all over the floor. Oh God. I'm so happy that I'm talking nonsense. Oh, Antonio. If you could only see yourself. You're almost better than before. Antonio, how do you feel? Answer me.

DOCTOR: Gently, madam, gently . . . he has to get used to speaking again . . . We have to go gradually . . . Remember that we have rebuilt his entire jawbone and palate.

ROSA: I get it. Now it has to be broken in, like a new car.

DOCTOR: Just leave it to me. Mr. Berardi, try opening your mouth slowly. Let's see if you can do it.

(The movements of the Double in bandages are aided by the Nurses.)

ROSA: It's opening. It's opening.

DOCTOR: Bravo. And now, try it with me. Repeat what I say: Ahaa . . .

DOUBLE: Ahaa . . .

ROSA: He said, "Ahaa."

DOCTOR: Please, madam, be quiet. Once more: Ahaa . . . Uhuuu . . .

ROSA: Come on, Antonio. Do: "Uhuuu," like the doc says.

DOUBLE: Uhuuu.

DOCTOR: No, first, "Ahaa," then, "Uhuuu." Pay attention to me, not your wife. Once more: Ahaa . . . Uhuuu . . .

DOUBLE: Ahaa . . . Uhuuu . . . Ehee.

ROSA: He said, "Ehee," all on his own. He's so smart.

DOCTOR: No, not at all. He shouldn't do that. Mr. Berardi, you must pronounce only the sounds that I ask you to make.

ROSA: OK, but if he wants to make an "ehee," what do you have to go and stop him for?

DOCTOR: Madam, you have to realize that the sound "ehee" requires the jawbone to extend to its maximum limit, with the risk that it might come out of its mastoid socket.

ROSA: Does that mean that my Antonio will have to talk without ever saying "ehee." What a disaster! He won't be able to sing the *Internationale*. *(She tries to sing it without "ehee")*

DOCTOR: No. He'll be able to say "ehee" too, but later. First he must make the intermediate sounds like: braa, broo, brii . . .

DOUBLE: Braa, broo, brii . . . *(His sounds turn into jazz scats)*

DOCTOR: There. That's perfect. And now say: gastric . . . gastropod.

DOUBLE: Gaastric, gaasopo.

DOCTOR: No, articulate it properly: Gas-tro-pod.

DOUBLE: Gasto, gasta . . . gestapo . . . Braa, bruu, brii . . .

DOCTOR: Silence. And now say: astronaut, manumission, concupiscence.

ROSA: Hey, doc. Are you crazy? What kind of words are you teaching him. He's a worker. For God's sake, make him say the words he's going to use every day, like wage freeze, layoffs . . .

DOCTOR: Listen, I'm doing the teaching here. Come on, Mr. Berardi: astronaut, manumission, concupiscence.

ROSA AND DOUBLE: Concu . . . concu . . . concu . . . screw you.

DOCTOR: What???

ROSA: See, now you've made him angry. *(The Double gets up and walks to the door)* I'll stop him. I'm his wife. Antonio, you can't go out. Antonio, stop. But look how he's walking. You must have done something wrong. Antonio, stop making like an elephant.

DOUBLE: Don't-you-start-too-madam.

ROSA: Doctor, did you hear? He called me "madam." He's pretending he doesn't know me. Antonio, dear, I'm your wife.

DOUBLE: Wife? What wife? Noooooooooo!

(He leaves, dragging the web of strings with him.)

ROSA: Did you hear that. Where's he going? Stop him, doc.

DOCTOR: No, let him take a little walk. Where can he go? He'll go to his room. And you, madam, don't be offended. Try to understand, after all these months of tension, with one operation after another . . . naturally his nerves are frayed. You should think about the happy outcome of this experiment . . . treatment.

ROSA: What happy outcome? I've been visiting him for months and he's never even looked at me. Then when he opens his mouth it's, "Braa, bruu, brii," and, "What do you mean 'wife?'"

(Inspector enters.)

INSPECTOR: Excuse me, professor, did you give the prisoner . . . sorry, the patient, permission to leave?

DOCTOR: Yes, let him go back to his room.

INSPECTOR: But he's not going back to his room. He's taking the elevator to the ground floor, to the exit.

DOCTOR: My God. He's losing his mind. Stop him.

INSPECTOR: Already done. I sent two of my men to nab him. Lucky we were on the lookout, or he'd have slipped away.

ROSA: What do you mean slip away? Have you seen the way he walks. He would have ended up in the zoo.

INSPECTOR: Yes, of course. Listen, madam, would you mind stepping outside for a moment? I'd like a word with the doctor, privately.

ROSA: OK, I'm going. People are always throwing me out. I'll go find Antonio . . . I'll give him some speech therapy on my own . . . I'll teach him to say: "I love you, Rosa. I'm leaving the bitch. I'm coming back to you." And you can stick your astronaut up your manumission.

INSPECTOR: Well, professor. It seems that everything went fine, right?

DOCTOR: Wonderfully, In a few days he'll be speaking almost perfectly.

INSPECTOR: Congratulations. I'd like to start right away with a few simple questions.

DOCTOR: All right, but only under my supervision. It's very dangerous to force things.

INSPECTOR: Yes, of course you can stay. In fact you can give us a hand. Would you mind if I invited the judge in? *(Calling offstage)* Your honor, step this way. *(Judge enters)*

PROFESSOR: . . . No, you can introduce yourselves. I'm very bad with names. *(Enter a Policeman with a typewriter)* This is my assistant . . . you know, to transcribe his testimony.

DOCTOR: What testimony? I still don't understand what you suspect him of . . .

JUDGE: Well, for a start we've discovered that the red Fiat 128 registered in Berardi's name is the same car that the terrorists . . . *(The Inspector signals the Judge to keep quiet)* But that's not important. What were you saying about the patient?

DOCTOR: Surely you don't think that the patient is ready. We must proceed gradually. It will be very difficult to get him to answer questions logically. Almost certainly, the trauma which caused his coma has flattened all his mnemonic-responsive anafracts. *(Doctor uses the head of the Policeman to demonstrate)*

INSPECTOR: "Mnemonic-responsive anafracts"? What does that mean?

(All though this speech, the Doctor is using the Policeman's head to make his points. The Policeman is on a rolling chair and his typewriter is on a rolling stand. He is propelled around the room by the Doctor's demonstration.)

DOCTOR: You see, in the central posterior parts of the brain, known as the mnemechaea, there is a space which we could call the memory warehouse. In this warehouse there are thousands of relays, which, when activated, switch on a number of tapes, on which are stored, memories, words, sensations, in short, everything that has happened in our lives.

INSPECTOR: So the trauma will have erased all his tapes? *(The Inspector also gesticulates on the head of the Policeman)*

DOCTOR: No, not all, but most of them. Perhaps only one, tiny, insignificant detail will pop up. Everything else will have been erased.

INSPECTOR: What if the subject just pretends he can't remember, or invents things to avoid telling the truth.

(The Judge and the Inspector continue alternately to bang on the head of the Policeman. He is pummeled into submission.)

DOCTOR: No, impossible. In this first phase, which we call the phase of innocence, the patient is incapable of practicing deceptions, because the fiction mechanism, which is the most exposed and ephemeral part of the brain, is always the first to be destroyed by any violent trauma.

(The Judge also tries to put his hands on the Policeman's head, but now he resists.)

JUDGE: To sum it up, they don't know how to pretend or lie. And does this happen in every case?

DOCTOR: Yes, in every case except that of politicians. Their fiction mechanisms are immune to trauma.

INSPECTOR: Here he is. They found him outside hailing a taxi.

(The Double enters walking like a wobbly flamingo. They sit him down on a wheeled office chair.)

DOCTOR: Here you are, Mr. Berardi. Just sit down and relax. These gentlemen would like to ask you a few questions. Please, don't press him. Let him free-associate.

INSPECTOR: Of course. OK, tell us where were you running off to in such a hurry?

DOCTOR: Come on, try to answer.

DOUBLE: Gasteronomical . . . gastero . . . could you repeat the question please.

INSPECTOR: Where were you running off to?

DOUBLE: Ruuuuuuuuuning ooofff. But I didn't want to run off . . . I oooonly waaaanted to goooo.

JUDGE: Go where?

DOUBLE: To headquarters.

INSPECTOR: What headquarters.

DOUBLE: To the headquarters . . . which . . . after . . . over theeere *(With a series of gestures he describes stairs, lifts, doorbells, etc.)* Fruut . . . tracht . . . drinn . . . sciacco . . . ploch. *(Gibberish)*

DOCTOR: No. Don't strain yourself. Calm down and relax.

JUDGE: Yes. Of course. Calm down. Relax. We only want to have a little chat . . . among friends.

INSPECTOR: To help you . . . so you can practice speaking.

DOUBLE: Practice speaking . . . among friends? Are these your frieeends, professor. And this one with the typewriter. Is he your friend too? What's he writing?

INSPECTOR: He's taking notes on what you say, so that we can monitor your progress.

DOUBLE: Ah . . . yes? And theen you'll let me read whaat I said . . . and what he has written?

INSPECTOR: Certainly, and sign it too.

DOUBLE: Sign? Why sign?

INSPECTOR: No reason.

DOUBLE: No. You're lying. Liar! Liar!

INSPECTOR: Stop that.

DOUBLE: Liar.

INSPECTOR: Now let's start with something simple. What's your name?

DOUBLE: Well . . . everyone calls me Antonio . . . even that awful woman . . . who drives me mad . . . Antoniooo . . . Antonioooo . . . Antonioooo.

JUDGE: Your wife?

DOUBLE: My wife? Yes, she says, "I'm your wife," . . . but I don't remember her. It's just as well I don't remember her, because . . . whoof . . . clacht . . . vruttt . . . Toniooooo. Bruuu. Antoniooo . . . Antonio . . .

DOCTOR: Calm down. We won't talk about your wife anymore.

JUDGE: We won't talk about your wife anymore.

INSPECTOR: We won't talk about her anymore.

DOUBLE: No more talking about my wife. Promise.

JUDGE AND DOCTOR: Promise.

INSPECTOR: What do you mean, "Promise"? We don't have much time.

DOUBLE: Promise, liar, promise.

INSPECTOR: OK. Promise. *(The Inspector crosses his fingers, like a child negating his promise, and continues angrily)* Now, what do you remember about the accident?

DOUBLE *(Goes crazy)*: Ahaa . . . fruutt . . . gut . . . gut . . . sgnach . . . bataplum . . . plaff . . . oeuh.

DOCTOR: No. I'm sorry, but you're doing it all wrong. You have to approach it more tactfully. Get at it indirectly.

JUDGE: You're right. Listen, Mr. Berardi, do you remember anything from your childhood?

DOUBLE *(To Doctor)*: He's taking the long way around. *(To the Judge)* Yes. My childhood. I liked cars . . . since I was little.

JUDGE: But all little boys like cars.

DOUBLE: I liked them more. I lived in a big mansion.

DOCTOR: Remembering our childhood, everything seems big.

DOUBLE: Sometimes later too.

POLICEMAN: Should I write down the part about the cars and the mansion?

INSPECTOR: No, leave out the stupid things that don't make any sense.

JUDGE: What do you recall about your mother and father?

DOUBLE: My mother . . . I don't remember . . . No . . . nothing . . . Mommy, no . . . At this moment of my mommy I have no recollection.

JUDGE: You don't remember?

DOUBLE: I'm trying to remember . . . my mommy.

INSPECTOR: Don't strain yourself.

DOUBLE: Wait a minute. I want to remember.

JUDGE: You don't have to.

DOUBLE: I want to remember. I loved my mommy. I don't remember my mommy. I don't have a mommy. I've looked all over my memory. I don't have a mommy. *(Rests his head on the Inspector's shoulder)*

INSPECTOR: What are you doing?

DOUBLE: I need a little tender loving support.

INSPECTOR: What do you mean, "tender loving support"?

DOUBLE: Just a little bit.

INSPECTOR: Please get a hold of yourself.

DOUBLE: Have a heart. Have a heart, for my mama.

INSPECTOR: That's enough. Let's go on to another subject. I don't give a damn about your mother.

DOUBLE: He said he doesn't "give a damn" about my mother. You better pray to God that my memory doesn't come back, because if my memory does come back and I remember who I am and who I was . . . watch out . . .

pscc . . . pscc . . . plat . . . But I do remember my papa. He always took me to see the cars.

INSPECTOR: Did he work at Fiat, too?

DOUBLE: Eh? Work? *(Rests his head on the Inspector's shoulder)*

INSPECTOR: Please, control yourself.

DOUBLE: My father was a little strange. I remember he put on a black shirt and then said Mussolini was a ball buster . . . Ha . . . Ha . . . Oh, look. I can laugh. Ah. It does me good to talk. I feel like I'm getting better already.

JUDGE: Sure. He was a worker, with a black shirt.

DOUBLE: Gastropod, astronaut . . . concupiscent . . . astronaut . . .

(The Policeman types frantically.)

INSPECTOR: What are you typing there? *(Policeman stops typing for a moment, then continues)*

JUDGE: Listen, do you feel up to telling us about the accident? Without straining yourself, though.

DOUBLE: Ahhh . . . Vrrr . . . peee . . . ooonly fragments . . . I remember I was in a car . . . and there was another car . . . two cars.

INSPECTOR: There were two cars?

DOUBLE: There was a race.

JUDGE: A chase . . . and you? . . .

DOUBLE: I was in the car.

JUDGE: Behind.

DOUBLE: Behind . . .

JUDGE AND INSPECTOR: The car behind. Wonderful.

DOUBLE: No . . . no . . . That's wrong.

INSPECTOR: What do you mean, no?

DOUBLE: I made a mistake.

INSPECTOR: The first answer is the one that counts.

DOUBLE: Liar . . . liar.

INSPECTOR: OK . . . let's not start that again.

DOUBLE: Imposters. Hypocrites.

DOCTOR: You shouldn't put words in his mouth. I already told you, let him free-associate.

INSPECTOR: OK. OK. Free-associate.

DOUBLE: Yes . . . I'm going . . . going fast . . . always faster . . .

buambamim . . . trum . . . slaff . . . then . . . enough . . . I can't remember anymore.

INSPECTOR: Try. Just a little more.

DOUBLE: There . . . yes flames . . . I'm burning. Aieuuuuu . . .

INSPECTOR: What's wrong. Calm down.

DOCTOR: I told you not to push him too far. *(Fixes the Double's dislocated jaw)* There, that's better.

DOUBLE: Thank you.

DOCTOR: Don't mention it.

DOUBLE: Ah, yes. Then I remember a voice shouting: "Agnelli. They're carrying away Agnelli."

INSPECTOR: Terrific. Write that down.

DOUBLE: Why is it terrific? What does it mean? Would you explain to me who this Agnelli is? Every once in a while, that word pops into my mind.

JUDGE: I bet it does.

DOUBLE: What?

JUDGE: Never mind. Now, what does the name Fiat mean to you?

DOUBLE: Fiat? Well, I feel like it's almost . . . how can I say it . . . like part of my family. Fiat.

JUDGE: Like part of your family.

DOUBLE: As if it were something that belonged to me.

DOCTOR: It's incredible how attached these workers are to Fiat.

JUDGE: And now could you tell us a little about your work.

DOUBLE: Work?

JUDGE: What work did you do at Fiat?

DOUBLE: Work?

INSPECTOR: Yes, work.

DOUBLE: At Fiat? Work?

JUDGE: Work . . .

INSPECTOR: Work.

JUDGE: Work . . . sweat . . .

DOUBLE: Sweat . . . work . . . sweat . . .

JUDGE: At Fiat . . .

DOUBLE: Work . . . sweat?

INSPECTOR: Yes.

DOUBLE: They're words without meaning . . .

JUDGE *(To the Policeman)*: Denigrates work!

INSPECTOR: And "profit," "production?" Do they mean anything to you?

DOUBLE: Oh yes . . . a lot . . . also restructuring . . . net worth . . . holding company . . . labor mobility . . . immediate downsizing . . .

INSPECTOR: And the word "terrorism?" What does that mean to you?

DOUBLE: It means: radical and accelerated development of the armed struggle with consequences which may be positive or negative depending on the general situation of conflictuality regarding the various combined interests.

INSPECTOR: Brilliant.

DOCTOR: Brilliant.

JUDGE: Brilliant. He expresses himself in the language of a terrorist!

DOUBLE: Did I say the right thing?

INSPECTOR: Exactly the right thing.

DOUBLE: I don't understand what I said. I'd like to know what I said.

INSPECTOR: Let's move on. Let's see if you remember any contacts . . . for example, with foreign groups . . .

DOUBLE: Yes, of course. Foreign groups. I remember.

INSPECTOR: Russians?

DOUBLE: Russians . . . Oh yes . . . Russians . . . many contacts.

JUDGE: Excellent.

DOUBLE: Did I guess right? You're pleased?

JUDGE: Yes very pleased. And with the Iranians?

DOUBLE: Iranians? Iran . . . Ah yes . . . I remember . . . I made a special trip to Iran. Men in uniform came to meet us.

JUDGE: And did you talk about secret activities?

DOUBLE: Yes, very secret . . . deals.

JUDGE: Deals for arms.

DOUBLE: Yes, arms, too . . . all kinds of arms . . . heavy and light . . .

INSPECTOR: Were you aware of why and for what purpose those arms were to be used?

DOUBLE: Water.

INSPECTOR: What?

DOUBLE: Mineral water. Noncarbonated.

JUDGE: What's he saying?

DOCTOR: It's simple. He's saying he's thirsty.

INSPECTOR: Wait a minute! Answer my question first.

DOUBLE: No. I'm thirsty. Noncarbonated mineral water. Cool, but not iced.

DOCTOR: Wait. I'll get it. I have some here.

JUDGE: All right. Bring him his water.

DOUBLE: I hope it's not carbonated, because if I burp, my nose'll drop off.

INSPECTOR: I'll have a glass, too.

DOUBLE: Oh, the funnel . . . Doc, do you have the funnel?

DOCTOR: Yes . . . yes . . . *(Gives him a funnel)*

JUDGE: A funnel? What for?

DOUBLE: To drink with. Otherwise I slobber all over. Doctor, could you help me screw the funnel in? Ah, no thanks, look, I did it myself. To your health, gentlemen.

DOCTOR: Bottoms up.

DOUBLE: It's cold. It gives me the chills.

INSPECTOR: Excuse me, but where'd you just pour that?

DOUBLE: Well, right into my esophagus.

DOCTOR: Of course, he won't be able to take in liquids or food through his mouth for a few more months.

JUDGE: Even his food goes through the funnel?

DOUBLE: Yes, they puree everything for me: appetizer, main course, dessert and coffee. No . . . not the coffee. I have special suppositories for that.

INSPECTOR: Listen, do you mind getting back to our little chat?

DOUBLE: Yes. Let's try again. You were asking me if . . . I remember arms . . . deals . . . who they were for . . . vaguely . . . I remember the word . . . North . . . Colonel . . . Ollie . . .

JUDGE AND INSPECTOR: North Colonel Ollie.

DOUBLE: Colonel.

JUDGE: Ollie.

INSPECTOR: Colonel.

JUDGE: North.

DOUBLE: Colonel Oliver North. That's right. And something about hostages . . . I can't quite remember . . . In Iran . . . Contras . . . Swiss bank accounts . . .

INSPECTOR: Swiss bank accounts? Whose bank accounts?

DOUBLE: There were lots of people making deposits and withdrawals. Lots of names. President Reagan. George Bush.

POLICEMAN: Deposits. Withdrawals. I didn't quite catch what he said after Iran-Contra.

INSPECTOR: Don't write it all down. Cross it out. Cross it out.

DOUBLE: It's starting to come back to me. The names of the people with the Swiss bank accounts. One of them was a judge.

JUDGE: Will you stop remembering!

INSPECTOR: Do something.

DOUBLE: If I make a little effort, I'll be able to put all the pieces together. I'm sure there's got to be some sense to it all. Hostages. Reagan. Arms deals. Swiss banks . . . *(The Judge and the Inspector try to stop him from revealing classified information, but he won't stop, so they signal to the Doctor who gives the Double an injection in his arm)* Cont . . . Contra . . . Con . . . Contras . . . Swiss Contras . . . Contra . . . I'm a Contra . . . You're a Contra . . . He's a Contra . . . *(Loses his power of speech and breaks down)*

DOCTOR: There you are, inspector. For ten minutes he won't be able to speak or hear.

INSPECTOR: And it's a good thing. There's no doubt about it. He's a terrorist. He condemned himself.

JUDGE: It's almost a crime to take advantage of his honesty, like this.

INSPECTOR: Don't forget, Your Honor, that he's the type of person that would shoot you in the back.

JUDGE: You're right. We must never forget it. As we suspected, he was part of the gang who kidnapped Agnelli. He was smashed up in the fighting. His colleagues thought he was finished, so they brought him here.

INSPECTOR: We'll have to put the word out that he's turned into a babbling idiot, because if they suspect he's talking, his terrorist comrades will be here to rub him out.

JUDGE: Unless the CIA beats them to it.

DOUBLE: I just remembered that . . .

JUDGE AND INSPECTOR: That's enough.

(The Doctor gives another injection to the Double. He collapses again.)

DOUBLE: Oh, well. Never mind.

JUDGE: It couldn't have worked out better if we'd arrested him on the spot . . . Let's whisk him away without letting anybody know, and lock him in solitary confinement, or even better, in a sensory-deprivation unit, like the antiterrorist squad does.

INSPECTOR: Yes, the antiterrorist squad.

DOCTOR: Yes, go ahead. That'll ruin all my work. He'll become completely deranged in jail.

DOUBLE: Now I'll tell you all the names. I just remembered.

JUDGE AND INSPECTOR: That's enough.

(The Doctor gives another injection to the Double. He collapses again.)

DOUBLE: What a hit.

DOCTOR: Listen to me. If you want to keep on talking, leave him alone for at least ten days.

INSPECTOR: Ten days. You've got to be kidding. We're holding the key to capturing an entire gang of terrorists, finding Agnelli—maybe even alive—and you . . .

DOCTOR: All right. Let's make it five days.

JUDGE: No, no. Two.

DOCTOR: Three.

JUDGE: Sold.

DOCTOR: But if his brain fizzles, the responsibility is yours. All right.

INSPECTOR: All right. Forty-eight hours.

DOCTOR: Seventy-two.

INSPECTOR: Sixty.

DOCTOR: Deal.

INSPECTOR: We'll be back.

DOUBLE: Now I remember the name of that judge.

INSPECTOR AND JUDGE: No more!

DOUBLE *(Pretends to leave, but comes back)*: Do you want to know?

JUDGE AND INSPECTOR: Shut up.

DOUBLE: OK. Then I won't tell you.

(Blackout.)

ACT TWO

SCENE 1

Rosa Berardi's apartment. There is a door on each of the three walls. The one on the right leads to the hallway, the one in the center goes to the bedroom and the one on the left goes to the kitchen. There is a table in the center of the room on which rests a white plastic head with a wig. There is a cabinet on the left and a television in the rear left. There is a rolling bureau of drawers on the rear right near a coat-rack. Next to the right wall is a rolling wooden chair with arms. On a rolling stand near the right wall is a plaster bust of a Greco-Roman figure with two faces. Hanging from a lampshade on a pole is a clarinet. Downstage center, between the actors and the audience, is a window mounted on a rolling tripod.

Rosa and Lucia enter stage right from outside. Rosa is carrying a bag with groceries.

ROSA: Oh, Lucia, I'm really sorry. How long have you been waiting for me here?

LUCIA: Oh, almost half an hour.

ROSA: Oh, goodness gracious . . . if I'd known, I would have hurried. Sorry for the mess . . . I was combing a customer's wig. *(She puts the wig on the table)*

LUCIA: Don't worry . . . Anyway, I'm the one who should apologize for showing up like this. I was very worried. I don't know what's going on with Antonio. They won't let me into the hospital. They say he's in an unstable psychological state, one crisis after another.

ROSA: Unfortunately, it's true. *(Opens the window)* A bit of fresh air. They only let me see him for five minutes, and as soon as I got near him he started shouting: "Go away. Go away. I don't want that ball breaker hanging around. Go away." He didn't seem like himself. He was possessed.

(The window rolls along the proscenium and disappears into the wings.)

LUCIA: How awful. What do the doctors say? Can they cure him?

ROSA: Well, they're doing what they can. They had this idea that they'd drive Antonio out to the Fiat plant and take him to his old department to see if it would jog his memory. When he got into the factory he seemed right at home. He was walking around the cars, cool as a cucumber, like he owned the joint. But when they put him on the assembly line, stuck a welding gun in his hand, and told him: "Come on, Antonio, weld." . . . it was like his brain exploded . . . his eyes bulged out of his head . . . he started shouting like a crazy man: "No. I'm not going to do this shit work . . . take me away from this infernal machine."

LUCIA *(Trying to hold back her laughter)*: Ha. Ha. Ha.

ROSA: Hey. What's got into you? Why are you laughing?

LUCIA: Excuse me. It's a nervous reaction . . . to think of a man like Agnelli, I mean Antonio, reduced . . .

ROSA: Yeah, it's enough to drive you crazy. You know they brought him here for a few hours. He went around the house, but he didn't recognize anything. Not even his two-faced bust of Plutarch and Suetonius. He used to be crazy about it. *(The statue rolls over to them and reveals its second face)* He didn't even look at his books. And here I was keeping everything in place for him. For when he comes back . . . after he gets tired of the bitch, I mean, Lucia . . . These things happen, you know . . . a man leaves his wife, moves in with another woman, then he gets tired of the other woman, and goes back to his wife . . . that's life. I even saw it in a film. A beautiful film. I saw it seven times. And she, the lover, gets terminally ill and dies a painful death . . . Come on, I was just kidding. Oh,

Lucia, even if he does get tired of you, he'll never come back to me. He's erased everything . . . his books . . . the furniture . . . Plutarch . . . Me!

LUCIA: Come on, Rosa, you'll see. Antonio will get better.

ROSA: No. Antonio won't get better. He'll never get better. I'm going to hang myself . . . do you want some coffee?

LUCIA: Thanks, but only if you're having some yourself.

ROSA: Yes, I'll make some coffee. I'll hang myself another day. *(Looks in the bag)* Where's the can? I just bought some. I must have left it at the store. I'll have to go back and get it. This story with Antonio is sending me over the edge. I'll have to go back to the store.

(Rosa exits. Lucia is alone. The phone rings, she answers it.)

LUCIA: Hello. No, she's gone out. I'm a friend of hers . . . ah, doctor, it's you . . . Yes, Lucia, the teacher. How clever. You recognized me. What? He's escaped? But how could he, with all those police around. No, he hasn't come here, I assure you, I would tell you . . . Don't worry, if he shows up, I'll call you. All right, yes, yes, good-bye, doctor.

(The real Antonio enters wearing a worn-out leather jacket.)

ANTONIO: Oh, Lucia. Good thing I found you.

LUCIA: Antonio. What are you doing here? Have you gone insane.

ANTONIO: And where am I supposed to hide out. I went to your house, but it was all locked up.

LUCIA: Good God, why didn't you just stay in the cellar. That was safe enough.

ANTONIO: Sure it's safe. Safe as a tomb. I can't take it anymore. I want to see people, to talk . . . you only come to see me once in a blue moon. *(He hangs his jacket on the coat-rack)*

LUCIA: But try to understand, I can't. The police follow my every step.

ANTONIO: Anyway, I'm not going back in there. I don't want to go mad.

LUCIA: All right, but you can't stay here. It's dangerous.

ANTONIO: Dangerous. Why? Who would dream that I'd come here to hide? I haven't been to Rosa's house in more than a year.

LUCIA: Yes, but all the same, you can't stay. Your wife will be back any minute.

ANTONIO: Well, maybe it's better that way. I'll tell her the whole truth. It's a rotten trick we're playing on the poor woman. And I'm paying the price for it . . . you have no idea what it's like, night after night, huddled up like an animal, with all the cockroaches.

LUCIA: Cockroaches?

ANTONIO: Yes, cockroaches. Yesterday I was so desperate that I caught twenty of them and put them in a circle. I stood in the center and pretended I was Judge Bork at the Senate Confirmation Hearings. I'm going mad.

LUCIA: I know. I know it's no fun, but be patient, don't give up now. Just a few more days and . . .

ANTONIO: Lucia, you've been telling me to be patient for months.

LUCIA: All right, it's a big mess, but what good do you think it's going to do to tell your wife that there are two Antonios? Just when she's convinced herself that the idiot Agnelli is you. In a few days, Agnelli will be better, and they'll send him here, and the two of them will live happily ever after.

ANTONIO: Agnelli's going to sleep with my wife?

LUCIA: Well? Don't tell me you're jealous.

ANTONIO: No. But the idea of it burns my ass. Him of all people. He's screwed me all my life. Now, I save his skin, and he screws my wife.

LUCIA: Antonio, don't be vulgar.

ANTONIO: What do you mean, "vulgar." He's the one who's a bastard. Now he'll get permanent disability pay. They send him home to a life of ease . . . in my house . . . with my life insurance money, and my pension too. That thief. No I'm sorry, I'm going to tell it all.

LUCIA: That's wonderful. And you'll end up in prison for at least four years—on suspicion alone. Do you really think Rosa will be able to keep her mouth shut, even for two minutes?

ANTONIO: Just leave my wife out of this, will you?

ROSA: I'm home!

(Rosa enters. Lucia pretends not to notice.)

LUCIA: Antonio . . . what do you mean you don't recognize me? Look at me . . . it's me . . . Lucia!

ANTONIO: Arrgh.

ROSA: Did they send him home?

LUCIA *(To Antonio)*: At least you recognize her, your wife? *(To Rosa)* No, Rosa. Stay there. Don't come too close to him.

ROSA: No. All right . . . I won't come too close . . . let's have a look at you. You've healed up well . . . you can hardly see the scars.

LUCIA: Go on. Antonio. *(Kicks him)*

ROSA: Why did you kick our Antonio?

LUCIA: Well, with psychologically unstable people you have to be firm . . . or they'll never get better. The professors at college always said: "A kick in the rear, will make your mind clear." Come on, Antonio. *(She kicks him again)* Look. You see. It works. Good. That's it. Now . . . hug her.

(Antonio hugs Rosa.)

ROSA: He hugged me. He didn't chase me away. Oh God, I'm getting all emotional. I feel weak. *(Asking Lucia)* Can I hug him back?

LUCIA: Of course, Rosa.

ROSA: Are you sure? With both arms?

LUCIA: Certainly.

(Rosa timidly embraces Antonio, who remains immobilized, embarrassed and moved by the situation.)

ROSA: Hello . . . how are you? . . . Do you remember me? . . . Who am I? Who am I?

ANTONIO: You're Rosa. You're my wife.

ROSA: His voice has come back. He recognizes me. And who is she? Come on. You recognize her, too. Don't you? *(She kicks him)*

ANTONIO: That's enough. Let's stop this charade. Listen, it's time for you to know what's really going on . . .

LUCIA: Stop it, Antonio. Don't be stupid.

ROSA: Give him another kick, another kick to calm him down.

(They kick him.)

ANTONIO: Ouch. Are you crazy? Stop it.

ROSA: We're doing it for your own good. "A kick in the rear, will make your mind clear."

ANTONIO: I want to tell you what happened.

LUCIA: Quiet. Wait a minute. *(The window rolls in from the wings on the right. It stops at center stage. Lucia peeks out of it onto the street)* Antonio, there's no time to lose. You're going to have to make a quick getaway.

ANTONIO: Why? What's happening?

LUCIA: I could be wrong, but something strange is happening down in the street. I bet it's the people from the hospital coming to get you.

ROSA: Why? Didn't they let him go?

LUCIA: No. He escaped. The doctor just called to find out if he was hiding here.

ANTONIO: It's not true! It's a pack of lies!

LUCIA: I swear, listen . . . let's get out of here and get to my house while there's still time. *(Gives him his jacket)*

ANTONIO *(Puts his jacket on the table)*: No. I'm staying here until I've finished telling everything to Rosa.

ROSA: Sit down. Bitch. You just want an excuse to steal my husband again.

(The Policeman, the Doctor and the Inspector break through the door.)

INSPECTOR: Here he is. What did I tell you, doc. I was sure we'd find him at his wife's house.

LUCIA: Are you happy now? And I'm a liar?

ROSA: Oh please don't hurt him. Don't frighten him. He's sick.

INSPECTOR: Nobody's going to frighten him. We're among friends. Right, Antonio.

DOCTOR: We were worried about you. How are you? Your pulse rate is a bit high. I'll prepare you a sedative.

INSPECTOR: Forget the sedatives. This guy's playing games, and wasting our time. I know what our dear friend Antonio really needs.

ANTONIO: But who are you? I don't even know you.

ROSA: You see? Making a scene like that, you've gone and made him lose his memory again.

POLICEMAN: Should we put the cuffs on him, inspector?

INSPECTOR: No. It's not necessary.

DOCTOR: No. Give me a hand. *(The Policeman helps him prepare an injection)*

ANTONIO: Listen, inspector, I want to tell you something. Listen, because I'm going to tell you . . . .

LUCIA: Antonio, are you crazy?

ANTONIO: Quiet, you. Inspector, listen to me.

(Antonio talks to the Inspector who is mistakenly injected by the Doctor.)

INSPECTOR: Aargh.

DOCTOR: Oh, excuse me. It's a sedative.

ANTONIO: Inspector, listen to me.

INSPECTOR: You're a real ball breaker. *(To Doctor)* Now he's going to tell me he's Agnelli again.

ROSA: Agnelli?

DOCTOR *(Prepares another injection)*: Yes! Ever since he made that unfortunate visit to Fiat, he's got it into his head that he's Agnelli.

ROSA: Oh. That's all we need.

DOCTOR: It's nothing to be alarmed about. It's a classic case of split personality. Come on, pull down your pants . . .

ANTONIO: My pants?

DOCTOR: It's for the sedative . . . over the past few months, while he's been stuck in bed, feeling trapped, he's developed such a hatred towards the man, who in his opinion, is responsible for his tragedy . . . Agnelli— *(To the Policeman)* Lift up his jacket—that he ended up identifying with him.

(The Inspector again gets the sedative intended for Antonio.)

INSPECTOR: Ahrgggaa.

DOCTOR: Take it easy, inspector. It's just another sedative.

ROSA: Oh, saints above! He's identified with Agnelli, and his personality is splitting. Like Doctor Jekyll, who first was . . . and then . . . so when he doesn't recognize me, it's because he's convinced that he's Agnelli.

DOCTOR: Exactly. *(Prepares a third injection)*

INSPECTOR: Excuse me, doctor. Would you mind coming here a moment? Now he says he's the one who saved Agnelli. Split personality or no split personality, he's trying to make fools out of us all.

(Antonio runs out.)

POLICEMAN: Aaargh. He's escaped.

INSPECTOR: Don't stand there like a potted plant. Go get him. Fast!

POLICEMAN: He's locked us in. The key was outside.

INSPECTOR: Then shoot the lock off. What are you waiting for?

ROSA: No, please. Don't shoot. I've got another key. Wait a minute. I'll find it.

INSPECTOR: No. There's no time. Fire. Fire. Fire. *(The Policeman shoots toward the audience)*

INSPECTOR: No. Not there. At the door.

(The Policeman shoots the door.)

ROSA: Antonio! Antonio was behind that door. You've murdered him.

(The door opens and the Judge walks in limping.)

JUDGE: My leg. There's a hole in my leg. Why did you shoot me?

INSPECTOR: Your Honor. What were you doing behind the door?

JUDGE: I was knocking. Do you always shoot at people when they knock at the door? *(Falls to the floor)*

INSPECTOR: Hurry, doc. He's fainted. *(To Lucia)* You, too, miss. Can you help out? If anyone says a word about this, I'll kill 'em. If it ends up in the newspapers: "Judge Kneecapped by the Police," I'll shoot myself.

(All leave with the Judge except Rosa.)

ROSA: What a madhouse. If I tell, nobody would believe me. Did you see that? Nasty little habit they've got . . . pulling out their guns at the littlest thing. You can't find the key—BAM—they'll take care of it. If someone reaches for his wallet—BAM—they stop him . . . forever. Poor Antonio. Let's hope they're not going to shoot him, too. *(Looks out window)* Oh God, there he is . . . that's him, hiding behind the bus. No, he's gone. Maybe it wasn't him . . . Oh, I hope they don't take him back to that hospital, because then he really will go bonkers, with a Doctor Jekyll split personality that's half wild and half Agnelli. Hey, but this is his jacket . . . he's gone off without his jacket . . . he'll catch cold.

(Double enters wearing an overcoat and scarf.)

DOUBLE: Maaay Iiiii? Excuse me.

ROSA: Ah. Who is it? Ah . . . it's you. You got away. You got away.

DOUBLE: Maaaaay I . . . cooooome . . . iiiin? Is aaaaany-booooooody hooome?

ROSA: Yes, nobody's home. They've all gone to take a gentleman to the hospital because he knocked at the door and they shot him in the leg . . . to open the door . . . and then he turned out to be a judge . . .

DOUBLE: Iiiiiiii . . . gooooooot . . . aaawaaay . . .

ROSA: Yes. I know.

DOUBLE: Thaaat . . . iiiiiimbecile . . . of an inspeeectooooor . . . is convinced that I kidnapped myseeeeeeelf. An auto-terrorist.

ROSA: Calm down, Antonio. Slow down and catch your breath. All that running is making your scars show again. They're all swollen up with fright. Look how you're sweating. Are you thirsty? Do you want something to drink?

DOUBLE: Yes, please. A little mineral water, noncarbonated, because otherwise I'll burp, and my nose will blow off.

ROSA: OK. I'll bring it right away. But what are you doing with that overcoat?

DOUBLE: It's cold.

ROSA: Do you have two overcoats?

DOUBLE: No, this one's a jacket.

ROSA: This split personality thing is getting to be a real obsession.

DOUBLE: Listen, madam. I have to tell you something . . . which evidently you don't know . . .

ROSA: But now you're calling me "madam"?

DOUBLE: Madam. I don't know you. I'm not your husband.

ROSA: Yes, dear, calm down . . . sit down. Now just drink your noncarbonated mineral water and try not to say silly things.

DOUBLE: But, madam, I'm not saying silly things, at all. I have never been so lucid and self-aware.

ROSA: Dammit. Then why don't you show it, and stop calling me "madam."

DOUBLE: All right. I'll stop calling you "madam." Would you be kind enough to help me screw the funnel into the tube. No, that's all right. I did it myself.

ROSA: The funnel? What for?

DOUBLE: To drink with.

ROSA: You drink through your neck?

DOUBLE: Yes. I can't drink through my throat yet . . . not until the scar tissue heals up completely on my glottis and epiglottis. Ah . . . it gives me chills. Just pour it straight from the bottle. It's easier.

(He mimes with head movements the pleasure he feels as the water goes down.)

ROSA: Oh, Lord. What am I seeing . . . my husband with a funnel stuck in him. You look like a beer barrel.

DOUBLE: And now, would you please sit down, so that I can tell my story . . . the real story.

ROSA: Again?

DOUBLE: For months after the accident, it was as if my identity had vanished . . .

ROSA: Yeah, I know.

DOUBLE: Then, that day when they took me to the assembly line at the Fiat plant, it was as if a bomb went off in my brain. Fifty electroshock treatments all at once. Suddenly I remembered that I was the one who had installed this criminal merry-go-round. That I was Agnelli, and that I didn't want to have anything to do with all this dust and shit and grime. And now I was there . . . me . . . Agnelli, hooked up to a welding gun that was spitting blinding sparks all over the place, shaking like I had a 220-volt plug up my bottom.

ROSA: Calm down, Antonio . . .

DOUBLE: I am not Antonio. I am not some prick of a worker who shakes all over. I am above all me! They think I've been kidnapped. But no . . . I've only been substituted.

And look at me now, with this ridiculous puppet's face. The face of one of my lineworkers . . . what a joke!

ROSA: Oh, Doctor Jekyll. Can we stop that. I've had it up to here with all this split personality stuff. Either you calm down, or I'll break your leg. *(She kicks him)*

DOUBLE: Ahh . . . but, you're insane.

(A siren sounds.)

The police. They're coming?

ROSA: No, it's not them. They're not stopping. In any case, it's not such a smart idea for you to stay here and wait for them to come back and nab you. I'll hide you. Take the scarf for your scars . . . You can sleep up in the attic. I've got it all fixed up, so I could rent it to a student. Come on. Come on. I'll show you the way. I even had running water put in. *(They exit, Rosa's voice continues from offstage)* Watch out for the steps. They're steep. Nobody knows this room is here, because I haven't reported it to the authorities yet. There you are. Come in. See, there's even a light.

(The real Antonio enters.)

ANTONIO: Rosa. Are you home, Rosa. Nobody's here. Well, it's a good thing, If they're all gone, maybe I can get some peace and quiet. Look how I'm sweating. I'm soaked. *(He takes off his shirt and jacket and leaves them on the floor)* I wonder if Rosa has a clean sweater for me to change into.

(Antonio exits. Rosa enters speaking to the Double, who is offstage.)

ROSA: Now stay there and behave yourself. Don't make any noise. I'll bring you something to eat right away. God, I'm so emotional. Who would have thought I'd be so emotional just to have my husband back home? *(Sees his clothes on the floor)* I'm so emotional I didn't even notice he'd taken his clothes off. That's what love does to you. *(Picks up the clothes)* And he's dumped them here on the floor, just like he always did. Oh, what a joy to have him back again. I'm so happy to have his nice dirty shirts to wash . . . to iron . . . and to cook for him . . . slaving like a servant . . . that's the life for me.

(Antonio reenters.)

ANTONIO: Rosa, are you back . . . are you back?

ROSA: What are you doing back here? Is something wrong? What are you doing back here?

ANTONIO: Why shouldn't I come back here? Would you prefer me to stay locked up like a criminal for the rest of my life?

ROSA: What do you mean, "The rest of your life"? . . . Just a few days. Until things get straightened out.

ANTONIO: No. No. Things will never get straightened out. If I go in, I'll never get out. I could be stuck in there for twelve years.

ROSA: Don't say silly things. You don't think I'm gonna keep you up there for twelve years.

ANTONIO: Up where? What do you mean "up there"? Rosa, what are you babbling about?

ROSA: Look, nothing's going right around here. I'm getting fed up. If you don't straighten yourself out, I'm going to pour twelve pints of bromide down your neck. *(Points a funnel at Antonio)* You're making everybody crazy. First it's black. Then it's white, then you change your mind and can't remember. Now go up in the attic . . . now!

ANTONIO: In the attic? But why?

ROSA: Because it's a safe hiding place.

ANTONIO: No. It's not safe at all. There's no way out of the attic. It's a trap. If you don't mind, I'd prefer to stay over there, in the other room, with a terrace, so if they come looking for me, I can jump on the roof.

ROSA: You'll fall and smash yourself to bits . . . then we'll have to start all over again . . . Bruuuu . . . braaaa . . . bray . . . astronaut . . . astronaut. But have it your way.

ANTONIO: Rosa, who is this astronaut?

ROSA: Stop it. Do what you want. It's impossible to reason with you. I'll go make something to eat.

ANTONIO: At last you've said something intelligent. I'm starving. *(Notices there are two coats on the coat-rack)*

ROSA: You're really lucky, you know. Today I cooked up the stew for the week, with a pig's foot.

ANTONIO: Whose is that?

ROSA: The pig's foot? It's ours . . . we'll eat it.

ANTONIO: I'm talking about the overcoat. Whose is it?

ROSA: Yours. Whose do you think it is?

ANTONIO: That one's mine. So whose is this one? The astronaut's?

ROSA: It's yours.

ANTONIO: Rosa, who is this astronaut that goes around leaving coats all over the place?

ROSA: Cut it out. It's yours. You had two of them. One on top of the other. Two overcoats. You were going around with two overcoats.

ANTONIO: Me? I had two overcoats, one on top of the other? I was going around with two overcoats. . . one on top of the other.

ROSA: Yes, you. *(Grabs a chair to hit him)*

ANTONIO *(Calming her down as if she's crazy)*: Yes, of course. And this is my vest.

ROSA: So. Should I heat it up?

ANTONIO: What? The coat?

ROSA: No. The stew. I knew the day of revenge would come. Well, how are you going to eat it? *(Antonio looks at her in amazement and starts backing away)* No, seriously, how do you do it? How do you swallow? Do you suck it down through the funnel? Or through the tube in your neck? And how are we going to get it down . . . there's no way it'll go through . . . even if I push it, because even if I cut the meat up into little pieces, it's still going to be too big . . . and since we can't let it touch your glottis or your epiglottis, which by the way are a couple of words I never heard of before . . . then how are you going to eat? Will you be sucking it down or not? But then, it won't go through the tube in your neck . . . it won't go through. Where are you going?

ANTONIO: Go on. You're right. Go on just like that. It's perfect. When it doesn't pass through the glottis . . . the tube is the best way . . . suck it through the funnel . . . the funnel is made especially for sucking . . . and as for me, my glottis is . . . and my epiglottis is a little less . . .

ROSA: Where are you going? This is serious. Come over here.

ANTONIO: Yes, yes. I'll be there in a minute. I'm going out for a minute to get the third overcoat that I left at the bar. I had three overcoats.

ROSA: Careful. Someone's coming . . . quick, go into the bedroom . . . I'll lock the door behind you . . . I'll give it two turns of the key . . . and you keep quiet.

ANTONIO: Yes . . . who is it?

ROSA: I don't know who it is. I'll go and see. *(Peeks through the front door)* Oh, hello. *(She comes back to the bedroom door)* Don't worry, it's nobody. Just the next-door neighbor . . . who I can't stand . . . he's such a busybody. He heard some noise, so he came to spy on me . . . I can't stand him . . . I'm . . . I'm going to report him. I'm going to report him for "morbid curiosity."

(Rosa goes into the kitchen. The Double enters.)

DOUBLE: Rosa, can I come in? Am I bothering you?

ROSA *(From the kitchen)*: A little patience, please. I'm dishing out the stew, and I'll be there in a second to open the door for you.

DOUBLE: Oh, you don't have to bother, I'm already in.

(Rosa enters with the stew.)

ROSA: But how did you get in?

DOUBLE: Through the door. Why?

ROSA: But it was locked.

DOUBLE: No, it was opened.

ROSA: What a dummy. I guess when I was turning the key just then . . .

(A siren sounds. The window rolls onto the stage; she looks out.)

There they are again. No, it's an ambulance. They're not stopping.

(The window rolls out again.)

DOUBLE: The police.

ROSA: Yes, but they're not stopping . . . oh, what a life. Sweetie pie, I would have loved to sit here all comfy and cozy to eat, you and me, but it's too dangerous. How about if we take the plates and silverware and go into the room?

DOUBLE: Oh, no please. I can't stand it anymore. That place in there gives me gruesome nightmares, like in the hospital . . . I start to throw up . . . I can't keep anything down.

ROSA: OK, we'll take a chance. But at the slightest suspicious noise, you'll have to get lost. Here you go, help yourself. Look, I brought you that mustard you like, and here's some green sauce.

DOUBLE: But Rosa, this is boiled beef.

ROSA: Yes?

DOUBLE: And boiled sausage.

ROSA: Yes?

DOUBLE: And even a boiled pig's foot . . .

ROSA: Yes?

DOUBLE: Everything's boiled . . .

ROSA: So? Is something wrong? Did you change your mind again?

DOUBLE: No, I like boiled stew very much . . . it's just that you've forgotten that my tube is very thin, and the food won't go through the funnel . . . especially a sausage that size.

ROSA: Haven't we been through this before. I could grind it up, but even then, it'd be too big to go through that little hole.

DOUBLE: No. It won't go through the hole in my neck. But it will go through the one in my nose.

ROSA: You eat stew through your nose?

DOUBLE: Yes. In the hospital they even made me suck spaghetti through my nose . . . with cheese sauce. Now I'll show you a little gadget that I brought from the hospital. There, you see, these tubes go up your nostrils. Then you connect this to the output socket from a meat grinder. I had a beautiful one in the hospital, electric . . . but I forgot it in the rush.

ROSA: Oh, what a dummy I am! I've got a meat grinder, too, but it's one of the old-fashioned kind, that you turn with a handle. Here it is.

DOUBLE: Let me see. The important thing is that the back end has to be the same diameter. Perfect. Size 12.

ROSA: Incredible. Antonio . . . even the color matches.

DOUBLE: Now I'll show you how it works. There, you see, the mask goes on like this. Then you put the tubes up your nostrils, and the meat grinder on your head. *(Takes off mask)* Dammit, I'm sorry.

ROSA: What is it, Antonio?

DOUBLE: I can't stand it. When the meat grinder starts grinding my head, I feel like my brain's being ground up. You have to help me control myself. Do you have any rope?

ROSA: Rope?

DOUBLE: Yes, rope. To tie me down.

ROSA: Tie you down?

DOUBLE: Yes, otherwise I won't be able to resist the instinct to pull the tubes out of my nose. But I have to eat!

ROSA: Well, we could try it with these straps. They're the kind kids use for their schoolbooks.

DOUBLE: Perfect. And this chair with the arms is just right. And you can use some belts to strap my neck to the back of the chair.

ROSA: Oh, it's awful. You look like you're in the electric chair.

DOUBLE: You said it. I am in the electric chair. Rosa, you're going to have to be strong. It's almost a question of life and death. I beg you, Rosa, don't let yourself be swayed if, at the beginning, I implore you to set me free. You have to be strong. You have to make me eat at any cost.

ROSA: Yes, of course. At any cost. I'll be awful. I'll make you eat everything. Oh God, the telephone . . . I can't answer it . . . I'm crying. *(Answers it)* Hello. Yes, doctor, it's me. No, I haven't seen Antonio. No, no, I assure you, he hasn't been here. I would tell you, doctor. I wouldn't tell the inspector—he's so uncouth—but I would tell you. Please let me know if anything happens. I'm in so much pain. Good-bye.

DOUBLE: What did he say?

(He has arranged the straps on the arms of the chair.)

ROSA: It was the doctor. I don't think he fell for it. They'll be here any minute. Quick, let's take everything upstairs, into the other room.

DOUBLE: No, for God's sake. Don't you understand. I can't wait anymore. I'm dying of hunger. Rosa, you've got to grind some stew up my nose or I'll go crazy.

ROSA: I'll grind you some in a few minutes. Go on, I'll meet you. Take the wine bottle and the glasses.

DOUBLE: Bread. I want bread. *(He jumps for the bread basket)*

ROSA: Leave the bread alone.

DOUBLE: But without the bread I won't be able to soak up the gravy.

ROSA: I've got grated bread crumbs. Go on. I'll bring up the rest of the stuff, including the electric chair. Hurry.

DOUBLE: All right, I'll wait for you. But you hurry, too. *(He leaves)*

ROSA: Wait a minute while I turn off the gas. There's some fruit here. Afterwards I'll make you a fruit salad. *(She reenters and places the food on the chair)* Look, what a pity. A nice piece of beef like that has to be cut up like it was meat for meatballs.

ANTONIO *(From the bedroom)*: Rosa, can we get moving? I'm still here waiting.

ROSA: Don't be so impatient. What am I supposed to do? Sprout wings. I'm loading up the electric chair.

ANTONIO: Loading what? Rosa, what are you babbling about now?

ROSA: Hurry. Come and give me a hand. I can't manage it . . . it's too heavy.

ANTONIO: I'd be happy to, if you come open the door.

ROSA: It's open. Push it and come out.

ANTONIO: Cut the crap, Rosa. It's locked tight. *(Rosa opens the bedroom door, Antonio enters)* Finally. Let's eat. Where have you been all this time?

ROSA: Antonio, please, you've got to explain to me how you managed to go into the bedroom, lock yourself in, and still leave the key on the outside of the door.

ANTONIO: What did I do?

ROSA: You locked yourself in the bedroom, with two turns of the key.

ANTONIO: I did? It was you, you who locked me in with two turns of the key.

ROSA: Yes, but that was before. But then you got out.

ANTONIO: I got out?

ROSA: Yes.

ANTONIO: How?

ROSA: Through the door. How else?

ANTONIO: I came out by the door?

ROSA: Yeeeeees!!!!!!!

ANTONIO: When?

ROSA: Before.

ANTONIO: Don't be ridiculous.

ROSA *(Lifts a chair, threatening to hit him)*: You did come out. You did come out.

ANTONIO: It's true. I wanted to keep it a secret from you, but obviously I failed. *(Mimes the actions he now describes)* I got out with an old trick that we use at the Fiat factory. When the foreman locks us in, we get out by sticking our hands under the door . . . First we put them under a pressing machine, our hands that is, to flatten them out . . . then we stick them under the door, and push them through up to the elbow. Then we turn the hand a little to make the rest of the arm go through more easily, right up to the shoulder. Then we grab the key. But the key is too thick. It won't go under the door. So, we stick our heads under the door, and push . . . and push . . . and opla. We get out. Are you satisfied. They call me the Flying Doormat. *(Rosa wraps the scarf around her head)* OK? Rosa . . . Rosa . . . what are you doing, Rosa?

ROSA: I have a headache.

ANTONIO: Well, maybe if we sit down and eat, it'll go away, Eh?

ROSA *(Goes to the chair and gestures)*: The electric chair . . . come on . . . let's go into the bedroom . . . and I'll do some grinding for you . . . I'll be ruthless . . . down to the last shred of meat . . . I'll grind for you . . .

ANTONIO: Stop it. You're driving me crazy. It's a trick, to drive me out of my mind. Stoooop it!

ROSA: I have to do my duty. In spite of everything. Antonio, we're going in there.

ANTONIO: In where?

ROSA: In the bedroom.

ANTONIO: To do what?

ROSA: To eat.

ANTONIO: Noooooo. For months I've been eating like a vagabond. Now for once I want to eat here, sitting like a Christian . . . sitting down like a Marxist. A Christian and a Marxist. Sitting down. A Marxist Christian, sitting down . . . and perplexed . . . because of what's happened in Poland. *(Rosa falls into a heap as he speaks)* What is it now? What are you doing. Rosa. Rosa, where have you been all this time? . . . You were in a cult, weren't you? And who was your guru? The astronaut?

ROSA: Antonio, I'm completely confused. Antonio, we've got to go in there . . . into the other room.

ANTONIO: Like that? Crawling?

ROSA: . . . because if the police arrive . . . *(The window rolls in and Rosa gestures threateningly toward it)* I said *if* the police arrive. *(The window rolls out, as if frightened)*

ANTONIO: Who cares? Close the door. Put on the chain. I had it specially installed. I'd like to see the police get past that. They'd have to break the door down. And while they're breaking the door down, I'll eat this wonderful beef. I have to say that when it comes to beef, Rosa, nobody does it like you do . . .

ROSA: You say that all the time.

ANTONIO: I could eat this with my eyeballs.

ROSA: You're going to have to eat it with your nose. *(Straps his arms to the chair)*

ANTONIO: Rosa, Rosa. What are you doing? Why are you tying me up?

ROSA: To make you eat, OK?

ANTONIO: Rosa, please. Later we'll have time to talk, and you can tell me all about the rituals in your cult. But not now . . . *(Rosa bangs the ladle on the table)* I know. That's the signal for mealtime.

ROSA *(Holding back tears)*: Stop it. We'll start with a nice helping of broth . . . to whet your appetite . . . But . . . Antonio, how are you going to eat it?

ANTONIO: I won't eat it, I'll drink it . . .

ROSA: Do you want it down your neck or in your nose? How do you like it best? It'll be better in your neck. Let's hope I get it in the right hole. *(Sticks the funnel into his neck)*

ANTONIO: You punctured my clavicle. Please, untie me. *(Rosa pays no attention to him. She straps his neck and pushes his head against the back of the chair)* Rosa, please . . . Rosa, it's true. I've been a louse. I've treated you badly, like a son of a bitch. I haven't respected you, but you have to be generous . . . and forgive me. I'll come back to you, Rosa. Please, let me go.

ROSA: Sweetie Pie. Sweetie Pie.

ANTONIO: Forgive me, Rosa. I love you, Rosa.

ROSA: I've waited so long to hear you say those words.

ANTONIO: Rosa . . .

ROSA: I love you, too. *(Puts the mask on his head and the tubes up his nose)*

ANTONIO: Rosa, Rosa . . . my nostrils are all blocked up . . . I feel like there's something in my nose. Rosa, I feel like an elephant . . . Why do you go see those kinds of films? . . . you know they just give you ideas.

ROSA: Quiet. Be quiet.

ANTONIO: That's enough now, Rosa . . . Let me go . . . Help! Help!

ROSA: Antonio, don't shout like that.

ANTONIO: Help.

ROSA: Antonio, don't shout. Don't you realize that you're torturing me.

ANTONIO: No, you're torturing me. Help! Help!

ROSA: Antonio, stop it. Antonio . . . stop playing elephant . . . the neighbor will hear. Stop it. Shut up. *(Stuffs a napkin in his mouth)* That's enough. You've got to eat. Be quiet. Antonio, stop it. All the neighbors will hear. *(Antonio's shouts are transformed into the sound of a foghorn by the tubes)* Stop it. I can't have you tooting like a tugboat. Oh, my God, you're turning puce . . . Oh, what a dummy, I blocked up all his holes . . . how's he going to breathe? . . . What should I put in instead of the napkin . . . ah, yes, the clarinet that you love so much . . . I'll hang it from this lamp, so you can breathe and play at the same time if you want . . . *(Antonio's shouts come out as clarinet blues, commenting grotesquely on the situation)* Now I can give you your broth . . . Don't be afraid, it's not hot . . . I put some cheese in and two drops of lemon to cut the grease

. . . there . . . that's good . . . all the way down . . . it's good for you . . . but . . . but . . . you're peeing in your pants? Ah, no . . . it's the broth running down your pants . . . I missed the tube . . . Well, we'll let it go . . . Let's get to the beef. We'll start with this nice piece of rump . . .

(Rosa puts the meat in the grinder. The lament of the clarinet becomes desperate rock music. Rosa continues grinding meat. There is a knock at the door.)

INSPECTOR: Open up. Police. Open up or we'll break down the door.

ROSA: There they are. I told you they'd be back. Be quiet. Don't move. Shut up.

(The Inspector and two Policemen break through the door.)

INSPECTOR: What are you doing?

ROSA: I'm feeding my husband.

INSPECTOR: With a clarinet in his mouth?

ROSA: Yes. It's the only way he'll eat. Would you mind giving me a hand. Keep grinding the meat. Meanwhile, I'll go fix him a nice fruit salad. But don't let yourself be moved, if he asks you to untie him . . . he has to eat . . . it's a matter of life and death.

(She leaves. The police takes the clarinet out of Antonio's mouth.)

ANTONIO: Help . . . I've got a piece of boiled sausage up my nose . . . have you got a nosepick?

INSPECTOR: What are you talking about?

ANTONIO: Help . . . let me loose . . . That woman's a horror . . . Take me away from here.

INSPECTOR: Take you away where? To prison, perhaps?

ANTONIO: To the zoo, if you want . . . just get me out of here . . . That woman's insane. She's killing me, sausage by sausage.

INSPECTOR: All right. We'll set you free, but first you've got to do a little favor for us. You're going to tell us a few things about the Agnelli kidnapping. You were there, weren't you? That night on the embankment.

ANTONIO: Yes, I was there, on the embankment . . .

INSPECTOR: Very good.

ANTONIO: But I didn't have anything to do with the kidnapping. In fact, I was the one who saved Agnelli.

INSPECTOR *(To a Policeman)*: Give the handle a little turn.

ANTONIO: No. No. Enough. Yes, it's true. I confess . . . I'm the head of the armed gang that kidnapped Agnelli . . . I'll tell all . . . I'll say anything . . . Just set me free.

INSPECTOR: What a wonderful little machine. We ought to have a gadget like this down at headquarters. OK, let him out.

(They set him free. Rosa enters.)

ROSA: Here, I've fixed you some fruit salad.

ANTONIO: No, not the fruit salad. *(He jumps up and seeks protection from the police)*

ROSA: But why did you set him free?

INSPECTOR: Don't worry, ma'am. We're just taking him down to the station for a while . . . .He's got a few little things to get off his chest . . . .Now you just sit down there, eat your fruit salad, and keep your mouth shut. Let's go. Let's go.

(Antonio leaves with the Policemen.)

ROSA: Oh, Antonio. Inspector, where are you taking him? Wait . . . his tubes . . . and the meat grinder.

INSPECTOR: No thanks. We use less sophisticated methods down at the station.

(The Inspector exits.)

ROSA: Oh God. Poor Antonio. What a terrible thing to happen. But why are they taking him to the police station? *(The window rolls in. She looks out)* Poor Antonio . . . There he is . . . They're loading him into the wagon . . . Antonio . . . Antioniooooooo.

(The Double enters.)

DOUBLE: Yes.

ROSA: He answered me. Antoniooooooo.

DOUBLE: I'm here . . . you don't have to shout. Since you took so long coming up, I came down. Now, please, hurry up and give me something to eat . . . I'm dying of hunger.

ROSA: Oh God . . . one Antonio here, and another Antonio there . . . Two Antonios . . . Your personality's completely split in two. *(She faints)*

DOUBLE: Ah, yes. One Antonio here, one Antonio there . . . if I can find a third one . . . I'll be God.

(Blackout.)

SCENE 2

Rosa's house. When the lights come up, no one is on stage. The bedroom door opens, revealing a character dressed as a secret agent with sunglasses, a flashlight and a pistol. The silent action is done to music: from an espionage ballet to a kind of rock tarantella.

The Group Leader sneaks around investigating with a walkie-talkie in his hand that squeals and squeaks. He goes to the door to signal three similarly dressed Secret Agents to enter. They set up hidden radio microphones around the room and search everything. They hide inside the furniture, and are responsible for its mysterious movement throughout the scene. The Group Leader begins talking into his walkie-talkie.

GROUP LEADER: Hello, hello, do you read me? Yes, we are setting up our observation post . . . The woman is still upstairs talking excitedly to a man in the attic . . . *(As he speaks, the Agents replace the cabinet with one that has space inside for him to hide; it has holes in its sides for his arms to stick out. The Agents replace drawers in tables with false drawers)* No, it's not her husband. He keeps calling her "madam." I don't know who it is . . . Yes, I've already searched the place . . . There were two hidden microphones. No, not our stuff. Must be the antiterrorist squad . . . Yes, we got rid of them . . . and your new microphones are in place. They're coming down now . . . I'm in position. Over and out. *(He hides inside the cabinet)*

ROSA *(Speaking to audience)*: Dammit, have you seen what's going on at Rosa's house? Rosa has finally discovered that there are two Antonios: one is her husband the other is Agnelli, who's useless around the house. He can't even change a light bulb. He thinks that manual labor is a Spanish waiter. And there's my Antonio in prison being kicked around by the police, and it's all his fault.

DOUBLE: All my fault?

ROSA: Where's my cigarettes? *(The Group Leader slips a pack into the drawer)*

DOUBLE: Calm down, please . . . before you say, "It's all his fault."

ROSA: Ah. Here they are.

DOUBLE: I would like to know, my dear Mrs. Rosa, if that generous Antonio of yours ever so much as lifted a finger when I was down there at the hospital having my face rebuilt to look like his. Did he ever lift a finger? Nosirree. He didn't give a damn. *(Lifts lid of soup bowl to throw away match and sees the head of a Secret Agent)* I'm not feeling well today . . . and then they say that we employers are cynical. *(Notices the television)* What's that if it's not cynicism? *(The television moves)* Excuse me, is it normal in this house for televisions to move around on their own? What channel is that? *(An Agent's face is in the screen)*

MAN *(Walks in from outside)*: Excuse me, does Mrs. Berardi live here?

ROSA: Do you always come into people's houses without even knocking?

MAN: Yes.

ROSA: What a sense of humor.

(Agnelli goes into the bedroom.)

MAN: Who's that gentleman? Your husband?

ROSA: That's my business . . . and what's this white thing? Your wife?

MAN: No, it's a washing machine. For you.

ROSA: For me? A washing machine? I didn't order a washing machine.

MAN: Then it must be a present.

ROSA: I never heard of such a thing. Take it away.

MAN: All I know is that it's for you, and I'm not taking it back. So long. *(He leaves)*

ROSA: Look, you're not gonna force me . . .

DOUBLE *(From within)*: What is it this time?

ROSA: They forced a washing machine on me!

DOUBLE: So what! We've been forcing our Fiats on all of Italy for eighty years, and nobody's ever said a word.

(They exit.

Musical interlude: an Agent pokes his head out of washing machine. Other spies hide in the television and other pieces of furniture. It is a slapstick ballet of espionage. One of the spies puts his head in the place of the Greco-Roman statue and pretends to be a statue.)

LUCIA *(Entering)*: Rosa, Rosa, are you home?

ROSA *(Offstage)*: What is it?

LUCIA: Big news.

ROSA *(Off)*: About Antonio?

(Rosa and Agnelli enter.)

LUCIA: No, not exactly, but indirectly. Good morning, Mr. Agnelli.

(The furniture reacts to the name "Agnelli.")

DOUBLE: No. Don't call me Agnelli. I told you before. Just call me Mr. Gianni.

ROSA: So, what's the big news?

LUCIA: On the radio, just half an hour ago . . . on TV too . . . didn't you hear it?

ROSA: On television? *(Secret Agent moves lips silently on screen)*

DOUBLE: No, we haven't heard anything.

ROSA: We never get any sound out of this damn thing. *(Bangs television and it goes off)*

DOUBLE: So, what did they say on television?

LUCIA: Prime Minister Spadolini has received a letter, supposedly from Agnelli.

ROSA: Cut the crap!

LUCIA: Yes, and another letter's gone to the Minister of the Interior, Rognoni.

ROSA: Well, obviously the letters are fakes. Where's he supposed to have written them from?

LUCIA: From the Red Brigade hideout where he's being held prisoner.

ROSA: But he's here.

DOUBLE: Yes, those letters are authentic. I wrote them.

(All the furniture moves closer to them.)

ROSA AND LUCIA: You? When?

DOUBLE: Three days ago. I wrote them and put them in the mailbox on the corner.

ROSA: But why? And what's in them?

DOUBLE: Just a moment, and you can read them for yourselves. Here they are. I made carbon copies for myself. I came straight to the point. I demanded an immediate exchange of hostages. My life in exchange for thirty-two political prisoners, all of them serving life sentences. The same demand that Moro made when he was kidnapped. You see, I signed them at the bottom. "Yours sincerely, Gianni Agnelli." *(A Secret Agent pops up as the wig head and examines the letters)* I don't feel well.

(The furniture moves even closer.)

ROSA: But why are you sending letters? You're not a prisoner. What's in it for you?

DOUBLE: Well, I want to find out what the government thinks of me, what value I have for them . . . I want to see whether they have the nerve to sacrifice me like they sacrificed Moro. So I have asked for thirty-two prisoners, all condemned for life, and we'll see what's what.

LUCIA: Excuse me, Mr. Gianni, but if I may say so, this presumptuousness of yours is disgusting. Who the hell do you think you are?

(The furniture lines up in homage to him as he speaks, almost as if bowing to him.)

DOUBLE: I am Gianni Agnelli. Two hundred seventy-five factories in Europe alone. Four in Poland. In Poland. With those Solidarity troublemakers. But I took care of them right away. I put one of my trusted foremen in charge . . . a certain Jarulzelski.

LUCIA: This is just a game of prestige and power you're playing. But it won't work. Tomorrow, the journalists and politicians will simply give the same replies they gave at the time of Moro, when he asked them.

DOUBLE: That remains to be seen.

ROSA: She's absolutely right. I can see the headlines now: "The State must make a show of strength by sacrificing one of its most outstanding citizens."

DOUBLE: I doubt it.

ROSA: That's just what they said at the time of Moro.

DOUBLE: Well, in case they do reply as you suggest, I already have my answer ready. My last will and testament.

ROSA: Your will?

DOUBLE: Exactly, my will. I'll read it to you. "Dear friends, gentlemen of the government: with my death you are all fired. At my funeral I want no one, no representatives of the government or the State. I want no priest, no one from my family, especially my bubbleheaded brother. I want to be cremated. My ashes are to be taken in a helicopter, which will fly over Turin, scattering them over the Rivolta, Stura and Mirafiori factories, so that the workers, when they breathe, will cough, and remember me. I may not stay in their hearts . . . but I shall rest in their lungs . . . forever!" *(Police siren sounds)*

ROSA: Oh God. What are we gonna do? They'll think we're the Red Brigade.

DOUBLE: You'll have to hide me.

ROSA: Quick, get in the washing machine.

(He obeys. The Inspector enters in his usual frenzy, accompanied by a Policeman. The Agent hiding under the table elongates it so that there is space in the middle for his head to emerge. Again he sticks out his head and pretends to be the wig mannequin.)

INSPECTOR: Good afternoon. Not disturbing you, am I?

ROSA: No. I'm very happy to see you, inspector, so I can finally see my husband and find out how he's doing.

INSPECTOR: Unfortunately, your Antonio's not doing well. He's feeling a bit swollen . . . Partly because he keeps tripping and having bad falls . . .

ROSA: Onto your fists, right?

LUCIA: Shut up, Rosa. Don't fall for it.

INSPECTOR: And partly because he keeps drinking like a fish.

ROSA: But how can that be? He's almost a teetotaler.

INSPECTOR: Exactly. He was only drinking water, with a little bit of salt.

ROSA: Water and salt?

INSPECTOR: Yes, by the bucketful, with a rubber tube. What a glutton.

ROSA: Shame on you. Torturer . . .

INSPECTOR: Eh, eh, madam. Watch what you say. *(He goes to lean on a table, but it moves)*

LUCIA: Don't pay any attention, inspector. You have to understand . . .

INSPECTOR: Of course I understand. I'm very understanding, so much so that I've taken the trouble to bring your man up here. *(Turns to the outside)* All right. Get moving. *(To Rosa)* He's your man. Maybe you can convince him to tell the truth. *(Bangs his fist for emphasis but the table moves)* What's going on here?

ROSA: I don't know, inspector. It's been going on all day. Must be the vibrations from the subway.

INSPECTOR: Anyway, up until now, your husband has been telling us a pack of lies. He even went as far as to say that you, Mrs. Berardi, have got Mr. Agnelli hidden here.

DOUBLE *(From the washing machine)*: For heaven's sake, don't give me away.

INSPECTOR: Which makes you, Mrs. Berardi, the person responsible for the logistical operations of the Red Brigade.

ROSA: My Antonio, said a thing like that, about me?

LUCIA: Of course, since they'd filled him with water, they could make him say anything they wanted.

(There are shouts from the hallway.)

INSPECTOR *(Looking out the door)*: What are you doing down there?

POLICEMAN *(From outside)*: We're not going to make it, inspector. He keeps trying to beat himself up and keeps falling down the stairs.

INSPECTOR: Well, tie him up with a rope then. Wait—I'll come down. *(To Rosa)* You come with me.

(The Inspector and the Policeman exit.)

ROSA: They're killing him.

DOUBLE: Don't contradict him. In fact, string him along as much as you can. You have to feed him the biggest whoppers you can come up with . . . the man's a psychopath.

ROSA: You mean I should say, yes, I am really responsible for the logistics of the Red Brigade.

DOUBLE: Tell him anything . . . you've got to give me time.

ROSA: But I'm not good at making up lies.

DOUBLE: Be inventive.

(Double goes back into washing machine. The Inspector and Policeman enter.

During the following scene the washing machine slowly rolls to the back wall where the Double takes advantage of a secret door to exit, and is replaced by a technician who continues to manipulate the washing machine.)

INSPECTOR: One more flight, and your husband will be here.

ROSA: Yes, and I could spit in his eye. I knew I should never have trusted that lug. He sang like a canary.

INSPECTOR: What . . . he's sung has he? So there's some truth in what he said!

ROSA: Yes, and now I'm going to sing: "There's no business like show business . . ."

INSPECTOR: That's not what I call singing.

ROSA: "Climb every mountain."

INSPECTOR: If you've got something to say, say it.

ROSA: All right. Up until yesterday, I knew where Agnelli was.

INSPECTOR: Oh yes? Where?

ROSA: In a blimp, you know, the one that advertises condoms over the football games.

INSPECTOR: You mean the rubber blimp? Listen, Mrs. Berardi, don't screw around with us, because there's a rubber tube full of water waiting for you, too.

ROSA: Who's screwing around? To begin with, here's the first piece of evidence. *(Puts a shoe on the table)*

INSPECTOR: What's that?

ROSA: Can't you see? It's a shoe. Agnelli's shoe.

INSPECTOR: Still screwing around, eh?

ROSA: Not at all. Size forty-four and three-quarters, handmade, Lenzuer Brothers, London.

LUCIA: They're specially made for him.

ROSA: If you don't believe me, call up Agnelli's house and ask if it matches.

INSPECTOR: I don't need to. *(To the Policeman)* Call headquarters. No, not with the telephone, with the radio. They've got all the data there. Check with the footwear division.

POLICEMAN: Hello, headquarters.

(When the Policeman uses his radio phone, antennae rise up out of all the pieces of furniture that hold the Agents inside.

Antonio enters.)

ROSA: Look, there's the stoolie. You'll get what's coming to ya.

LUCIA: Please, don't be so hard on him.

ANTONIO *(His belly is inflated)*: But, Rosa . . . glug, glug. *(Spits out a fountain of water into the Inspector's face)*

ROSA: You dirty rat. Go gargle somewhere else.

INSPECTOR: Take him to the bathroom, before he drowns us all.

POLICEMAN: Inspector, headquarters tells me that the size and the brand match . . . Agnelli was the only person to wear that kind of shoe in Italy . . . him and the pope.

INSPECTOR: Good God! *(Grabs the shoe)* Take a picture of it!

ROSA: Yes. With all of us. Around the shoe. *(Everyone poses for a group photo around the shoe)* So, now do you believe that we're on the level.

INSPECTOR: Well, yes, it is evidence . . . but fairly, how should I say, insubstantial.

LUCIA: What do you mean, insubstantial?

INSPECTOR: Well, one of Agnelli's shoes doesn't prove that you have the rest of him.

ROSA: What about two shoes. *(Bangs the other shoe down)*

INSPECTOR: Well, of course, two shoes . . .

ROSA: And that's not all . . .

INSPECTOR: Three shoes?

ROSA: No, the original carbon copies of the letters to Spadolini and Rognoni, written in Agnelli's own hand. *(Gives them to the Inspector)*

INSPECTOR: The original carbon copies? Are you sure of that? Watch out, because if this is a joke, it could cost you plenty.

(The furniture comes closer. The Policeman bumps into a table that is moving and excuses himself. The Agent hiding underneath pops out and says, "No problem," and disappears back underneath.)

POLICEMAN: Wait a minute, inspector. I've got the evening editions of two newspapers. This one has the letter sent to Spadolini. It's an enlarged reprint.

INSPECTOR: Well, yes, the handwriting is very clear and it looks pretty much the same to me. *(The furniture crowds in for a look)* Stop crowding me!

POLICEMAN: It's not me, inspector. It's the washing machine, the TV and the table.

INSPECTOR: That subway is getting carried away . . . It looks like a pretty good forgery to me.

LUCIA: What do you mean forgery? Forged by who? Nobody's ever seen a single line written by Agnelli up until now. And this newspaper just came out an hour ago.

POLICEMAN: It looks pretty authentic to me.

ROSA: Well, that's enough of that now.

(Rosa grabs the paper and gives it to Lucia. The furniture follows her. Another espionage ballet with furniture moving like a carousel, as music plays.)

INSPECTOR: Stop it! My head's spinning!

(The furniture stops moving and all goes back to its original position.)

Listen, lady. You're under arrest. Talk. Where are you hiding Agnelli?

ROSA: No, if you arrest me I won't talk. I'm not talking until I'm free and have got guaranteed immunity, repentant terrorist, special category A1, C31.

LUCIA: That's right. Without immunity, she won't talk.

INSPECTOR: You'll talk or I'll blow your brains out.

ROSA: All right, you talked me into it. I'll talk, but only in front of a judge.

INSPECTOR: He's on his way. I already sent for him. You know the judge I mean—the one who was here last time.

ROSA: Oh yes. The one you shot in the knee.

INSPECTOR: Shhh. Please.

ROSA: OK. We'll wait.

INSPECTOR: No. We're not waiting for anybody, understand? Because I'm going to kill you.

(The furniture reacts.)

ROSA: Inspector, don't shoot, don't shoot. I'm not a car at a road block. Don't shoot! OK. I'll talk.

INSPECTOR: Oh, you've finally come around. Now you're going to talk loud and long, and God help anyone who interrupts. *(To the Policeman)* Is the waterlogged thug still in the toilet?

POLICEMAN: Yes. I locked him in . . .

INSPECTOR: Wonderful. Then go keep an eye on him. *(To Rosa)* OK, now you can go on. Be precise, and don't deviate. When did you first decide to kidnap Agnelli? *(To the Policemen)* You write and you tape it.

(Agnelli prompts Rosa from the washing machine.)

ROSA: The idea of kidnapping Agnelli came to me about the time we were preparing the Via Fani operation . . .

INSPECTOR: I want details. Names, dates, addresses, everything.

(The furniture moves closer.)

ROSA: It all started in early January . . . 1978 . . . I was in Milan, it was a nice day. A pale sun shone dimly through the fog that hung over the city . . .

INSPECTOR: Listen, forget about the pale sun and the fog . . . We're taking your testimony, not writing a novel . . .

ROSA *(To the Double)*: Look. See what a fool you're making of me? *(To the Inspector)* OK, no poetry. Just the facts. Nothing but the facts. The strategy meeting for kidnapping Agnelli took place in a . . . movie theatre. *(She comes up with the idea herself; Agnelli hides)*

INSPECTOR: A strategy meeting in a cinema?

ROSA: Yes. The Splendor Cinema . . . a nice little theatre near my house. We have the meetings there so I don't have so far to walk, because my feet . . . *(Continues to improvise)*

INSPECTOR: All right. Get on with it.

ROSA: Yes. So there we were in the Splendor Cinema, watching the movie, when the door burst open and who should walk in but . . . Mr. Big.

INSPECTOR: No.

LUCIA: Rosa, no.

INSPECTOR: Mr. Big. So he really does exist. Who is he?

ROSA: My friend Lucia is right. I don't think it's right at this point to keep talking. We're getting into names, places and the people who are too important . . . I can't talk.

INSPECTOR: Trying to be clever, eh?

ROSA: OK, inspector. Do you want to die? Are you ready to give up your life for knowing things that are too important to know? *(To the Policeman)* Hey, you. Are you ready to write this down for the last time? Are you ready to listen, inspector, because it may be the last thing you ever do?

LUCIA: Rosa, if you're going to talk, then I'm going . . . I don't want to die.

POLICEMAN: Excuse me, inspector. I've got to go, too.

INSPECTOR: Go where?

POLICEMAN: I have to take my wife to the hospital and I've got an abscess on my tooth, and I've got to go and have my gum lanced.

INSPECTOR: You cowards. The abscess isn't on your gum, it's on your ass.

(The Policeman leaves, followed by the furniture.)

ROSA: Inspector. My furniture. It's moving on its own. Stop it. Come back. Come back.

INSPECTOR: Oh God. I feel sick . . . my heart . . .

ROSA: Do you feel sick? See what happens when you want to know too much? Lucia . . . officer . . . Come quick . . . the inspector is sick.

LUCIA: What's happening?

POLICEMAN: Look, the newspapers have printed a special edition. This stuff is unbelievable.

DOUBLE: Pass me one, too. *(The Policeman gives him a copy)* Thanks.

POLICEMAN: Hey, but that's the prisoner, what's he doing in there?

DOUBLE: Just keeping my hands clean . . . Listen, the whole Cabinet has met and issued a communique. Here it is. The headline reads: "Kidnap Chaos. Cabinet Caves In."

ALL: No.

DOUBLE: Yes. "In the Moro Case, the State answered: 'No exchange.' This time it must answer: 'Yes.'"

ALL: No.

DOUBLE: Yes. "The prisoners requested in the exchange will be set free today."

ALL: No.

DOUBLE: Yes. "And in order to prevent an unlimited number of further prisoners being released . . ."

ALL: Well?

DOUBLE: "The Cabinet, with the approval of the various organs of State, has decided to free all political prisoners."

ROSA: Hallelujah. So my Antonio is free!

DOUBLE: Yes. Everyone's free.

INSPECTOR: No. Impossible. Have they all gone mad?

DOUBLE: Maybe. Listen, inspector, this is for you. "All antiterrorist proceedings have been dropped as well." You can retire in peace.

INSPECTOR: All the work I've done, my hard work, flushed down the toilet. It's disgusting. Bastard politicians.

(The furniture responds with agitation.)

ROSA: Bastard politicians is right. They let Moro be killed like a lamb led to slaughter. And now with Agnelli, they flip-flopped and gave in . . . the dirty scum.

DOUBLE: They can't sacrifice me. I am power! Don't you understand? Of course not . . . These days only we corporate executives read Karl Marx . . . especially the part of "Das Kapital" that says: "The only true power is financial-economic power, holding companies, markets, banks, commodities . . . in other words, capital." And then he adds a sentence which children should memorize and sing in the playground: "The sacred laws of this state . . . the economic state . . . are written on watermarked paper money. So government and state institutions are nothing more than support services for the real power, which is economic power." How could they even consider sacrificing me in order to save the State? I am the State!

INSPECTOR: What's he saying? Who do you think you've turned into this time?

DOUBLE *(Standing on top of the furniture)*: I am Gianni Agnelli. And don't let my face fool you. It's only plastic surgery.

INSPECTOR: Listen, I'll give you plastic surgery if you don't stop . . .

ROSA: Calm down, inspector. He really is Agnelli.

POLICEMAN: Inspector. There's another Agnelli in the toilet. The spitting image of this one . . .

ROSA: Yes. Only that one is my Antonio. And this one is Agnelli.

(The Agents emerge from the furniture.)

AGENTS *(In chorus)*: Yes, inspector, we can assure you. We have been listening in on their conversations for quite some time.

INSPECTOR: What's this? Who are you?

AGENT 1: CIA.

AGENT 2: FBI.

AGENT 3: CNN.

GROUP LEADER: It turns out that this gentleman really is Mr. Agnelli, whose face has been mistakenly rebuilt in the image of Antonio Berardi, one of his workers. It was he who wrote the letters to the government, and mailed them from this house, pretending he was held prisoner by terrorists. He concocted the whole dirty mess.

(The Inspector, as if hypnotized, slowly climbs up toward Agnelli, who touches him with his finger as if he is God from Michelangelo's Sistine Chapel.)

DOUBLE: I created you. Go forth.

INSPECTOR: You're mocking me. You're pulling my leg. I don't care if you are the State. I'll shoot the State . . . Right in the balls . . . I'll shoot this State of shit . . .

ALL: Stop. No. You're crazy. Think of what you're doing. Stop him.

(They grab the Inspector, whose gun goes off just as the Judge walks in the door.)

JUDGE: What is it? What's happening? *(The Judge is shot in the leg)* Ahiaauuuuuu. They got me in the other knee. This is getting to be a bad habit.

(Blackout.)

THE END

ELIZABETH:
ALMOST BY CHANCE A WOMAN

BY **DARIO FO**

EDITED BY **FRANCA RAME**

TRANSLATED BY **RON JENKINS**

SUBVERSIVE SLAPSTICK

When Dario Fo wrote the first version of his play about Queen Elizabeth, Franca Rame declared it unworkable and urged him to rewrite the central character. The result was *Elizabeth: Almost by Chance a Woman*, a tragicomic portrait of a queen with the heart of a woman who is forced to wield power like a man. In the play, Elizabeth believes that Shakespeare has written *Hamlet* as a transvestite parody of her indecisive policies. The theme of sexual identity and power reversal is heightened by Fo's role (played in drag) as the Queen's comic maidservant, who administers secret beauty treatments to ease her mistress's insecurities. At the same time that the Queen submits to leech-sucking as a method of weight reduction, and to bee stings as a breast enlargement technique, she battles fiercely against the conspiracies of men who are jealous of her power. Confronting kidnapping plots and assassination attempts, Elizabeth makes political pronouncements that echo the clichés of modern Italian politicians, and also of Ronald Reagan, who was in office at the time of the play's premiere, in 1985.

In performances of the play, Rame (playing Elizabeth) and Fo occasionally toy with the boundaries between past and present, which are written into the script by partially slipping out of character and improvising dialogue in which the arguments between the Queen and her servant resemble arguments between the husband-and-wife team who has created the work. At one point, as Elizabeth changes her gown behind a screen, Fo jokes that the people in the balcony are getting a view of her underwear. When Rame senses her husband's improvisation going on too long, she chastises both Fo and his character: "Stay in your place and try to be quiet," she admonishes, as the monarch, "because now I'm the Queen, and for once, at last, you are the Servant. So shut up. Is that clear?" Fo responds with a mock threat to assert his authorial authority: "Dario Fo wrote this play, and he wouldn't like to see you treating me like this," he quips. "One word from me and he'll cross out 'Queen' next to your lines and write in 'The Maid.'" Fo then steps completely out of character to address the audience directly: "She's really been immersing herself in the role. At home she answers the telephone: 'Hello, this is the queen speaking.'" The self-parody that Fo and Rame slip into their play enables the spectators to see the bickering of a modern couple overlapping with the squabbling of a sixteenth-century servant and her mistress. The distant past is made more immediate and the play's complex tapestry of social, literary and political themes becomes more accessible to contemporary audiences.

On another level the improvised banter (some of which eventually becomes fixed into a form that is repeated every night) is emblematic of the creative partnership that Fo and Rame have evolved over their half-century of collaboration. Rame plays the role of the beleaguered editor, reining in the excesses of Fo's overenthusiastic stage impulses. Fo, in turn, plays the role of the writer with a wounded ego, while he is actually responding happily to Rame's suggestion with an improvised speech that weaves them both into an epic tapestry of sexual politics that transcends the barriers of traditional theater. Instead of a period play that would fit easily into the category of tragedy or comedy, the couple has created a unique theatrical event that fuses contemporary political satire, historical costume drama, parody of new-age medicine, old-fashioned melodrama, transvestite farce, Brechtian social critique, postmodern celebrity gossip and the resurrection of traditional commedia dell'arte, with Fo playing his usual Harlequin role in drag.

The complexity of Fo and Rame's theatrical teamwork is also revealed in their shared moments of physical comedy. When Fo as the maidservant begins recounting the plot of *Hamlet*, Rame as Elizabeth tries to stop him, insulted by what she perceives to be Shakespeare's satiric portrait of herself and her family. Silenced by the Queen, Fo begins pantomiming the action with his hands, and when she grabs his hands he continues to enact the story by gesticulating with one foot in the air. This slapstick physical duet becomes a vivid visual metaphor for censorship. The Queen's authority is used to silence a powerless underling who refuses to submit and continues speaking with his body even after his words have been taken away. Every attempt to suppress the servant's expression is met with a wacky form of physical resistance. The scene is comical on the surface, but the serious issue of censorship emerges clearly in the aftermath of the laughter. Fo and Rame have fought battles against censorship repeatedly throughout their careers. In 1962 they were fired from Italy's most popular television show, *Canzonissima,* after refusing to alter the political content of their scripts. In the 1970s Fo was barred from state-controlled television stations for performing religious satire that the Vatican deemed offensive. In the early 1980s Fo and Rame were repeatedly denied visas to enter the United States under the McLaren Act, which is used by the State Department to bar entry to foreigners perceived as a threat to national security. In 1983 Fo was briefly jailed in Sardinia for refusing to alter his scripts in compliance with the government censorship office, and Rame's 1973 kidnapping was of course an extreme attempt at censorship through violent intimidation. In this context the physical comedy of the seemingly lighthearted routine in *Elizabeth* can be read as an allegory linking the personal struggles of Fo and Rame to the decades of political turmoil through which they and their audiences have lived. The physical suppression of speech and the visceral need to speak out against oppression were expressed with precision in the couple's slapstick *pas de deux*.

—Ron Jenkins

This essay is excerpted from the book *Dario Fo & Franca Rame: Artful Laughter* by Ron Jenkins (Aperture, New York, 2001).

PRODUCTION HISTORY

Elizabeth: Almost by Chance a Woman had its American premiere at the Yale Repertory Theatre in May 1987. It was directed by Tony Taccone. Set design was by Tim Saternow, costume design was by Marina Draghici and lighting design was by Michael Giannitti. The cast was as follows:

ELIZABETH	Joan MacIntosh
MARTHA	Mary Lou Rosato
EGERTON	Tom Mardirosian
BIG MAMA	Joe Morton
THOMAS	Daniel Chace
ASSASSIN	Peter Lewis
GUARDS	Jim MacLaren
	Erik Oñate

CHARACTERS

ELIZABETH, Queen of England
MARTHA, the Queen's maidservant
EGERTON, chief of the Queen's police
BIG MAMA, Mistress of Herbal Medicine (played by a man)
THOMAS, the Queen's young lover
ASSASSIN, a fanatic
GUARDS, palace soldiers

TIME

Elizabethan England in the palace of the Queen

NOTE

All song lyrics were written by Dario Fo. As there is no musical score, it is suggested the lyrics be set to traditional English folk music. The songs are intended to be recorded and played offstage as background music.

PROLOGUE

THE ACTOR PLAYING BIG MAMA: Before we begin I want you to know that the author, Dario Fo, sends you all his best wishes. He remembers that for many years the U.S. State Department had refused him permission to perform in this country because of some confusion about his plays and his politics. So to avoid any future problems he asked me to assure the American public that there is absolutely no subversive satire in this play that could in any way be construed as being critical of the United States.

First of all, Elizabeth is a play about despotism, and we all know that there is absolutely no historical, metaphorical or allegorical relationship between the power-hungry imperialism of Elizabethan England and the benign policies of the world's greatest democracy today. It is also a play about hostage deals, secret national security police and covert foreign policy initiatives conducted by swashbuckling advisors, and we all know that things like this happened only in the past, and that the world today is much more civilized.

The author would also like the State Department to take note that his play is not entirely critical of despotism. In fact it could even be seen as a play in defense of despotism. Mr. Fo does admit that some of his earlier plays might have lashed out a bit too severely at despots through the ages, but after deeper reflection Mr. Fo now finds himself in agreement with the United States' humanitarian support of poor despots everywhere.

In recent years Mr. Fo has come to have great sympathy for the problems of despots. He understands how difficult it is for them to maintain their palaces, suppress rebellions and supervise their substantial investments abroad. They have taken on an exhausting job in the service of their subjects, and they deserve more support. The author hopes that everyone who sees this play will leave with a deeper understanding of the extenuating circumstances that forced poor defenseless Queen Elizabeth to cut off the head of her cousin, Mary Queen of Scots. Being a queen is a dirty job, but someone has to do it, and despots like Elizabeth should be appreciated for their efforts, not satirized by wisecracking clowns with no respect for authority.

Mr. Fo also wants to assure all the Shakespeare scholars here in the audience that he has deep respect for the great work they have done in interpreting and deconstructing Shakespeare's plays. He shares their views of Shakespeare as a great artist who would never stoop so low as to write political satire. Mr. Fo wants to underline the fact that the notion of Shakespeare as a satirist is presented only as one of Elizabeth's demented fantasies and should not be taken as the view of the author who understands that great art never refers to current political events.

Finally to make intentions perfectly clear, Mr. Fo has asked me to read you a letter that he mailed personally (on the occasion of this play's American premiere in 1987) to President Ronald Reagan:

> Dear Friend and Fellow Actor:
>
> I am sorry to read about all your problems in the White House, and hope you find time to cheer yourself up by coming to see my play. I can get you complimentary tickets. It's the least I can do after all the free publicity you have given me by refusing to give me a visa for all those years. As a true man of show business, I know you realized all along how much extra interest would be generated in my work by the

controversy over my visa. For all the sold-out performances I enjoyed when I was finally allowed to perform in America, I want to personally thank you and your press agents at the Department of State.

After all the help you have given me, I don't want you ever to think that I would be ungrateful enough to satirize you in any of my plays. I know you are a sophisticated man of theatre who understands the use of allegory and anecdotes to make a point, so I don't want you to leap to any false conclusions about possible parallels between the story of Elizabeth in my play, and your own presidency. Just because my play is about an aging leader whose advisors don't tell her what they're doing behind her back, a leader who tends to get confused and forgetful about certain details—don't think for a minute that it has anything at all to do with you. Everything in this play happened a long time ago to a queen who was at the end of her reign, and there is absolutely no parallel to the current situation in America. I know that America will never give up its world dominance the way the Elizabethan empire did.

Also be assured that the minor urinary problems Elizabeth suffers in the play have nothing to do with your well-publicized prostate operations, and that her obsessive concern with her image and with cosmetic beauty treatments has no relation whatsoever to the dying of your hair, your face-lifting, or the polyps that disappeared mysteriously from your nose.

And don't let anyone try to convince you that Elizabeth's love for horses has anything to do with your image as a galloping cowboy. Elizabeth never chopped wood at her ranch, and I made sure she wore dresses in every scene, so that no one could possibly get the two of you confused.

And when Elizabeth begins hallucinating and talking in a delirium about things that never really happened, as if she were watching reruns of old movies in her head, please don't think I am trying to suggest that you mix up the movies and real life. I know that you have a firm grip on the difference between the two. You handle affairs in the White House with a style that could never be equaled in the movies.

Finally, dear friend, the scene in which Elizabeth's female confidante helps her to remove leeches from her skin contains no allegorical reference to Nancy and her reputation for helping you to get rid of parasites on your staff. If I had wanted the Queen's confidante to be a caricature of Nancy, I could have called her "the dragon lady" but I'm not interested in cheap laughs like that. I personally have been shocked by people who suggest that Nancy hides under the table at all your cabinet meetings to make your decisions for you: that she pulls on your right pant's legs when she wants you to say yes, on your left pant's leg when she wants you to say no, and that whenever there is a doubt about the right answer she pulls on the middle, and that this was the origin of your prostate problems. Rumors like these are absurd, and I would never sink to using them in one of my plays.

So now that we've got all these misconceptions out of the way, I hope you enjoy my play, and that you come to share my sympathetic view of the poor misunderstood monarch Elizabeth. She is a failing leader, losing her memory and her health as her empire collapses around her. We are all lucky that awful things like this only happen in the past.

With all best wishes,
Your loyal friend and fellow actor,
Dario Fo

ACT ONE

The action takes place in London at the beginning of the seventeenth century. Elizabeth's bedchambers. The interior of a large room in the style of the Renaissance. Running along the back wall are eight windows. There is an inner balcony stage right which has a door leading out of the chambers. There is a stairway leading down from the balcony into the bedchamber. On the ground floor there are doors leading out of the bedchamber on the right and left sides.

In the center there is a bed modeled after the one owned by Frederick of Montefeltro. It is constructed to look like an armoire, so that the bed inside its walls cannot be seen. The space on stage left is hidden by a double curtain made from two parallel tapestries, one behind the other, on rollers. Behind the second tapestry is hidden a life-sized wooden horse mounted on wheels. Between the tapestries is a dressing table with a mirror on it. Next to the mirror is a candelabra. There is also a lectern with a manuscript and a pen. Several chairs and tables.

In the center of the stage there is a mannequin for clothing. On it is a black formal gown with white trimmings.

"Candia" is sung offstage or on tape:

The moment you stop loving me, to Candia I will go
And on the ship's sail I'll paint your eyes
So that when we're at sea and the waves beat against the bow
The water will splash against the mast

And fall like teardrops from your crying eyes
Eyes that never cried for me.

And on the prow I'll carve a masthead with breasts like yours
So that your face and chest will meet the waves
And you'll be embraced by the sea
You who never wanted to be held in my arms.

And when we arrive at the bright lights of Candia
And the people on the dock
Ask why this mariner has the eyes of a woman on this sail
I'll answer, "Because this is my love,
And I hold her close, so that perhaps I'll be able to forget her."

(When the song ends, Elizabeth enters with papers in her hand. It is so dark that she heads straight toward a mannequin dressed in one of her formal gowns.)

ELIZABETH: Where's everyone gone? . . . Martha . . . It's time to start the day . . . *(Bumps into the mannequin)* What's this? . . . Martha! . . . Why is it so dark in here? *(Opens one of the drapes to illuminate the mannequin. Elizabeth screams)* Damned Stuart! You don't scare me. *(Turns toward a curtain at her right, which is moving. She lunges at it with her dagger)* And neither do you. I saw you . . . bastard . . . I'll stab you.

MARTHA *(From behind the curtain)*: Help . . . Stop . . . Elizabeth!

ELIZABETH: Who are you. Come out or I'll kill you.

MARTHA *(Coming out)*: It's me, Martha . . . what's got into you.

ELIZABETH: Martha? And what were you doing back there. Spying on me?

MARTHA: What are you saying? I heard you shouting. What's wrong?

(Martha uses a stick to open the curtain so that the mannequin is illuminated again. Elizabeth lets out another shout and throws her papers at it.)

ELIZABETH: There. There. It's Mary. The Stuart.

MARTHA: No, it's only her dress . . . calm down.

ELIZABETH: Who brought it here and put it on that dummy with no head.

MARTHA: You ordered it to be taken out of the wardrobe . . . as a gift for someone . . . I don't know who.

(Martha takes the clothes off the mannequin and carries them offstage.)

ELIZABETH: It's not true. I only wanted to have the dress aired out. That's all.

MARTHA: Then it was obviously just a misunderstanding.

ELIZABETH: Obviously, my ass. They brought it here on purpose . . . and put it on that dummy with no head . . . to scare me to death. Whose idea was it? I want him here. Now!

MARTHA: OK . . . I'll start immediately . . . I'll call all the servants . . . and we'll have a nice little investigation. That way everyone will know that Elizabeth is still obsessed with the ghost of Mary of Scots.

ELIZABETH: I'm not obsessed . . . I don't give a damn about that whore of a queen from Scotland.

MARTHA: Good. Then prove it. Calm down and get back to bed. *(Moves toward the bed to open its panels)*

ELIZABETH: Stop. Don't open the panels to my bed.

MARTHA: Why? Do you have a guest? With all the racket you've been making, he must be awake already.

ELIZABETH: He's not awake . . . because he's not there. I didn't bring anyone to my bed last night.

MARTHA: Then I can open it?

ELIZABETH: No. I didn't bring anyone to bed last night, but the one I brought three nights ago might still be there.

MARTHA: For pity's sake! OK . . . you're impossible this morning. What's gotten into you? Look . . . you've scattered these papers all over the place. *(Picks up some of them)*

ELIZABETH: Ah, yes. Give them to me.

MARTHA: What is this stuff?

ELIZABETH: You tell me. Who is this bastard? Does he write this stuff on his own, or is he just a front man? Where does he get his information? I stayed up all night trying to figure it out.

MARTHA: Elizabeth, will you please calm down? I don't understand. Who are you talking about?

ELIZABETH: Shakespeare. Who is this Shakespeare?

MARTHA: Shakespeare. Him again? What did he do to you this time?

ELIZABETH: I told you to find out about him a month ago. I want to read every page he's ever written . . . how much of this poppycock has he managed to put on the stage . . . who prints it . . .

MARTHA *(Pointing to the pages she's gathered up)*: And you, with all the real tragedies swirling all around you, how can you get yourself all worked up over these worthless melodramas. You're forgetting that there's a difference between real life and the stage.

ELIZABETH: I know. "Elizabeth is losing touch with reality." I've heard it before. But just sit down and look at this, and tell me if this *Henry IV* and this *Richard III* aren't reflections of me and my way of governing.

MARTHA: But he didn't invent any of that. It's history.

ELIZABETH: Of course, I can't get angry at history for copying my life, but I can get angry with this infamous bastard for putting it all upon the stage to make the allegories more clear.

MARTHA: I see you're also the queen of the imagination.

ELIZABETH: Oh, you think it's my imagination. Look at this. *(Shows her another page) Hamlet*. Isn't that a spitting image of me. Tell me it isn't.

MARTHA: *Hamlet*, a portrait of you?

ELIZABETH: Yes. Don't look at me with that dumfounded expression. Have you read it?

MARTHA: No . . . I barely know the plot.

ELIZABETH: Then read it . . . carefully. You'll find my words . . . my lamentations . . . my curses . . . spoken here in this room. How does this Shakespeare know about them? Who is his spy?

MARTHA: Listen, if you think it's me . . . just say so, and I'll pack up my bags right now.

ELIZABETH: No, not you. You haven't got the imagination for it.

MARTHA: Thank you. In any case, if you got into the habit of screaming in a slightly lower voice, you might not be overheard by everyone from the corridor guards to the pimps passing by to some young boy who happens to find himself tucked into your bed.

ELIZABETH: So now you're putting yourself on the side of the gossips?

MARTHA: What gossips? Are you forgetting that I'm the one who makes your bed every morning.

ELIZABETH: That's true.

MARTHA: In any case, if you really want to find out what's behind these plays, why don't you ask your chief of police?

ELIZABETH: Who? Yes, I forget about him. What's his name? . . . Egerton? Where is he?

MARTHA: In the corridor where he's been waiting for you since dawn. With your permission, I'll let him in.

ELIZABETH: Let him in? Why? So he can see how monstrous I look when I've just woken up. If that damned spy gets a look at me, tomorrow all of London will be talking about how awful I look "au naturel."

MARTHA: OK, as you wish. I'll wait until you put yourself together. *(Ironically)* I'll tell him to come back in about four hours, this afternoon.

ELIZABETH: Ha. Ha. Very funny. Let him in, but bring me something that I can hide behind . . . no, you go . . . I'll do it . . . all I have to do is roll out my horse. *(Opens the curtains to reveal a wooden horse. She rolls it out to the middle of the stage)*

MARTHA *(At the door)*: Come in, Egerton. Make yourself comfortable. Her Majesty awaits you.

(Egerton enters with a folder under his arm.)

EGERTON: Thank you. *(Looks around, seeing only the horse)* Good morning Your Highness.

ELIZABETH: Good morning, Egerton.

EGERTON *(To Martha)*: Where is she?

ELIZABETH: I'm back here . . . behind the horse. And I warn you Egerton, if you start poking around this beast to sneak a look at me, I'll shoot you right between your spying eyes. *(Points a pistol at Egerton over the horse's neck)* What news have you got for me?

EGERTON: Your Majesty, I'm mortified. I know that you're angry with me.

ELIZABETH: Being angry, Egerton, is a small thing. I'm furious. First, why haven't you found out anything about that beast who shot at me from the riverbank while I was out in my boat. I don't know if he was an Irishman, a Puritan, a Papist or a hunter who mistook me for a wild duck. At least he missed me.

(Martha leaves, then returns with a pan and towels. She begins washing Elizabeth's feet.)

Second, I'm still wondering what kind of criteria you use when you read plays that are submitted to you for performance licenses. You're supposed to be the chief of my Intelligence Service . . . not the stupidity service.

EGERTON: Your Majesty, I am prepared to accept all insults. But permit me to assure you that the assassin in question has been captured and he has confessed.

ELIZABETH: Freely?

EGERTON: Yes, with a lit torch under his feet . . .

ELIZABETH: For the love of God, Egerton, are you still using these inhuman criminal methods.

EGERTON: But, my lady, the world being what it is, a policeman who wants to obtain a confession is compelled—

ELIZABETH: Compelled, my foot. How should I say this. We are no longer in the era of my father Henry VIII, when torture was a commonly accepted form of entertainment. No, today, we live in a free and humane country, where I am supposed to be indignant, to insult you, to turn you over to a special prosecutor if I catch you in the act. Your duty, on the other hand, is to continue engaging in these illegal activities without telling me about them. For God's sake, Egerton, you're ruining my day.

EGERTON: You're right. Excuse me. But at least we have ascertained that the Earl of Essex had nothing to do with it.

ELIZABETH *(With emotion to herself)*: Oh, Robert, Robert. *(To Egerton)* You're just saying that to please me. You know I'm crazy about him.

EGERTON: No, my lady. It's the truth. The shot was fired by a fanatic. An isolated lunatic.

ELIZABETH: How could he be isolated? There were two of them.

EGERTON: Uh, yes . . . two isolated lunatics.

ELIZABETH: Great . . . in a little while you'll discover that there were three of them . . . four . . . the national association of isolated lunatics. You're pathetic and monotonous. Anytime someone is caught engaging in dirty business, you try to cover up the names of those who are really responsible, by coming back to this idiotic refrain of isolated lunatics.

EGERTON: Maybe you're right, my lady . . . we do repeat ourselves. But I assure you that, in this case, the Earl of Essex is not involved.

ELIZABETH: In this case. Does that mean in other cases he is involved? Come on, speak up.

EGERTON: I'm afraid that he might be engaged in a very foolish enterprise.

ELIZABETH: Yes. And you, Egerton, along with my advisors, are overjoyed.

EGERTON: My lady, please . . . we . . . the fact is that the Earl is allowing himself to be used by a band of radical extremists. They are persuading him to organize a full-scale popular rebellion, backed up by a supporting invasion.

ELIZABETH: A supporting invasion? From where?

EGERTON: They are trying to bring in your cousin, the King of Scotland.

ELIZABETH: James?

EGERTON: Yes, so that he can support them with his troops when the rebellion erupts.

ELIZABETH: How could they be such ball busters . . . those bastards . . .

MARTHA: Now, now, Elizabeth. You're still a lady, as well as a queen.

ELIZABETH: And I'm also the pope of my religion, so be quiet or I'll excommunicate you. Out. Out.

(Martha leaves carrying the basin and towels.)

It's not true, Egerton. Lies. Proof. I want proof.

(Martha reenters.)

EGERTON: Here it is, my lady. *(Takes some papers out of his folder and hands them over the horse to the Queen without looking at her)* A letter written in the hand of the Earl of Essex. *(He leans toward her, but she stops him with her pistol, drawn from her dressing gown)*

ELIZABETH: Stop or I'll shoot. *(Reads letter)* "Act now. Right away. A better time will never come. The whole country is fed up, convinced that the queen is completely dominated by her advisors, and that their infamous policies are destroying the nation." *(Laughs, shows the letter to Martha)* Martha, come and look. It's a fake, a bad imitation of Essex's handwriting. It's a fake, Mr. Intelligence.

EGERTON: Impossible. The messenger is one of our men . . . He assured us . . .

ELIZABETH: Silence. I said it's a fake. Or perhaps, Egerton, you doubt my word, and prefer to believe a common traitor who is probably working for James.

EGERTON: For pity's sake. Of course . . . what can I say . . . uh, these things should always be double-checked.

ELIZABETH: Bravo, Egerton. Double-check him. Interrogate him. And arrest him. Yes, arrest him, your faithful collaborator, and give him Royal Immunity.

EGERTON: Royal Immunity?

ELIZABETH: Yes, it was my brother Edward's idea. First you scare the hell out of the prisoner by showing him the gallows . . . then all of a sudden you promise him liberty and money, if he talks . . . You'll find that he'll begin denouncing people right away, so many people in fact that you'll have to stop him to keep the prisons from overflowing.

EGERTON: Of course, Your Majesty . . . I'll have the information for you right away.

ELIZABETH: Keep me informed, Egerton.

EGERTON: Immediately. *(He rises to go)* Majesty, your devoted servant. *(Gestures good-bye to Martha and leaves, forgetting his folder on a chair)*

ELIZABETH: "Devoted servant," my foot! *(Pushes horse back to its original position)*

MARTHA: Excuse me, Elizabeth, I just glanced at the letters, but I was shocked by your certainty. Don't you have any doubts?

ELIZABETH: No doubts at all. I'm absolutely sure that Robert of Essex wrote that letter himself.

MARTHA *(Taken aback)*: Ah. But then?

ELIZABETH: Quiet. Can I condemn him to death? Should I have his head cut off? Then what am I going to do with a headless man? I love the wretch. And even you said that maybe it was my fault that Robert was doing crazy things.

MARTHA: OK, protect him. Save him. Your jack of hearts . . . just be careful he doesn't pick up too many trump cards . . . or even the joker . . . that would be something to laugh at. *(Leaves. She returns with a tray and cups to serve the Queen)*

ELIZABETH: The joker. You don't understand anything. Robert already had the joker in his hand. It was me. I'm the joker. But the cretin didn't know how to play me . . . He threw me away like a two of spades. And then he tries to organize a rebellion against me with a band of idiots, even more idiotic than him. Egerton, Cecil and Bacon infiltrate his band with spies and provocateurs, and this poor little ball buster of mine doesn't even realize it. What does he think he's accomplishing. The simpleton. And then to think that last night he mounted an attack.

MARTHA: Who, Essex . . . with his men?

ELIZABETH: Yes, fifty of them attacked the old armory, and stole a cache of weapons. Egerton clearly knew about it already, but he didn't say a word. Luckily I have a second secret police force that tells me everything . . . and I've infiltrated his police force with spies from mine . . . *(Ironically)* "Separate bodies of the State" . . . They attacked my armory, stole my weapons . . . they even got two cannons . . . I'm very possessive about my cannons . . . they used a strategy that I have to say was ingenious.

MARTHA: Wonderful.

ELIZABETH: You're overjoyed? Look at her . . . you pretend to be stern, but you're rooting for the jack of hearts, too, aren't you.

MARTHA: No, wait a minute . . . I was just applauding his courage and intelligence . . .

ELIZABETH: Whose intelligence? Robert of Essex? His head is so empty that if an idea ever got in, it would die of loneliness. *(Offers Martha a cup)* Drink your tea. You're forgetting about Egerton's infiltrators. They are the intelligent ones. This attack on the armory was planned here at the palace . . . at the table of my advisors, to cut off Robert's balls.

MARTHA: That's right. So Egerton must have known about Essex's plans to steal the weapons.

ELIZABETH: Yes, but he let them do it. You always let a sucker win the first three hands, so that you can crush him more easily in the end. Cecil, my beloved advisor . . . Bacon . . . Lesly, and all the Lords of the Crown wanted to punish me. They will never forgive me for having given the boy so many honors and land and appointments . . . I love him . . . And that dwarf had the insolence to shout at me: "One of these days your Robert of Essex is going to put a saddle on your rump, like a heifer." Do you understand? He called me a heifer.

MARTHA: Who would have dared? What dwarf are you talking about?

ELIZABETH: Cecil, my beloved advisor . . . I paid no attention, as if he hadn't spoken. I remained quite indifferent. I only spit in his eye. Right on target, Martha, a bull's-eye. Pum. It wasn't by chance. I spent three months training to put out a candle at three-meter's distance. Then I kicked them all out on their asses, cursing like a Turk.

MARTHA: No wonder they want to get even. *(Takes the tray to leave)*

ELIZABETH: They'll bring me Robert's head on a plate like John the Baptist. If I could only talk to the scoundrel.

MARTHA *(Embarrassed)*: I talked to him.

ELIZABETH: You? When?

MARTHA: Three days ago. I went to look for him. But of course, I only did it for you. I heard you crying all night . . . you were calling him . . .

ELIZABETH: How did he receive you? . . . Come on now.

MARTHA *(Even more embarrassed)*: I told him a little lie.

ELIZABETH: What kind of lie?

MARTHA: Don't be angry with me . . . promise?

ELIZABETH: I promise. Queen's honor.

MARTHA: I told him that you sent me.

ELIZABETH *(Kicks the tray held by Martha and sends the cups flying all over the room)*: Whore, bitch . . . mother . . .

MARTHA: You promised: "Queen's honor."

ELIZABETH: Who gives a damn . . . I'll break your bones . . . I'll kill you . . . (Picks up a pot to hit her)

MARTHA *(Shouting to ward off the blow)*: Calm down, Elizabeth . . . Robert didn't believe me.

ELIZABETH *(Changing her tone, as if nothing had happened)*: Martha, why are you shouting, dear. Just say, "He didn't believe me," that's all. Sometimes you make we want to break my pot over your head. *(Continuing the story)* He didn't believe you. *(Distracted, she picks up Egerton's forgotten folder)*

MARTHA: No, he's still pouting about the other time . . . he said that you humiliated him in front of everyone. What could you have said that was so offensive?

ELIZABETH: I called him a gigolo and a kept man. *(Opens the folder and glances at its contents while continuing to talk to Martha)*

MARTHA: A kept man? You're crazy.

ELIZABETH: Yes, but he insulted me first. With a shit-eating grin he called me a "barren, withered old carcass." What do you think of that?

MARTHA: Not very kind. *(Picks up the cups)*

ELIZABETH: No, not very kind. But I punished him. I took back the earring that I had given him . . .

MARTHA: You did the right thing.

ELIZABETH: Along with a piece of his earlobe.

MARTHA: That seems a bit excessive.

ELIZABETH: Yes, but then I gave it back to him . . . the earlobe.

(Immerses herself in the contents of the letters from Egerton's folder)

MARTHA: In fact, when I tried to warn him about the infiltrators and provocateurs . . . you're not listening to me.

ELIZABETH: Yes, yes. I'm listening . . . go on.

MARTHA: What are you reading?

ELIZABETH: It's Egerton's folder . . . he forgot it . . . or maybe he left it here on purpose . . . they are the letters from the various ambassadors to their respective superiors . . .

MARTHA: No kidding . . . and Egerton unglued the envelopes?

ELIZABETH: Of course. He's in the Intelligence Service. He has solvent saliva . . . one lick and it's open, copy, and send them off again. Oh, look. This one is all about me. Listen, listen to the compliments from the ambassador from Venice: *(Reads)* "The Queen of England shows off by quoting old anecdotes in Latin and Greek, but above all she loves to laugh in a manner that is gross and vulgar. She tells jokes that would make a whore blush. She curses . . . and has learned from an Italian clown how to blow raspberries, which she bestows on Lords who have fallen out of her favor . . . I even saw her spit at one of them . . ." *(Laughs)* He was there, too.

MARTHA: You've got an international reputation.

ELIZABETH *(Reading)*: "She dances like a madwoman, making incredible leaps and sweating so much that when she spins, she sprays the air around her like a wet dog shaking off water."

MARTHA: Well, that's true; when you get excited you do tend to splash and spray.

ELIZABETH: The ambassador from Portugal thinks I'm charming. Listen to the way he describes me: "A wooden doll, a bloodless mannequin . . . with a thousand frills and ornaments . . . a pompous robe with a head of glass." Disgusting wretch. Shit-faced papist. That's not in the letter. That's what I think of him. *(Passes the paper to Martha)* Go ahead, you read it.

MARTHA: "It is said of her that she is too feminine to be a man . . ."

ELIZABETH: What?

MARTHA: ". . . but too masculine to be a woman."

ELIZABETH: So I'm a hybrid . . . an hermaphro-monarch.

MARTHA: "Like all self-respecting monarchs, she loves funerals."

ELIZABETH: Of course all monarchs love funerals . . . so what?

MARTHA: "During the services the high notes of the chorus are drowned out by her wailing sobs."

ELIZABETH: Yes, I do suffer.

MARTHA: "The same night she will go to a party, embracing her Essex, and moaning like a . . . *birrocha encalorada* . . ."

ELIZABETH: What does that mean? *(Grabs the paper from Martha)* "*Birrocha encalorada*"? . . . Seems like an insult to me . . . *(Studies the paper)* . . . Oh, look. There's an asterisk . . . with Egerton's translation . . . how considerate! ". . . moaning like a mule in heat"?! *(Calmly)* This doesn't bother me at all. It would be beneath my dignity to even notice it. "A mule in heat."

(Lets out a terrifying scream. She knocks over anything within her reach, the furniture scatters. She kicks the horse, which moves forward. In response to the movement she pulls out her pistol and shoots at it. The horse returns to its position.)

Don't move! If I don't stop him with the gun, he wanders all over the house! Now stay put. *(Puts the gun back in her bodice)*

MARTHA: Don't exaggerate. The things this ambassador is writing about Essex are the same things you've been saying to yourself . . . with much more colorful language than he uses.

ELIZABETH: But I love Robert, so I can say what I please. *(Noticing for the first time that the furniture is scattered all around the room)* Who made all this mess? Clean it up, Martha. I'm dying of love for this sweet scoundrel who won't even give me a word . . . a letter . . . but his voice is always in my head . . . his eyes in my eyes. I'm dying of love . . . I love him.

MARTHA: Now, now, Elizabeth . . . be strong . . . you'll get over it.

ELIZABETH: But, Martha, I don't want to get over it. I'm fine like this *(Mocking Martha's voice and gestures)* "You'll get over it." . . . Dying of passion makes me happy. *(Puts her hand over her breast where she had deposited the pistol)* Oh my God!

MARTHA: What is it? Are you feeling sick? . . . Your heart? . . . Sit down.

ELIZABETH: No, it's the pistol . . . I put it in here . . . but it's slipped . . . the bullet's going to fire . . .

MARTHA: But it's empty . . . you just shot it off . . .

ELIZABETH: No, it has two bullets . . . there's still one shot left . . . the trigger is cocked . . . it's going to fire . . . mama . . . I'm going to shoot myself.

MARTHA: Now calm down . . . I'll just loosen your corset. *(Gets a stool)* Get up slowly so I can get it to your waist . . . Stand up on this stool . . . Where do you feel it?

ELIZABETH *(Gets up slowly onto the stool. She is terrified that the gun will go off any moment)*: God, how awful. I have to climb all the way up here just to die. I'm already on my tombstone.

MARTHA: There, I've loosened it . . . *(Reaches into the Queen's clothes)* Now we have to slip it down under your armpit to your back . . . just a minute while I call someone to help me . . . *(Runs to the door)* Guard!

ELIZABETH: Are you crazy? With me half-undressed . . . you're letting in a stranger . . .

MARTHA: It's your choice. A bullet in your stomach or an indiscreet glance.

ELIZABETH: A fortune-teller once told me that I'd have problems with a cock, but I never imagined that it would be the kind that was attached to a pistol.

(Martha reappears with two guards.)

MARTHA: Careful men. It could go off any second. We have to move it around to her back.

ELIZABETH: "Careful, men"? How many of them are there? Why don't you call in the whole army?

MARTHA *(As the three of them begin to fish for the pistol)*: Keep up your courage . . . Reach around there with your hands, men . . . that's it . . . do you feel the pistol?

ELIZABETH *(Beginning to enjoy it, she looks at the young men with new interest)*: Good morning. Go right ahead . . . yes, like that . . . yes . . . keep looking, boys, you'll find it . . . *(Changes tone)* But if that gun goes off and I survive . . . I'll have you all shot!

MARTHA: That's good, Elizabeth . . . Oh, no!

ELIZABETH: There. I knew it. It's slipped away . . . now it's down by my belly.

MARTHA: That's all right . . . in fact, it's even better . . . come on, let's move around to the back . . .

(The two guards move behind the Queen and continue their search.)

ELIZABETH: Hey, take it easy back there . . . that's my gluteus maximus . . . *(Languidly)* Yes . . . at least you could whisper something affectionate every now and then . . . Pigs!

MARTHA: That's it . . . keep going . . . we've almost got it . . .

(A shot goes off.)

ELIZABETH: Oh, God. Martha. I've assassinated myself. *(Terrified)* Blood . . . I feel blood running down my leg . . . Oh, God . . . I'm dying . . . My Essex . . . I want him here . . . Now . . . Robert . . . I want to see him for the last time.

MARTHA *(To the guards)*: Leave . . . Go away . . . Out! *(The guards leave)*

ELIZABETH: Shot in the butt. What an undignified end for a queen. I beg you, Martha. Tell them it was you. Take the blame. *(Martha reacts)* I know they'll cut off your head, but the Catholics will make you a Saint. Saint Martha the butt-buster.

MARTHA *(Goes to Elizabeth and lifts up her gown)*: Let me look at this . . . Help me lift up your skirt . . . I don't see any blood.

ELIZABETH: Are you sure?

MARTHA: Yes. There's a hole, but it's in the dress.

ELIZABETH *(Changing tone)*: Ha. They missed me. But if the shot went out into the air, then I must have peed all over myself. *(Desperate)* Oh, I did, Martha . . . I did. *(Gets down from the stool to look at the puddle)* And so much! Oh, how humiliating. The guards poking around into confidential places . . . the pistol going off by itself . . . piss all over everything.

(Martha exits. She comes back with a basin and a towel.)

. . . And Robert doesn't love me anymore . . . I want to see him . . . Martha . . . go and bring him here. Tell him to stop organizing rebellions against me . . . and that if he comes back, I'll grant him a contract for sweet wines . . .

MARTHA: Yes . . . yes . . . dear . . . I'll find him. I'll bring him here. Meanwhile, come here so I can wash you.

ELIZABETH *(Takes the basin from Martha)*: Let me do it myself . . . You go and look for him . . . but don't tell him that I sent you.

MARTHA: Then what can I tell him?

ELIZABETH: Tell him that I'm sick . . . that I'm dying . . . yes, that's it . . . that I shot myself with a pistol . . . but don't tell him about the pee . . . please. *(Martha exits. Elizabeth puts down the basin and shouts)* Stop, Martha. *(Martha returns)* I can't let Robert see me like this. Where is my little mirror? . . . I want to see if I'm getting better . . . *(She looks at herself in the mirror)* I'm not any better. No, not any better at all. Martha, how could I have gotten so old in these last thirty-five years . . . I can't let him see me like this . . . I can't . . . I'm ugly, horrible . . . old. *(She takes leaves out of her pocket and pops them into her mouth over and over again)* I'll kill myself . . . Oh, what a life!

MARTHA: For a start . . . you can spit out those disgusting leaves.

ELIZABETH: No, they give me a lift . . . they rejuvenate me.

MARTHA: Yes, and they stupefy you, too . . . and rot your teeth—go on, spit it out. *(Offers her a bowl)*

ELIZABETH: No, I won't spit.

MARTHA: If you don't, you'll get dragon breath. Spit.

(Elizabeth spits.)

ELIZABETH: I might as well have the breath of a dragon. I've already got the skin to go with it. If I met Saint George, he'd try to stick a sword in me.

(Martha carries the basin out and returns.)

MARTHA: Of course, if you decided to fix yourself up a little . . . a nice astringent compress . . . spruce up your color.

ELIZABETH: Again . . . with that hag . . . what's her name?

MARTHA: Big Mama . . . yes, that's her . . . she's the only one who can help you.

ELIZABETH: Yes, help me into a pile of excrement . . . the miraculous compresses that hag gives me are disgusting.

MARTHA: Don't be ridiculous . . . It's not excrement, it's medicinal mud, organic waste in varying states of decomposition.

ELIZABETH: There, you said it. The scientific definition of shit. Yes, I know all about it. She comes in. She slaps on some compresses of "organic waste"—that's your name for it—and it makes you look younger, about twenty minutes younger . . . and in exchange for this you go out of the house smelling like a dunghole . . . People say: "Oh, how young she looks!" . . . And TACH! They faint dead away!

MARTHA: I understand. You just don't feel like it today. And you're right. Why submit yourself to that kind of torture? For whom? It's not worth it.

ELIZABETH: Yes, it's not worth it. Go out and get Big Mama right away.

MARTHA: Yes, but . . .

ELIZABETH: Go.

MARTHA: You're not going to change your mind and make me send her away like you did last week.

(Martha exits. She returns with a mop.)

ELIZABETH: Go get her, I said! You big-mouthed gossip. What are you doing now?

MARTHA *(Pointing to the wet floor)*: Wait a minute while I dry this up.

ELIZABETH: Are you crazy? That's sacred pee. I made it myself. I'm the pope! Go.

MARTHA: OK, I'll let her in. *(Goes to the door)*

ELIZABETH: Let who in?

MARTHA: Big Mama. She's right out here.

ELIZABETH: Already? How could it be?

MARTHA: I took some initiative, and called her myself.

ELIZABETH: Stop. Just a minute . . . Wait . . . I'm not ready . . . I'm afraid.

MARTHA *(Looks out the door and comforts Elizabeth)*: Think how much a chicken suffers to squeeze out a simple egg. You have to give birth to a new queen . . . Be strong . . . Here comes Big Mama!

(A gigantic woman enters wearing a white mask similar to the ones worn in the Venetian carnival. She carries a basket in her arms.)

BIG MAMA: Maxima domina te exelle nobis . . .

ELIZABETH: Stop right there! Why are you wearing that mask?

BIG MAMA: Wear it I do only to cover up the ugly, ugly that be beneath it, my lady mine.

ELIZABETH: Take it off, immediately. I want to see your face.

MARTHA: Why fuss about it? She's doing it to save you trouble. You know what kind of reputation she has. If word got around that you were getting cosmetic treatments from Big Mama . . . a half-witch . . .

ELIZABETH: Take off the mask, I said.

BIG MAMA: I hope not to frighten you, my ladyness. *(Takes off the mask)* Here I be naturalistically.

ELIZABETH: Dieu, sauve moi! Qu'elle est horrible!

MARTHA: Je t'avais prevenue.

BIG MAMA: It's useless to parlez-vous francais. Understand it I do quite well, magnificent lady mine. I know that like a monster I look, and not a very pretty one at that. But shame me not, kind Queenie, and be not afraid, because I'm a good creature, and am here to offer you much help.

(Big Mama goes toward the door and carries onto the stage a strange wooden machine.)

ELIZABETH: I hope so, Big Mama. *(To Martha)* Why is this crazy woman talking like that?

MARTHA: I don't know. I think it's the slang they use on the other side of the Thames.

ELIZABETH: What is this round contraption?

BIG MAMA: This be called a rickety-rick, a stroller-roller . . . for learning you to walk on platform shoes, like all the fancy whores do, without falling in the off.

ELIZABETH: Platform shoes? Like the whores?

(Big Mama shows her two shoes made of cork and leather.)

MARTHA: These! Look! The soles are almost a foot high!

ELIZABETH: They look more like stilts than shoes.

BIG MAMA: The courtesans in Venice all be wearing them to look more tall.

ELIZABETH: Did you hear that, Martha. I'm making a career change. From queen to whore . . . *(To Big Mama)* I don't need to look any taller. I'm fine as I am.

BIG MAMA: If you prefer it, Queenie, we can just take up your dress so your ass looks smaller.

ELIZABETH: Hey, watch your tongue! I'll throw you out of here.

BIG MAMA: Calm thyself, my lady magnificent. *(Slips)* Oh. On what did I slip? . . . What is this wetness? . . . I could be mistaken, but to me it seems to be . . .

ELIZABETH: It was . . . my horse.

BIG MAMA: A wooden horse that pees? That be good luck!

ELIZABETH: What do you know about it? It's a royal horse.

BIG MAMA: Oh! Rise, Your Magnificence, rise. Come on into the rickety-rickety roller-stroller. That's it. Let's close you up in the behind. Can you be helping me too, Miss Martha.

MARTHA: With pleasure.

BIG MAMA: Oh look what a queenlike queen she be. It's the miracle of Your Highness's Highness.

ELIZABETH *(Laughing)*: At my age . . . in a baby buggy.

BIG MAMA: Would you like a pacifier in your mouth, Your Highness.

ELIZABETH *(No reaction)*: Don't I look a little silly way up here. I'm taller than my horse.

BIG MAMA: Yes, but you are beyond comparing to that wooden pisser!

MARTHA: Walk. Practice.

ELIZABETH: You can be sure that once I learn to walk on these prostitute platform shoes, I'm going to go looking for that

Portuguese ambassador, Mr. Mule in Heat, and walk all over him. I'll make him my doormat.

(While Elizabeth practices walking, Big Mama carries a platform onto the stage and puts an armchair on it.)

BIG MAMA: Walk. Walk, my sweetie longlegs!

ELIZABETH: Of course when I'm in the arms of my Essex . . . After he stops organizing these rebellions, of course . . . won't he be surprised at how tall I've grown . . . I'll ask him for a kiss . . . *(Laughing)* And he'll kiss me on the belly button . . . *(Changes tone)* Get me out of this thing.

BIG MAMA: Come, come Queenie. Be putting your sweet butt here on this chair while I be preparing the ointment to smear all over you.

MARTHA: Why don't you relax and play your lute while you're waiting. I'll go get it for you.

ELIZABETH: No, give me those papers from the desk over there.

MARTHA: The ambassadors' letters.

ELIZABETH: No, the manuscript of *Hamlet*.

MARTHA: That stuff again? *(Gives the manuscript to Elizabeth)*

BIG MAMA: Oh, *Omelette*. I be knowing it well. I've seen it at the glub-glub theatre put on by actors emoting grandly: "Get thee to a nunnery, Ophelia . . . amen, amen . . . because if ever you got married, your husband would be one hell of a sorry old cuckold . . . Get thee to a nunnery! Amen, amen!" Ha. Ha. Ha. *(Gets a cream out of her basket and spreads it on the Queen's face)*

ELIZABETH: Do you always laugh like that?

BIG MAMA: No, my voice is being a little hoarse today.

ELIZABETH: What did you put on my face . . . it's pulling my skin off.

BIG MAMA: Rock juice.

(Big Mama begins tying back the Queen's hair.)

MARTHA: What are you looking for in that manuscript?

ELIZABETH: Proof that this was written to mock me, that the seeds of Robert's rebellion are planted inside these plays.

MARTHA: Come on. You mean that Hamlet is a libelous piece of propaganda?

ELIZABETH: Don't make fun of me, Martha. *(To Big Mama)* And you, take it easy. You're pulling me up like a skinned rabbit.

(Martha takes off Elizabeth's platform shoes.)

(To Martha) And you, get it into your head that I'm serious about this. This entire play is an attack against my character and my politics. Every night at the Globe this theatrical tub-thumper spits in my eye.

MARTHA: Listen, Elizabeth, by chance I happened to see a performance of Hamlet a few days ago, and I assure you that I saw absolutely no attack against you.

ELIZABETH: You saw it, and you didn't suspect a thing? Then it must be true: "The frog at the bottom of the well believed that the bucket hanging above him was the sun."

MARTHA: What are you saying?

ELIZABETH: I was just paraphrasing Shakespeare.

BIG MAMA: Pretty. How goes it? "The frog, croak-croak, in the bottom of the well, thought the asshole of the bucket was the sun, plop-plop." Magnificent.

MARTHA: Quiet. The only thing I understand is that you're calling me a frog, but what's the rest of it about?

ELIZABETH: That's the way Hamlet talks.

BIG MAMA: Now I be understanding. It's like seeing backwards in a mirror, tervsy-topsy . . . versy-vicey . . . insy-outsy.

MARTHA: Shut up.

ELIZABETH: No, she's got it right. It's just like a reversed image in a mirror.

BIG MAMA: See. Miss uppity-uppity fartface.

MARTHA: Don't talk to me like that.

BIG MAMA: Just be quiet, and be putting the whore shoes away. *(To Elizabeth)* What servants you have, my lady sublime.

ELIZABETH: To sum it up, this charlatan, William Shakespeare, to disguise . . .

BIG MAMA: Unblouse yourself and be getting your clothes off.

ELIZABETH: I wouldn't dream of it.

BIG MAMA: Of what are you embarrassed. We all of us be women . . . The only masculine one here be that wooden horse pisser.

ELIZABETH: All women? *(Looks intently at Big Mama)* I'm not so sure. I have some doubts about one of us, dear Big Mama.

BIG MAMA: Why you shouldn't be so hard on yourself. You still be a good-looking woman.

ELIZABETH: I'm not getting undressed.

MARTHA: I have an idea.

(Martha leaves and returns right away with a screen that she puts in front of Elizabeth to cover her, leaving only her head exposed. Elizabeth takes off her blouse assisted by Martha and Big Mama. Martha takes the Queen's clothes away and comes back with a big sheet that she wraps around Elizabeth.)

ELIZABETH: I was saying that Shakespeare, in order to disguise his political allusions, has simply changed the sex of his characters.

MARTHA: In what sense?

ELIZABETH: He just changed the female characters into men, and vice versa.

BIG MAMA: He added the game of transvestites to switcheroo the sexes in the mirror.

ELIZABETH: Yes.

MARTHA: Give me an example.

ELIZABETH: That's easy. I'm a woman . . . and Hamlet is a man.

MARTHA: I see, because Hamlet is a parody of you. I forgot.

BIG MAMA: Listen, you've got to stop mocking this woman. AOOOOOOOUUUUUUUU.

(The screen improvisation: Big Mama, while undressing Elizabeth, inadvertently uncovers her breast.)

ELIZABETH: Oh, excuse me. *(Covers herself with the screen)*

BIG MAMA: Oh, boy. Why be you pulling so strong?

ELIZABETH: Please, there's people in the back row, you know.

BIG MAMA: And this be the reason why so many of them is up there.

ELIZABETH *(Tries to continue acting her lines, but is continually interrupted by Big Mama, who continues talking, pretending to speak to a spectator in the balcony)*: So I was saying that I am a woman . . . *(Angry, she stops)* What is it?

BIG MAMA: They be standing up for a better view. Sit down!
ELIZABETH: Stop it. Let me continue. I was saying . . .

(Big Mama continues to talk to someone in the balcony.)

. . . I was saying that I am the queen . . .
BIG MAMA: Pervert!
ELIZABETH: Will you let me go on? Stay in your place and try to be quiet. Because, now I'm the queen, and for once, at last, you are the servant. So, shut up. Is that clear?
BIG MAMA: Dario Fo wrote this play, and he wouldn't like to see you treating me like this. One word form me and he'll cross out "Queen" next to your lines and write in "Maid." *(To audience)* She's really been immersing herself in the role. She answers the telephone: "Hello, the Queen speaking." So she called me a servant. We'll just have to have a servant's revolt. Let's sing the "Revolting Servant's Theme Song." *(Sings. Then to Martha)* You can join in, too.
MARTHA: Never.
ELIZABETH: Now, can we please go on?

(Screen improvisation ends unless Big Mama can get away with interrupting the Queen a few more times with her "Servant's Song.")

ELIZABETH *(To Big Mama)*: Cut it out. *(To Martha)* So, are you listening? I'm Hamlet. The sweet Ophelia is a woman . . . and my beloved Robert is a man. Hamlet's father was assassinated . . . my mother was assassinated. The ghost of Hamlet's father pursued him night and day . . . just like my mother has always shouted for vengeance in my dreams.
BIG MAMA: Look how it all works out to be the same. One over here. One over there.
ELIZABETH: Hamlet's mother remarries her brother-in-law . . . and my father Henry VIII also married the widowed wife of his brother, his sister-in-law.
BIG MAMA: How nice that the family stays so cozy-close.
ELIZABETH: It's exactly my story, dear.

MARTHA: Calm down, don't cheat. Your father personally executed Ann Boleyn, but Hamlet's mother is innocent.

ELIZABETH: Who says so. Read the text closely . . . the Queen pleads innocence, but Hamlet condemns her. My father also pretended to disagree with the Lords who condemned Ann Boleyn to death. Oh, if you could have seen how he despaired and shed tears of blood over the headless corpse of my mother . . . just like Hamlet's mother.

BIG MAMA: A mirror image in versy-vicey. Exacto.

MARTHA: Elizabeth, I'm sorry, but tell me what serious, concrete evidence do you have for believing that Hamlet is you?

BIG MAMA: Answer that, can I?

ELIZABETH: Go ahead, we're listening.

BIG MAMA: Okeydokey. The Queen of Elizabeth here in England, as everybody knows, has a bad awful habit: whenever a moving curtain she sees, her dagger is always ready . . . "A ghost," she cries, and whip-whip-slice . . . And whoever is behind it . . . is behind it . . . too bad. *(Mimes the action of the stabbing)*

MARTHA: Yes, this morning she almost killed me.

BIG MAMA: What a shame she missed you. In any case, Hamlet had also this bad awful habit . . . a scene there is with a moving curtain . . . whip-whip-slice-ping . . . and behind it is Polonius.

ELIZABETH: Polonius who plays the figure of my chief advisor, Cecil.

BIG MAMA: Oh, I love a good allegory. Get it? There's this Polonius who be the allegory of Cecil, standing in the behind of the curtain, and Hamlet be there talking to his mama, saying the most god-awful things . . . I was so shocked . . . like when he said: "How could you marry a wimp-weeny like that . . . you, whore." Just like that he said it . . . And then the curtain moved . . . Aaahaahaa . . . A rat . . . whip-whip-slice . . . there in Denmark, you know, the rats are always five-and-a-half-feet tall . . . five feet minimum . . . slice-slice . . . the knife . . . 'bye-'bye . . . Polonius . . . one more allegory bites the dust. *(To Martha)* . . . And the next allegory will be you.

MARTHA: Oh, what a brilliant explanation. Indisputable.

BIG MAMA: You're still not convinced. OK. I'll give you another try. In the fin-fin finale of *Hamlet,* who is arriving to restore order to the whorehouse of a kingdom?

MARTHA: Fortinbras.

BIG MAMA: Fortinbras of Norway. Good, and in this whorehouse of the Queen's England, who, according to the Puritans, is the Fortinbras of the North who'll be coming down the mountain to restore the order of the kingdom?

MARTHA: James.

BIG MAMA: James of Scotland, the big bagpiper who is on the border perched, ready for to pounce down on the queen's noggin. *(Pulls violently on the Queen's hair)*

ELIZABETH: Eh, Big Mama . . . take it easy.

BIG MAMA: Excuse me, my excessivity of enthusiasm.

ELIZABETH: And you're pulling my ears and eyes back so far that I'm going to end up looking like a Mongol.

BIG MAMA: But what a Mongol! You're splendiferous. Look, I even made disappear your double chin.

ELIZABETH: How can you say such a thing. I never had a double chin.

BIG MAMA: Right. You had a double neck.

MARTHA: Excuse me, you're confusing her with Hamlet. He's the one with the double chin . . . and a potbelly . . . and flatfeet.

ELIZABETH: Your subtle irony eludes me.

BIG MAMA: But me it eludes not. Shall I tell her?

MARTHA: No, be quiet.

BIG MAMA: Yes, tell her I will: the fact be that the actor who plays the part of Hamlet, goes by the name of Richard Burbage, and alas, poor Burbage, I know him well. He's forty-two years young, but on a good day he doesn't look a day over sixty-two . . . sixty-four . . . he's a fat old guy with a bit of flip-flop belly pot . . . and he's very short of breath . . . so that every time he starts acting, he gets an asthma attack . . . and during the duel with Laertes . . . Laertes is young, jump-jumping, leap-leaping all around . . . but Burbage be fighting the duel . . . he never even moves . . . but he still gets short of breath . . . and the Queen be saying: "Oh, Hamlet, thou art not a boy no more, you're breathing through your asshole." Oh, that Shakespearean rag . . . what a poet . . . that line was censored . . . but that be just the way he wrote it . . . meanwhile, this Burbage is oozing with sweat . . . pant-pant . . . puff-puff—

MARTHA *(Interrupting)*: And his face is oozing with pimples . . . and he has not one, but two double chins . . . and he walks like a cross between a chicken and a duck.

BIG MAMA: Yes, it be true. He does have a bit of a bowlegged strut, with his feet out-turned and his belly hanging out . . . but when he acts: "Be it to be or not to be . . ." he has a power that inebriates the audience with drunken joy . . . *(Acts out a bebop, jazz, scat version of Hamlet's "To be or not to be" monologue)* . . . "To bebop or not to bebop, that be the question . . . bop bop, bo diddley, bebop . . . slings and arrows, arrows and slings, bebop bi doodly, come on and shake that thing . . . to die, to sleep, to sleep no more, bebop, ba-dabba-babba, tear up the floor . . . shake it, shake it, shake it, shake it Shakespeare . . ." *(Gets increasingly carried away with the rhythm of the performance)* . . . And everybody understands what he's saying . . . he's a natural phenomenon . . . who cares if he's gay.

ELIZABETH: Ah, he's a homosexual.

MARTHA: It hardly shows.

BIG MAMA: It shows. It shows . . . all he needs is a feather in his ass . . . and why do you think they gave the part to this gay cavalier. There be at least five other actors in the company who could have played it better . . . younger, stronger, smoother . . . why give the part to an aging queen?

ELIZABETH: They chose him precisely because he was a withered, old, washed-up actor . . . so that there would be no doubt that he was a perfect double of me. "Queen of radiant beauty," they flatter me as if there were no wrinkles in my face . . . "Goddess of youthful zest," as if I were not falling to pieces.

BIG MAMA: No, no. You can't say things like that anymore. At least not about your face. Look how firm that kisser be.

(She gets Elizabeth out of the chair, and takes it off the platform.)

ELIZABETH: What are you doing to me now?

BIG MAMA: You want to get rid of that belly flab, don't you?

ELIZABETH: Belly flab? What kind of muck have you got this time?

BIG MAMA: Little bellysuckers. *(Shows her one from his jar)*

ELIZABETH: Leeches.

BIG MAMA: No. Leeches suck blood. These only suck fat . . . straight out of your skin . . . look how cute they are . . . with their little blue eyes . . . hello . . . slurp-slurp—

ELIZABETH: How disgusting! No, no, please. Get them away from me.

(Martha forces Elizabeth to stand on the platform while Big Mama puts the leeches on her.)

BIG MAMA: See, you can also use them on your flabby hips and thighs.

ELIZABETH: For pity's sake.

BIG MAMA: On your shoulders . . . your arms . . . your neck.

ELIZABETH: Oh, God. I'm going to throw up.

BIG MAMA: On your back . . . on your buttocks . . . they're slenderizing! Look at that little monster . . . what a glutton . . . slurp-slurp . . . Attlia . . . Caligula . . .

ELIZABETH: OK. Go ahead. Just don't let me see them. Where were we?

MARTHA: Talking about an old washed-up actor.

ELIZABETH: Right, and he's probably impotent too. Hamlet's always horny, but he never does any screwing.

BIG MAMA: What a dirty-mouthed queen. And in front of the little bellysuckers . . . they're so shy . . . look, this one is blushing . . . suck, darling, suck . . .

ELIZABETH: But what really gets on my nerves is that this bastard makes me out to be the ruination of the country: "Something is rotten in the state of Denmark . . ." Don't you understand . . . he's talking about England. "Denmark." Who does he think he's fooling?

BIG MAMA: Ah. Now I see how his mirror game works. When he says, "All of Denmark is a prison . . ." he's not really talking about Denmark . . . he means that America . . . I mean England's a prison.

MARTHA: You're obsessed with double meanings.

ELIZABETH: You think so? Let's look at what happens at the end of *Hamlet*.

MARTHA: A massacre.

BIG MAMA: Yes . . . what a finish . . . bodies everywhere . . . Laertes chopped up over here . . . whip-whip . . . the Queen is poisoned over there . . . gag-gag . . . the King is throwing up here . . . puke-puke . . . and Hamlet is breathing his last breath there . . . gasp-gasp . . .

ELIZABETH: And who's to blame?

BIG MAMA: Hamlet is. Everyone knows that it be all his fault. The boy couldn't make up his mind. He could have settled it all right away with a little dagger in his uncle's back . . . slip-slip . . . while he was praying . . . amen-amen. *(Becomes Hamlet and mimes out the actions as she recounts them)* "Now I'll stick you good . . . Wait—he says to himself—I'll be doing him a favor if I kill him now . . . whip-whip . . . purified, with his sins forgiven . . . amen-amen . . . he'd sail straight on up to heaven . . . flap-flap . . . My father died full of sins . . . hubba-hubba . . . and he went straight down to hell . . . sizzle-sizzle . . . I'll wait till he's in my mother's room screwing around . . . hootchy-kootchy . . . then I'll pull out my knife . . . shup-shup . . . not now . . . tomorrow . . . we'll see . . . the day after tomorrow . . . I don't know . . . maybe next week." Oh, boy, what a wimp. He could have fixed everything fine in the very first scene when the ghost of Hamlet's daddy came up to him and said: "Hamlet . . . let . . . let . . . let—the father ghost talks in echoes, like all avenging phantoms—your uncle . . . uncle . . . uncle . . . is the assassin . . . ass . . . ass . . . ass . . . kill the creep . . . creep . . . creep . . . creep . . ."

ELIZABETH: But if he had killed his uncle in the first scene, he never could have written a five-act tragedy.

BIG MAMA: Fooey . . . I prefer something clear . . . one act . . . but clear . . . Daddy ghost says: "Hamlet, there's your man . . ." "Oh, yeah." Knife. Stab. Curtain. Much better than: "Now I'll think about it, now I'll wait, change my mind, procrastinate . . ."

ELIZABETH: And isn't that what they accuse me of doing, too? *(Accidentally squashes leeches as she turns)*

BIG MAMA: Ahhh.

ELIZABETH: What happened?

BIG MAMA: You squashed my bellysuckers. What butchery . . . It's just like the last act of Hamlet. You even squashed the Queen.

ELIZABETH: Isn't that what they accuse me of doing, too?

BIG MAMA: Of squashing bellysuckers? They're right.

ELIZABETH: No, of not eliminating my enemies . . . of not taking direct action . . . The Puritans complain that the Spanish are crushing the Flemish on our doorstep, and that I am too timid to stop them. The Irish are rebelling, and I, instead of organizing the proper kind of scorched earth repression, hold myself back, make treaties, change my mind and procrastinate. I negotiate with the pope who excommunicated me, and don't even talk to the Protestants who elected me their pope.

BIG MAMA *(Playing with Elizabeth's ear)*: Its because you be too soft in letting them complain. If I was queen: ZACH! *(Makes the gesture of cutting off heads)*

ELIZABETH *(To Big Mama)*: What are you doing with your finger in my ear?

BIG MAMA: I isn't doing nothing with my finger. One of the bellysuckers got loose in there.

ELIZABETH: Oh, Jesus, Mary and Joseph . . . Get it out.

BIG MAMA: I can't help it if these little suckers like greasy holes.

ELIZABETH: God, I'm going to be sick.

BIG MAMA *(Digging the worm out of her ear)*: He's slipping away . . . there he is . . . oooplah . . . got him . . . Look how fat he is . . . and such pretty eyes . . . smooch-smooch.

ELIZABETH: Damned witch . . . get out of here . . . go away.

(Martha takes Elizabeth offstage to get dressed behind a curtain.)

BIG MAMA: Oh, the little suckers are all over the floor . . . Look at this fat one . . . what a feast he's had . . . so fat it's disgusting . . . I'll take him right to my husband's house . . . he's a fisherman and he goes wild over big fat worms like this . . . a fishing he will go . . . he'll stick this bellysucker on his hook . . . ouch-ouch . . . throw it in the water . . . splash-splash . . . to the bottom of the river . . . glub-glub . . . and as soon as they see this worm, the fish will start running . . . *(Mimes the arrival of the fish family)* "Yum-yum, it's a bellysucker." UARGH! UARGH! And tonight we'll eat an enormous fish. AHHHHHHH. No, we won't really be eating a fish, because this sucker has been sucking on the queen, and the fish was sucking on the sucker . . . so we in the end will be eating the queen. *(Looks around, content)* What a subtle idea, is it not? See what an allegory can do . . . But if the truth must be told, I didn't make it up myself . . . not me . . . not me . . . It was Shakespeare . . . He was the one who hatched this baby allegory . . . When he had Hamlet say that a king sits down to a banquet not to eat but to be eaten, because when he dies the worms will eat his corpse. A fisherman will pass by . . . take a handful of the kingly worms . . . and put them on his hook. He catches a big fish. And a beggar, the lowest of the low, find the fish and eats it. So in the end, the beggar eats his king. Its gives you goose-bumps. What a mind, that Shakespeare. You can't have an idea that he hasn't thought of before.

ELIZABETH *(Behind the curtain)*: Big Mama, I could be imagining things, but I feel thinner.

BIG MAMA: Oh, no, your majesticness, it be not your imagination. You surely have been slenderized. Be it enough to see how fat these bellysuckers have become. They look pregnant. *(Passes a leech around the side of the curtain to Elizabeth)*

ELIZABETH *(Behind the curtain)*: I told you to keep them away from me. They're disgusting. *(Changes tone)* Listen, do you think you could perform another little miracle, for my breasts. They look like two-dried out mozzarellas.

BIG MAMA: You call that a small miracle! If you give me time, I'll resurrect your tits. I'll make your boobs so big that when you cross your arms you'll think you're leaning on a shelf. Then you can put a vase of flowers up there and water them every morning . . .

(Elizabeth comes out from behind the curtain wearing a ceremonial gown and a crown on her head.)

Oh, how beautiful! What an outfit!

ELIZABETH: Oh, it's just something I threw on to wear around the house. How do I look? Do you think Robert will like it?

MARTHA: He'll be dazzled.

BIG MAMA: Yes, he'll be stupefied. Kind of like me after I heard this story about you being the double of Hamlet. Bebop, bebop, do-bee.

(Martha and Big Mama put the platform shoes on the Queen.)

MARTHA: It's intrigued me, too.

ELIZABETH: Ah, so I've finally gotten through to you.

MARTHA: More than anything, I'm perplexed. You understand that if what you suspect is true, there must be an organized campaign behind it all.

ELIZABETH: Of course there is.

BIG MAMA: Excuse me, Queenie, but I do not agree. Come on. A revolution organized by theatre people. I can see it now. Actors with wooden swords, and cannons loaded with talcum powder. "Ready for the revolution. OK. Load the cannons. Fire!" Puff-puff . . . cough-cough . . . fizz-fizz . . . end of the revolution. *(Mimes the explosion of a cannon loaded with talcum powder and suffocates)*

ELIZABETH: The theatre people are only the bit players. But there's someone behind them . . . using real bullets. And I'll prove it to you if you give me the manuscript of *Hamlet*. I'll read you this monologue replacing the masculine with the feminine. *(Reads:)*

Why what an ass I am.
This is most brave.
That I, the daughter of a dear mother murdered,
Prompted to my revenge by heaven and hell,
Must like a whore unpack my heart with words
And fall a-cursing like a very drab . . .

(Egerton enters with another folder.)

EGERTON: May I? Am I disturbing . . .

(Big Mama goes toward Egerton and motions him to be quiet. Elizabeth gets up and walks on her platform shoes as she reads.)

ELIZABETH: Quiet in the gallery. *(Continues reading:)*
How stand I then, that have a mother killed, a father stained
Excitements of my reason and my blood,
And let all sleep? While to my shame . . .

EGERTON: Who's she talking to?

BIG MAMA *(In a whisper that gets louder and louder)*: She's playing the part of Hamlet . . . he's the transvestite with a feather in his ass who's been making fun of the queen . . .

ELIZABETH *(Trying to interrupt Big Mama)*:
O Most pernicious woman . . .

(Big Mama explains the plot of Hamlet to Egerton in gibberish and mime, and finishes with:)

BIG MAMA: Curtain. Act One. *(To the Queen who is annoyed because she is distracting her audience)* My Majesty, I have to explain it to him because about Hamlet he knows not a thing. He must be one of your Intelligence Officers. *(Continues explaining the plot in mime and gibberish)* . . . Curtain. Act Four.

ELIZABETH: Quiet, Big Mama.
O Most pernicious woman . . .

(Standing between Egerton and the Queen, Big Mama continues her one-woman synopsis for Egerton, while trying to hide her actions from the Queen who sees her gesturing.)

(To Big Mama) Give me your hand.

BIG MAMA: We've almost finished the fifth.

ELIZABETH *(To Big Mama)*: If you don't stop, I'm going to call the guards and have you thrown out.

O most pernicious woman!
O villain, villain, smiling damned villain . . . it cannot be
But I am pigeon livered, and lack gall
To make oppression bitter . . .

Why are you looking at me like that, Egerton? *(Referring to her platform shoes)* Do I look taller? Don't you know that people keep growing until age seventy. *(Serious)* Now tell me, if someone had the audacity to make a monkey of your queen with insults like these, what would you do?

EGERTON: My lady, who would dare to show you such lack of respect?

ELIZABETH *(Handing him the manuscript)*: He would. There's his name and his insults, word for word. If you went to the theatre a little more often, dear Egerton . . . to the Globe, for example . . . tonight in fact . . . you would hear it all repeated.

BIG MAMA: Do you realize that Hamlet is a transvestite who's making a mockery of the queen . . . Dressed as a frog in the bottom of a well looking at the bucket's asshole and saying, "What a sunny day."

EGERTON: That's impossible.

MARTHA: It's true. These third-rate actors insult her . . . And the people applaud.

ELIZABETH: And all you think about is setting traps for Essex and his good-for-nothing followers.

EGERTON: Is it true that they say these things at the Globe? The sheriff is there every night and the never mentioned anything to me about allusions to you.

ELIZABETH: My wooden horse has more brains and imagination than you and all your men put together.

BIG MAMA: And he pees more, too.

ELIZABETH: Give me the manuscript, Egerton. Now listen, and try to understand the real meaning of what I'm reading to you.

BIG MAMA: It's no use. *(Referring to expression of stupefied bewilderment on Egerton's face)* This man just don't understand.

ELIZABETH: Quiet, Big Mama.

BIG MAMA: But look at his face. There's no light in his eyes. Nobody's home!

(While Elizabeth reads, Big Mama mocks Egerton's facial expressions of stupidity, imitating them.)

ELIZABETH: Enough. Listen. This is Hamlet speaking:

. . . To take arms against a sea of troubles . . .

Big Mama, I'm reading Shakespeare, and I will not allow you to interrupt.

BIG MAMA: I'm not interrupting. He just don't understand.

ELIZABETH *(Continues reading)*:

To die, to sleep—
No more, and by a sleep to say we end
The heartache and the thousand natural shocks
That flesh is heir to; 'tis a consummation
Devoutly to be wish'd. To die, to sleep;
To sleep, perchance to dream. Ay, there's the rub;
For in that sleep of death what dreams may come
When we have shuffled off this mortal coil,
That makes calamity of so long life . . .

EGERTON: I don't understand.

ELIZABETH: Bravo, Egerton . . . That should be your motto. Repeat it every once in a while. It helps me. Come on. Say it again.

EGERTON: I don't understand.

ELIZABETH: You don't understand? He's saying that the only reason that poor people put up with their miserable lives is that they are afraid of life beyond death. If it weren't for that, everyone would kill themselves. Thousands of people would throw themselves off of cliffs, into the sea, into the fire. Say it again, Egerton, your motto.

EGERTON: I don't understand.

BIG MAMA: He's a natural. *(Moves toward Elizabeth and looks at the manuscript)*

ELIZABETH: Bravo. You don't understand. But it's so clear:

For who would bear the whips and scorns of time.
Th'oppressor's wrongs, the proud man's contumely,
The pangs of despis'd love, the law's delay,
The insolence of office, and the spurns . . .

Take note, that I'm not making any of this up, Egerton.

Who would fardels bear,
To grunt and sweat under a weary life . . .

EGERTON: Yes, I don't think he likes us.

BIG MAMA *(Referring to Egerton's sudden insight)*: Lightning strikes.

ELIZABETH:

But that the dread of something after death,
The undiscovered country, from whose bourn
No traveler returns, puzzles the will,
And makes us rather bear those ills we have
Than fly to others that we know not of?
Thus conscience does make cowards of us all . . .

BIG MAMA: Outrageous. Now I see what he's up to. This Shakespeare is telling people: "What's up? Why don't you move your asses? Why do you let yourselves be treated like slaves and animals? Just because you're afraid of burning in hell? Don't you idiots realize that hell is here on earth. Not down there. Don't be afraid to stand up for yourselves. Beat the shit out of your screwed-up government." *(Begins singing a protest song)*

EGERTON *(Shouting)*: You're right. You're absolutely right. He's inciting the people to revolt, to start a revolution!

BIG MAMA: Take it easy. You'll bust your brain if you try to think it through all at once. Let it sink in slowly.

MARTHA: Wait a minute. I think you're exaggerating . . . I don't see any incitement to revolt here . . . Maybe a little questioning . . . some discontent, but . . .

BIG MAMA *(Mocking Martha, she mimes a chicken laying an egg)*: TACH! The egg of peace. And there's a teeny-weeny Jesuit inside. *(Mimes a tiny creature flying away)*

EGERTON: In any case, Your Majesty, I'll arrest him and close down the theatre immediately.

ELIZABETH: You'll do nothing of the kind, dear Egerton. Instead, you'll start an investigation to find out if this Shakespeare is part of Robert of Essex's conspiracy . . . then we'll see.

EGERTON: I'll appoint a special prosecutor, right away.

ELIZABETH: Speaking of investigations, have you verified the authenticity of that letter, the one you thought was written by Robert of Essex.

EGERTON: Your Majesty, I am mortified, but I must tell you that you were right. The letter was a forgery. The seal was also counterfeit.

ELIZABETH: That's quick work for such a thorough investigation.

EGERTON: No, all we had to do was hang the courier who gave us the letter from his feet by a hook, and he admitted everything.

ELIZABETH: Lovely. You see, Martha, in our country, the balance of justice hangs from a butcher's hook.

BIG MAMA: What a beautiful line. What an allegory. Shakespeare? . . . Oh, that Shakespearean rag!

ELIZABETH: No, Big Mama. It's mine.

BIG MAMA: But it's so Shakespeariano.

ELIZABETH: In a few days you'll find the line in one of his plays. He gets all his best ideas from me. What is it now Egerton? What are you hiding in the folder. Bad news, I suppose.

EGERTON: Evidence, Your Majesty.

ELIZABETH: Evidence of what?

EGERTON: That the Puritans are funneling secret funds to the conspirators.

ELIZABETH *(Laughs)*: Your trap is turning against you, Egerton. You used the armory as bait so that Essex and his conspirators would feel confident enough to start shooting . . . You thought you could finish him off that way . . . But now the Puritans are snatching up the same bait . . . How entertaining to watch the cannon-loader sit on his gunpowder by mistake and shoot himself in the air.

BIG MAMA: Ah . . . how beautiful. Shakespeare.

ELIZABETH: It's mine.

BIG MAMA: Yours. That crook. Can't this Shakespeare write anything on his own? The crook!

EGERTON: I don't know why you're so happy about it, Your Majesty. It seems you are enjoying the idea of our defeat.

MARTHA: He's right. You're crazy. You're forgetting that it would be your defeat as well.

ELIZABETH: Yes, yes . . . I got carried away. All right then, what are you waiting for.

EGERTON: Your Majesty, at the moment they are scattered in small groups . . . We're waiting for them to reunite, and then we'll attack them on their way to Parliament and the palace.

ELIZABETH: Which palace?

EGERTON: This one. Yours.

BIG MAMA: Got that, Queenie. These miscreants have the gall to come here and kill you.

MARTHA: Just like that.

EGERTON: Therefore, Your Majesty, I believe, and Cecil concurs, that you would be safer someplace else.

ELIZABETH: In other words, I have to make a quick getaway.

BIG MAMA: And after I was going to make that nice little shelf with the flower vases on top.

ELIZABETH: Quiet.

EGERTON: Yes, Your Majesty. All your advisors agree that you should move your quarters to Fort Kenilworth . . . with an armed escort, of course.

ELIZABETH: An armed escort? But why me? What has all this got to do with me? Personally I've read lots of scribbling on the walls of London in these past few days, and none of them say anything bad about the queen. My popularity with the people is as strong as ever. It's my advisors that they criticize. The insults and death threats are all directed against Bacon, Cecil and even you. You and my advisors should take an armed escort to Fort Kenilworth. You're the ones who need protection.

BIG MAMA: You tell him, Queenie.

MARTHA: Elizabeth, you're pitiless. But tell me how you could have seen those writings on the wall? You haven't left the palace for weeks.

EGERTON: Exactly. Unless Your Majesty has been out alone at night walking the streets.

ELIZABETH: Big Mama, pass me that tube.

(Big Mama gives her a telescope that has been leaning against the wall.)

I went out on the streets with this.

EGERTON: What is it?

ELIZABETH: A gift from the Venetian ambassador. *(Hands it to Egerton)* It's called a telescope. You just put it up to your eye like this. An amazing gadget.

(Egerton looks out at the audience with the telescope.)

EGERTON: It's fanstastic . . . everything looks so close. Incredible . . . as if you could touch those people out there with your hands.

MARTHA: Could I take a look for a moment?

EGERTON: Of course, go right ahead. *(Hands telescope to Martha)* It certainly would be wonderful to have one of these gadgets for my security police.

MARTHA *(Looking through the telescope)*: Magnificent.

ELIZABETH: Certainly. I've already ordered a case of them for you. Then you can check up on everybody at all times: what they're doing, who they're with, even through their windows into their homes. You can watch them in bed when they're making love, and when they're relieving themselves . . . Everything under surveillance . . . a truly modern nation . . . the voyeur State.

BIG MAMA *(Takes the telescope from Martha)*: Oh God. I can't believe my eyeballs.

ELIZABETH: What is it?

BIG MAMA: Down there, at the end of the street, it seems that your beloved Essex . . . oh what a hunk . . . and his men . . . oh what a hunk . . . are advancing towards the palace . . . and there are people applauding them . . . oooh-oooh.

MARTHA: Give me that. *(She looks)* Yes. They're armed . . . they're waving . . . they're inviting people to join them.

EGERTON: Dammit! I didn't expect them so soon! *(Takes the telescope from Martha)* Let me see.

ELIZABETH *(Arrogantly takes the telescope)*: It's mine. I'm the queen.

BIG MAMA *(Goes to get another little telescope from her basket and looks out toward the audience with it)*: Uh-oh, Queenie . . . Looks like we're in for it this time.

ELIZABETH: Big Mama, where did you get that telescope?

BIG MAMA: It's mine. I brought it from Venice. The street vendors sell them in the square. If you buy ten toy gondolas, you get one free. Military secret. O sole mia . . . *(Mimes a gondolier)*

ELIZABETH *(Looking through telescope)*: Look, there's another group coming across Saint Bartholomew's Bridge . . . and another advancing from Trygham.

EGERTON: Excuse me, but I have to go immediately to find Hellington and organize the counterattack.

ELIZABETH: Stop. You're not going to organize anything. The orders are: nobody moves. We'll allow them to let off some steam while they lap up the applause of the shop-keepers in the marketplace.

BIG MAMA: Good move, Queenie. Then when the first cannon fires, they'll pee themselves wetter than your piss-piss wooden horse.

ELIZABETH: One thing you can do, Egerton, is to go to Cecil with orders to send the leader of Parliament and the chief justice to Essex with this message . . . write it down.

BIG MAMA *(Goes to the desk and takes up a feather pen)*: I'll write it up, right away.

ELIZABETH *(Dictates)*: We come on behalf of . . .

BIG MAMA: Wait. Let me be getting the address . . . "To Mister Earl Essex . . . Palace number . . ."

ELIZABETH: I'm sending two Lords to deliver the message. The address is unnecessary.

BIG MAMA: Yes, but if the Lords get lost, there goes the message. What does it cost you to stick on the address?

ELIZABETH: All right, but hurry.

BIG MAMA: "To Mister Earl Essex . . . into his hands . . . at the end of his arms . . ."

ELIZABETH: We come . . .

BIG MAMA: "We come . . ."

ELIZABETH: . . . on behalf of the queen . . .

BIG MAMA: ". . . on behalf of the queen . . ."

ELIZABETH: . . . and we want to know . . .

BIG MAMA: ". . . and we want to know . . . on the other hand . . ."

ELIZABETH: Don't be ridiculous . . . and we want to know the reason . . .

BIG MAMA: ". . . and we want to know the reason." Period. That's telling them.

ELIZABETH: Why a period. I didn't finish the sentence.

BIG MAMA: You didn't?

ELIZABETH: No. It continues.

BIG MAMA: Then it's a comma.

ELIZABETH: No comma.

BIG MAMA: Semi-colon?

ELIZABETH: No semi-colon.

BIG MAMA: Exclamation point?

ELIZABETH: No. I told you. There's no punctuation.

BIG MAMA: Well, I've got to do something with this little period here. Maybe I'll draw a little flower around it. Ah-AHH. A dragon. Puff-puff. Saint George on horseback. Grr-grr . . .

ELIZABETH: All right! Put in a comma! . . . —We come on behalf of the queen and we want to know the reason . . .

BIG MAMA: Comma.

ELIZABETH: . . . the reason for these assemblages . . .

BIG MAMA: ". . . for these semblances . . ."

ELIZABETH: Assemblages!

BIG MAMA *(Stubbornly)*: "Semblances!"

ELIZABETH: Assemblages.

BIG MAMA *(With the air of having finally understood)*: Ah! "Sandwiches." It's a metaphor. Ah ah. "Sandwiches." Ah-ah.

ELIZABETH: The queen . . .

BIG MAMA: Another one.

ELIZABETH: No.

BIG MAMA: The same one as before. "The queen, the same one as before . . ."

ELIZABETH: No, that's understood.

BIG MAMA: Do they have to guess?

ELIZABETH: Silence. The queen assures you . . .

BIG MAMA: "The queen is sure of you . . ."

ELIZABETH *(Correcting her; emphases the letter "A")*: Assures you.

BIG MAMA *(With the air of saying it's the same thing)*: "Is sure of you."

ELIZABETH: Assures you!

BIG MAMA: Oh, another metaphor. "Ah. Sure it's you." "Ah sure it's you."

ELIZABETH: . . . that you will be . . .

BIG MAMA: ". . . that you ah will be . . ."

ELIZABETH: No. There's no "ah" there. . . . that you will be . . .

BIG MAMA: Oh, it's the exception to the rule.

ELIZABETH: Exception to what rule? Stop it!

BIG MAMA: ". . . that you will be . . ."

ELIZABETH: . . . paid attention to . . .

BIG MAMA: ". . . paid tention to . . ."

ELIZABETH: Attention.

BIG MAMA: "Ah. Tension."

ELIZABETH: . . . and . . .

BIG MAMA: ". . . a . . ."

ELIZABETH: Not "a," "and" . . . *and* there will be . . .

BIG MAMA: Ah. "will be." Another exception? Two exceptions?

(Elizabeth looks at her threateningly. Big Mama writes.)

". . . will be . . ."

ELIZABETH: . . . there will be justice.

BIG MAMA: ". . . that you will be paid ah! tension to and there will be . . ." *(Comes to the end of the page and can't fit in the rest of the sentence)*

ELIZABETH: . . . justice!

BIG MAMA: ". . . just . . . just . . ." *(Turns the page)*

ELIZABETH: Big Mama, what are you doing?

BIG MAMA: There's no space left for "justice."

(Big Mama goes to Egerton and reads the whole letter to him in nonsense language, echoing all the "Ah's" and punctuations.)

ELIZABETH *(Trying to interrupt and finally shouting)*: Big Mama. Pig of a whore! The signature.

BIG MAMA: I did it already . . . "Yours truly . . . pig of a whore!" *(Gives letter to Egerton)*

EGERTON: With your permission, my lady. I'll return shortly. *(Looks quickly at the letter, asks Big Mama)* What language is this written in?

BIG MAMA: Onomatopissian. It's understood everywhere.

ELIZABETH: Egerton, declare a twenty-four hour truce. And as soon as the Lords have spoken with Essex, bring him here to me. Thank you.

EGERTON: Of course, Your Majesty. Right away. *(Exits)*

BIG MAMA: Ah, Queenie . . . did you see Egerton turn white when you told him about the threats that were written on the wall. I bet that Cecil and Bacon are scared shitless.

MARTHA: Please, Big Mama, watch your language.

BIG MAMA: It's from hanging around the queen that I learned all these dirty words. Pig of a whore.

ELIZABETH: Big Mama. Did you hear . . . in a few moments Robert will be here. You promised to make a miracle for my breasts.

BIG MAMA: I'll do it, but I warn you that it might sting a little.

ELIZABETH: Sting?

BIG MAMA: Yes, we'll use these.

ELIZABETH: What are they?

BIG MAMA: Buzz-buzz.

ELIZABETH: Buzz buzz? Do you mean bees? What do you have in mind?

BIG MAMA: First of all, you, Martha, take this piece of sandalwood to smoke up some smoke. I'll open the jar with the bees right on your breast. Buzz-buzz . . . Then I'll put a little smoke around. Buzz-buzz . . . The bees inside will get angry and . . . ping-ping-ping . . . they'll sting you. In a little while your breasts will blow up to enormous proportions . . . Vavoom-vavoom . . . hard, firm, watertight.

ELIZABETH: You're crazy. You want to inflate my breasts with a bee. With all the pain . . .

MARTHA: Sounds like a great idea . . . I never thought of it.

ELIZABETH: If you think it's such a great idea, why don't you let the bees bite your breasts.

BIG MAMA *(Referring to Martha's small breasts)*: She needs a hornet.

MARTHA: But I don't have Robert to hold against my watertight breast, dear Queen. In any case, you can always say no. We'll just stuff some cotton into your bodice.

BIG MAMA: Yes, you can do it with cotton, but the results be not the same. There's an old proverb that says: "Tits stuffed with cotton, will soon be forgotten."

ELIZABETH: Are you sure they'll blow up big and firm.

BIG MAMA: Well, they'll not be balloons, but they'll be beautiful. Mama's honor.

ELIZABETH: All right, go ahead. Subject me to this new madness, as well.

(Big Mama gets the jar out of her basket.)

MARTHA: Bravo. Go to it, Big Mama.

BIG MAMA: Let's rub on the honey and myrrh. Help me. *(Gives Martha the sandalwood)*

ELIZABETH: Wait. How long will the swelling last?

BIG MAMA: Oh, three days . . . maybe five. It depends on how long we leave in the stinger.

ELIZABETH: Ah, because if you take out the stinger after half an hour . . .

BIG MAMA: No. Half-hour is too long. Your tits would swell up like watermelons. Like this. Phaloop-phaloop. Slurp-slurp.

ELIZABETH: Just what I need.

BIG MAMA: Sweet Queen, take a deep breath.

ELIZABETH: Robert, my love, I'm doing this for you.

BIG MAMA: You, Martha, shake that smoker.

(Martha takes the lid off a smoke-filled jar, and places the open jar onto the Queen's breast.)

ELIZABETH: AHHIUIUIU. That hurts.

BIG MAMA: Wonderful. He stung you right away . . . WO-WO-WO-WUUUU.

MARTHA: Wait. I'm choking.

ELIZABETH: I'm going crazy. The stinging!

BIG MAMA: Hang on, Queenie, hang on. I'll put a little camphor on it.

ELIZABETH: No more, no more . . . pull out the stinger.

BIG MAMA: No, just a little bit longer . . . hang on, Queenie . . . look, look it's getting bigger already.

ELIZABETH *(Happy)*: Bigger. Bigger. OH-OH . . . it hurts.

MARTHA: Hold out a little longer . . . think how splendid you'll look. I'm almost ready to try it myself. *(Pointing to the second jar)* What's wrong with the bee?

BIG MAMA: He's done lost his sting and died. I'll get another jar with a new bee.

ELIZABETH: Wait, at least let me catch my breath.

BIG MAMA: No, they have to bubble up both at the same time . . . to stay a matched pair . . . you don't want one to blow up fat and juicy while the other one lies there flat as a mat. Fizzle-flop. Fizzle-flop.

ELIZABETH: All right . . . go on . . . *(She stops, immobilized and embarrassed)* . . . Oh God.

MARTHA: What's wrong?

ELIZABETH *(Ashamed)*: I peed on myself again.

BIG MAMA: It's normal. Bee stings always have this side effect. Bang-bang, piss-piss. Pee as much as you want. We can always say it was the horse. All right, here comes the second one. Is it biting, Queenie?

ELIZABETH: No, it's not biting.

BIG MAMA *(To Martha)*: Smoke it, smoke it. *(Turns hopefully to the Queen)* Is it biting?

ELIZABETH: No, it's not biting.

BIG MAMA: Oh, what a bee. To bee or not to bee. A bee that's not a bee. You don't want to sting, bee? I'll beat the bee-jeezus out of thee. Hee-bee, gee-bee, hee-bee, gee-bee. *(Shakes up the jar)*

ELIZABETH: And what happens now. Am I supposed to walk around with one breast up like a watermelon and the other a dried mozzarella?

BIG MAMA: No, no. Here's one that will bite you for sure. *(Takes another jar out of his basket)*

ELIZABETH: How do you know?

BIG MAMA: It's from Ireland.

ELIZABETH *(Jumps up to her feet)*: An Irish hornet? Now I understand. You're trying to assassinate me with a hornet.

BIG MAMA: Don't be afraid, sweet Queen. The sting is gentler than a bee's. Calm thyself. Hold her down, Martha.

(Martha pushes Elizabeth back onto the chair, where she had unthinkingly left the burning wood.)

ELIZABETH: AH-I-U-HA? What's that?

MARTHA: I'm sorry . . . it's my fault . . . I put the smoker there by mistake . . .

BIG MAMA: Evil woman. Burning the queen's ass. *(Gets a bucket)* Sit down in here and let the water cool your buns. *(When getting the bucket, she inadvertently puts a bee jar on Elizabeth's chair)*

ELIZABETH: Get away. All I want to do is sit down on something soft. *(Sits and screams again)* AH-I-AH-AH!

MARTHA: What is it now?

ELIZABETH: The burning wood again?

BIG MAMA: No this time you sat on the bee. The pervert. He didn't want to bite your breast, but he bit your bottom good. A Catholic hornet! A Democrat!

ELIZABETH: Oh what a mess. One big breast. One bitty breast. One bun's punctured and the other one's fried. What a miserable muddled-up queen. And I'm still peeing all over myself.

(The lights go down. "Crazy Queen Elizabeth" is sung offstage or on tape:)

Crazy Queen Elizabeth
To make her breasts pretty
To make herself young again
Had herself stung by a bee.

Bitten on her breasts
By a bee with yellow stripes
One breast like a ball
And the other like a melon.

Big Mama, Big Mama, Big Mama, so much pain
Big Mama, Big Mama, Big Mama, so much pain.

One breast swelled up like a whale
The other as flat as a flounder
And the bee doesn't want to bite
Because he doesn't like the taste of fish
The rancid breast he doesn't want to bite.

Big Mama, Big Mama, Big Mama, so much pain
Big Mama, Big Mama, Big Mama, so much pain.

So she sat on the bumbling bee
The queen with the big breasts
And a backside like a barn
Boobs like a whale, tits like a flounder
One buttock shriveled, and the other blown-up fat
So scared and confused, she pees in her pants
With lopsided breasts, she pees in her pants.

So she sat on the bumbling bee
The queen with the big breasts
And a backside like a barn
Boobs like a whale, tits like a flounder
One buttock shriveled, and the other blown-up fat
So scared and confused, she pees in her pants
With lopsided breasts, she pees in her pants.

ACT TWO

"Isabella the Redhead" plays while the curtain is down. As the curtain rises the lights go up. In the center of the stage the Queen is seated on the wooden horse looking at the audience through binoculars. She has the same clothes that she wore in the first act and is without her wig. The mannequin is clothed in a white ceremonial gown. On a chair is a hoopskirted undergarment. On the bed/armoire is a wig, which is identical to the wig Elizabeth usually wears.

The prisoner has been taken down from the tower
Oh my God, oh my heart
His head is cut off
My life is over
It's the end of my love.

Isabella the redhead had three young men
The first spent the night on her doorstep
The third came at night to sing songs
And the other hid in her bed making love
In the bed making love with the queen.

Isabella, don't do it, it's a terrible mistake
You are blushing
Making love in secret
This young man is dead
Entombed by your love.

Go away, it is dawn, they'll discover you here
They will kill you, from the gallows you'll swing

The first spent the night on her doorstep
The third came at night to sing songs
And the other hid in her bed making love
In the bed making love with the queen.

ELIZABETH: Are you still awake? Yes, yes, there are the lights in your window. *(Shouting to the wings)* Martha! *(Back to front)* For the love of God, Robert, that's enough. *(To the wings)* Martha!

(Martha enters.)

MARTHA: Here I am, dear. What's wrong?
ELIZABETH: Where are you going? I'm not in bed.
MARTHA *(Amazed)*: What are you doing up there?
ELIZABETH: I'm up here because it's the only way I can see the window of Robert's room.
MARTHA: Did you go to bed at all?
ELIZABETH: No. I couldn't even close my eyes. I'm tense. Like a drum.
MARTHA: Now, now. Relax. Do you want some warm herbs?
ELIZABETH: Warm herbs. You don't understand anything. I'm as tense as a drum because you pulled back the skin on my forehead so tight that I can't close my eyes. I'm sitting up here like a haunted old owl. Bring me Big Mama.
MARTHA: Right away.
ELIZABETH: Tell her to bring me something to cool my breasts. They're burning. You could iron a shirt with them.
MARTHA *(Yells offstage)*: Hurry up Big Mama.

(Big Mama enters carrying a basket.)

BIG MAMA: Here I be. How splendid. Up on your wooden horse that pees so in the morning early.
ELIZABETH: What do you have in your little basket?
BIG MAMA: More wasps, my dearie.
ELIZABETH *(Frightened)*: Again? Get them out of here. The last one that stung me felt like a knife wound. It even left a lump on my left breast.
BIG MAMA: Good. It's called the Lump of Venus. Now hold onto your horse, and backwards we go. Go weeeeeeeeee! *(Pulls the horse back)*

ELIZABETH: And when you made my breasts round, you made them strange. They don't stay still anymore. They move up and down, here and there. They wiggle.

BIG MAMA: Yes, dearie. It's a little erotic game. Vavava-voom. Vavava-voom. It makes men wild. Now let's fall down your hair. *(Big Mama and Martha let down Elizabeth's hair)*

ELIZABETH: Thank you. Fix it so I can close my eyes one time before I die. What a night I've had. Ahhh, how marvelous. I feel so good. *(Changes tone)* Big Mama, I feel so bad. I've had an awful night. Last night I heard screams coming from Robert of Essex's palace, as if there had been a raging battle.

MARTHA: A raging battle?

BIG MAMA: No. Trust me, trust me. There was no battle. I was walking around myself, around the town, myself around. Looking for wasps. And I didn't even hear the woof-woof of a dog. It was so quiet you could even hear the flies flying. The flies that were flying last night in London.

ELIZABETH: And I heard shooting. Musket shots.

MARTHA: It must have been a nightmare.

ELIZABETH: A nightmare. Yes. I had an awful nightmare. I dreamt about Mary Stuart.

BIG MAMA: No!

ELIZABETH: She was walking around without her head. There in my room, as if it were hers.

BIG MAMA: No!

ELIZABETH: And she had her head in her hand.

BIG MAMA: Alive. The head was alive. Like Saint John the Beheaded Baptist. Oh ho. How convenient. You can see all around you without straining your neck. You can look over here. You can look over there.

ELIZABETH: It was terrifying. The eyes moved. The mouth spoke. It sneered at me, and said, "Ugly bitch. Ugly bitch."

BIG MAMA: Oh no!

ELIZABETH: "Your plans have gone wrong. It's not my head that's coming off. It's Robert's. Ha ha!" And PACH! She gave me a raspberry.

BIG MAMA: A raspberry from a headless head.

MARTHA: How terrible.

ELIZABETH: Then all of a sudden she started to play with the head as if it were a ball. She was throwing it in the air. She was catching it. And then, TAN-TAN-TAN. She was bouncing it.

BIG MAMA: She was bouncing?

ELIZABETH: The head.

BIG MAMA: And then.

ELIZABETH: And then the head jumped out of her hands and shouted, "Christ . . . you're destroying me. I'm not a ball."

BIG MAMA: Well, she was right. You can't treat a head like a ball. That woman just didn't have her head on her shoulders. Of course not, she had it in her hand. Don't worry. I understand what it all means. This dream means that the Earl of Essex has lost his head.

ELIZABETH *(Frightened)*: What do you mean?

BIG MAMA: That his head he lost for love . . . of you.

ELIZABETH: Ah, would that it were true.

MARTHA: Yes, everything will turn out fine. You'll see.

BIG MAMA *(To Martha)*: Speaking of good news, tell her who's on his way.

MARTHA: Ah, yes. I almost forgot. It's probable that the leader of the conspiracy will arrive here today.

ELIZABETH: Robert.

BIG MAMA: Robert of Essex has got it in his slaphappy head to come and show you his respect. Are you happy?

ELIZABETH *(Aggressively)*: Why did you try to hide important news like this?

MARTHA: I was going out of my head . . . with all those stories about nightmares.

BIG MAMA: Be careful not to lose your head . . . it might end up somewhere. *(Mimes bouncing a ball)* Bouncing, bouncing, bouncing.

ELIZABETH: Come on, Big Mama. Bring me down.

BIG MAMA: Yes, ma'am. *(Helping her down)*

ELIZABETH: Tie up my hair. Robert will be here soon and I want my skin to be pulled smooth, And you, Martha, keep a lookout with the eye-tube.

(A knock at the door.)

They're knocking. Don't let anyone in. I'm a mess.

BIG MAMA: It's useless to knock. The queen doesn't want to see anybody because she's a mess and looks disgusting. *(Looks through the peephole)* My lady, it's the head of the police, the big spy.

ELIZABETH: Egerton. Let him in. Maybe he has news about Robert.

BIG MAMA: My lady, are you sure you want to let him see you looking such a mess.

ELIZABETH: Blindfold him.

BIG MAMA: Blindfold the head of the big spies?

ELIZABETH: Pull his hat down over his eyes.

BIG MAMA: That's an idea. Come in. *(Opens the door and pulls hat down over Egerton's eyes)* Master Egerton. The queen orders me to cover up your eyes under the cover of your hat because . . . oh, what a head, my lady his head is so big that his hat can't cover it, a head so big that if it ever fell into the executioner's hands, he would faint for joy . . . Look. *(Mimes execution)* There it goes. Come along dear. *(Pulls Egerton down the stairs by the seat of his pants)*

ELIZABETH: Help him down the stairs. I don't want him to fall and hurt himself.

BIG MAMA: There's plenty of others who could take his place.

ELIZABETH: What news do you have for me, Egerton?

EGERTON: Your Majesty . . . I hope you have had a . . . good night.

ELIZABETH: I've had a miserable night. I would like to know why I have not yet seen the delegation of Lords going to Robert of Essex.

BIG MAMA: Respond, my lord.

EGERTON: Sir Keeper Lesly was unavailable, Your Majesty, and because of his indispensability—we thought it best to postpone it until today.

BIG MAMA: Oh, what a smooth tongue.

ELIZABETH: I see. You make plans, you cancel them, and you say nothing to me. What are you hiding in that envelope?

EGERTON: I am mortified, Your Majesty, but I have to admit once more that your doubts were justified. *(Opens the envelope)*

ELIZABETH: What doubts?

EGERTON: This theatrical . . . what's his name? *(Tries to read under his hat)*

ELIZABETH: Shakespeare.

EGERTON: Yes, that's him . . . he's in with them.

ELIZABETH: In with who?

EGERTON: The conspirators.

BIG MAMA: Conspirators. Speareshaker's a revolutionary. What news.

ELIZABETH: Are you sure?

EGERTON: More than sure, Your Majesty. This Shakespeare is under the patronage of the Earl of Southhampton, who is also his theatrical impresario and the co-owner of the Globe.

ELIZABETH: So?

EGERTON: But, Your Majesty, Southampton is one of the leaders of the conspiracy.

BIG MAMA *(Shocked)*: No. My lady. Actors in politics? Unthinkable.

ELIZABETH *(Even more shocked)*: Southampton, my only living relative. I've always shown him affection, friendship, and now to discover that he's mixed up with these pigs who want to screw me . . . of course it's all tied in with the story of the letters to James of Scotland.

MARTHA: No, Elizabeth. Calm down.

ELIZABETH: Silence. I'll exile them. I'll search every house . . . I want them hung. Butchered. Disemboweled. *(Can't control herself anymore)* I want them left hanging until they rot! I want to see all the birds in England rip out their intestines. I feel sick. Martha, I'm going to throw up. *(She bends over holding her stomach)*

MARTHA: There, I knew it . . . come . . . come over here. *(They leave)*

BIG MAMA: Away she's gone. *(Lifts up Egerton's hat)* Breathe a little breath.

EGERTON: I'm sorry to have precipitated this crisis.

BIG MAMA: Lucky for you that you didn't see her eyes bulging big. Evil. Terrifying, like the eyes of her sister, Bloody Mary, when she set up the courts of the inquisition.

EGERTON: I feel sorry for Southampton. His days are numbered, poor man. Shakespeare's, too . . .

BIG MAMA: The head of the poet in the basket will also fall. Do you know, my lord, why all the coffins in England are shorter than coffins abroad.

EGERTON: No, why?

BIG MAMA: Because everyone to be buried comes with their head in their hands.

EGERTON: Very funny.

(Elizabeth and Martha return.)

BIG MAMA *(Quickly putting the hat back over Egerton's eyes)*: Not too loud. It's the queen. *(To the Queen)* How be you? Better?

ELIZABETH: Much better, thank you. Egerton. Enough. I can't stand it anymore. I'm fed up with all these secret plots popping up all over the place. Do we understand each other, Egerton? Every time one faction in power wants to get rid of another faction, they inevitably drag me into it. What do I have to do with it. Enough. I'm sure if all of you put your minds to it, the whole sordid mess will go away, and in a few days no one will be talking about it anymore. Then we can go on with a clean slate. And as every actor knows: all is well when the play ends between the white-washed sheets of a nice clean double bed. *(She laughs)*

(Shouts and the footsteps of running men are heard outside the door.)

VOICE FROM OUTSIDE: An intruder. Guards. There he is. Over there. *(They knock on the door)*

ELIZABETH: What is it now? *(To Martha)* Go see.

(They knock again violently.)

MARTHA: What's got into you. I'm coming. *(She opens the door slightly and speaks to the guards)* One moment.

BIG MAMA: The voice it is of the head of your guards.

MARTHA: Yes, it's him. He says that they've seen a man trying to climb in . . . should I let him in.

ELIZABETH: Let who in? The one who's climbing or the captain of the guards. We're losing our minds. Egerton, start a search, but do it outside of my room. Immediately.

EGERTON *(Without lifting up his hat, he moves decisively toward the audience)*: Right away.

BIG MAMA *(Blocking his way)*: Stop. There be a big drop to bottom there. *(Leads him to the door. Egerton exits)* Not yet the time for your short coffin. It's true what the proverb says: "Where justice is blind, soldiers are cross-eyed." *(Worried)* In let the guards, my lady. Danger there is.

MARTHA: She's right. There really is an assassin around . . .

ELIZABETH: There's no assassin. It's a diversion for putting the palace into a state of confusion and keeping me from seeing Robert, but I'm not falling for it. *(Goes to the bed)*

MARTHA: Or maybe you just want to stop them from putting their noses between your sheets. Tell the truth. Do you have someone in bed?

ELIZABETH: Be quiet, you witch. *(Opens the doors of the bed)* Wake up, Thomas, hurry. Wake up. *(A semi-nude youth appears)*

MARTHA: Oh, look what the Easter Bunny left behind.

BIG MAMA *(To Martha)*: No innuendos, little gossip with a mind of soot, that knows not what happened really. A miracle, miraculous. This morning in the early almost night, in fact it was last night in the almost late morning, Elizabeth heard a little bird cheep-cheeping in the garden. Crying it was, and down she went, and found the little bird shiv-shivering from the cold. Shiv-shivering, she put it cheep-cheep between her breasts. And good samaritan that she be, Elizabeth, brought it shiv-shivering to her bed and placed it cheep-cheep between her sheets, where she breathed on it whispers of warmth, whish-whish. And jumping out of a sudden was this beautiful youth. The queen down fell on her knees. Oh, oh. "Saint Rosalie," she cried. She cried, "Saint most beautiful that there be. What should I do with this beautiful youth, whish-whish-

whish?" And the saint answered, "Mmmmmmmmm-mmmm. Hold the birdie close to your little bird's nest." So she did. Cheep-cheep, shiv-shiver, whish-whish, oh-oh, mmmmm-mmmm. And that's what really happened.

ELIZABETH: Thomas, cover yourself up with this quilt. *(To Martha)* Where can I hide him.

MARTHA: Let him climb out the window.

BIG MAMA: Good. That way they'll mistake him for an assassin. Bang-bang. He comes back a little cheep-cheep.

ELIZABETH *(To Thomas as he gets dressed)*: Don't get dressed, Thomas. There's no time.

THOMAS: My lady, I can't go out like this . . . with a quilt . . .

ELIZABETH: Go out? And let the guards discover that you've been in here with me?

MARTHA: Why don't you dress him up as a woman.

THOMAS: Be quiet.

BIG MAMA: Yes, good, like a lady. Like a lady. That's the idea.

ELIZABETH: Like a lady?

BIG MAMA: Yes.

ELIZABETH *(To Martha, pointing to some clothes on the chair)*: Give me those clothes. *(To Thomas)* I'll pass you off as one of my ladies in waiting. It'll be easy with your cute little ass.

THOMAS: It's not right, my lady, to mock me like this, dressing me up in women's clothes.

ELIZABETH: Stop whining, Thomas.

THOMAS: Don't make me do it, please. I'd rather throw myself out the window just as I am.

ELIZABETH: Wonderful. Then people will say that the queen takes in young men, gives them a squeeze, then throws them nude out of the window. Put them on. Go over there and do it. That's an order. *(Thomas leaves the stage reluctantly)*

MARTHA *(Referring to Thomas)*: How nice. Epicurus says that sleeping next to young men is good for your complexion.

BIG MAMA: Shame, shame. Watch out for your head. *(Mimes bouncing a ball)* Bounce. Bounce.

ELIZABETH: You're a hyena. I just wanted to try an experiment. Robert of Essex will be here in a few hours and I wanted to see I was ready to withstand the caresses of a man.

(While Elizabeth speaks, Big Mama goes up on a step and looks out the window)

BIG MAMA: A warm-up boy, to test her tits.

ELIZABETH: It was a disaster. A total failure. I couldn't stand him touching me anywhere. He hurt me all over. You ruined me, Big Mama. I would have yelled, "No. Stop. What pain." But I didn't have the strength, so all I could say was, "Oh, ooo, darling, nooo." The cretin, convinced I was moaning with great passion, kept going for more. Kept going for more. I could have murdered him.

BIG MAMA *(Alarmed)*: My lady, it's a man . . . down there in the garden . . . in the labyrinth . . . the guards . . . grrr . . . are chasing him with the dogs, woof-woof.

MARTHA: Who's in the labyrinth?

BIG MAMA: Must be the bastard who was trying to climb up here to murder kill the queen. Now he's somewhere elseplace.

ELIZABETH: Go down, run . . . order them to bring me him alive. *(Martha runs out the main door)* I want to interrogate him myself.

BIG MAMA: Alive. Then like a woman, she can dress him up, too. Cheep-cheep. Whish-whish. Oh-oh.

ELIZABETH: Follow me, Big Mama. Let's go watch from the balcony.

BIG MAMA: Go us yes. How sweet it be. What a party marvelous be it here at the court. Every moment a change of scene. From the window you see a man chased by dogs. In the bed there be a man with no clothes. *(As she runs after the exiting Queen, shouts)* It's like being in the theatre.

(Almost at the same time, an embarrassed Thomas comes back into view from behind the bed. He's dressed as a woman from the waist down, he wears petticoats but his chest is bare.)

THOMAS: My lady, I'm sorry, but I just don't feel like myself.

(Thomas looks around for the Queen. From behind a curtain a man appears in priest's clothes. It's the Assassin.)

ASSASSIN: You stupid, son of a bitch. What are you doing?

THOMAS *(Frightened)*: Who is it? Ah, it's you, father. Careful, the queen can't be far away . . . and there are guards all around.

ASSASSIN: Exactly. And you choose a time like this to start complaining about a little house dress and a bonnet.

THOMAS: It's humiliating.

ASSASSIN: Imbecile. What's more important: your dignity or the success of our cause.

THOMAS: I know, but when they spit in your face and drag you down to the level of a transvestite queen . . .

ASSASSIN: Well, that's what you get for rolling in the bed of a bastard murderess, and letting her drool kisses all over you.

THOMAS: But you ordered me to let her take me into that bed.

ASSASSIN: Yes, but I didn't expect you to have so much fun at it. Never forget, Thomas, that she was Mary's murderer.

(From outside there are new shouts and some shots.)

THOMAS *(Pointing to the window)*: Who is that scoundrel they're chasing after?

ASSASSIN: Scoundrel? Would that you had half his courage. He created a diversion to give me time to climb up here undetected. Now you get moving and do your part. Stay in this room as long as possible to help me. As soon as we've taken care of the queen, sound the alarm and send the guards up to the attic, so I can escape down below.

THOMAS: And what if we fail? In a little while this room will be filled with people . . . I heard that Essex is on his way . . .

ASSASSIN: No, Essex isn't coming . . . unless it's for an attack.

THOMAS: An attack? But the chief justice himself is going to bring him in . . .

ASSASSIN: Listen closely, Thomas: if Essex arrives here, he will be armed and accompanied by his army . . . and behind him will be marching the entire city . . . they'll throw out Cecil, Bacon and half the advisers . . . but they'll save the queen . . . and we can't permit that . . . so let's get moving . . . Follow my orders without questions. Understood? Even if I ask you to stand on your head with a lighted candle in your ass.

THOMAS: No, not lighted, no.

ASSASSIN: Enough! I'll hide here, inside the horse. *(Approaches the animal from the side)*

THOMAS: But how will you get in?

ASSASSIN: There's a hidden door here . . . Come on, give me a hand. *(Lifts the false opening; to the audience it appears that he is getting into the side of the horse)* This horse belonged to Henry, Elizabeth's father . . . he hid his lovers inside . . . my mother was one of them . . . Nobody knows about this secret compartment, not even Elizabeth. Come on, help me in. No, wait. Maybe, it would be better for me to hide in this fireplace. Now, when the right moment comes, give me the signal by playing on this flute . . . is that clear? *(Gives him a tiny flute)*

THOMAS: Yes, but hurry.

ASSASSIN: And make sure no one lights a fire.

THOMAS: Who's going to want a fire? It's springtime. Go on.

(The Assassin gets into the fireplace and climbs up the chimney. There are more shots outside.

Elizabeth, wearing a ceremonial robe, wig, crown, jewels, etc., enters with Big Mama.)

BIG MAMA: I'd like to know how that man suicided himself.

(Martha comes in from the gallery.)

ELIZABETH: Martha, who fired the shot?

MARTHA: He did it himself.

ELIZABETH: That bullet was meant for me. Now we'll never know who sent him. *(Notices an uncomfortable Thomas)* What are you doing still dressed up like that? The guards will be here any minute . . . that bastard probably had an accomplice . . . Do you want to compromise my reputation?

THOMAS: All right, Your Majesty. I'll put on the rest of the dress too.

ELIZABETH: No, put this one on instead. *(Points to the dress on the mannequin)*

THOMAS: But that's your dress.

ELIZABETH: Martha, help him. I want to see how it looks. I've never tried it on.

THOMAS: But don't you think it would look better on your governess?

(Martha and Big Mama dress Thomas in the platform shoes, wig and crown.)

ELIZABETH: No, it's not her size. Besides I want you to understand what it's like to play the role of the queen.

(Thomas is now dressed in the Queen's clothes.)

That's what I wanted to see. How do you feel?

THOMAS: Suffocated, caged-in . . . it's hell. Especially the humiliation. Please don't tell anyone about this.

(Smoke comes out of the fireplace.)

ELIZABETH: What's happening over there? . . . Why is there smoke in the fireplace?

BIG MAMA: Oh no. The candelabra fell in the fireplace.

ELIZABETH: Put out the fire!

(Big Mama takes a pail of water and throws it in the fireplace.)

BIG MAMA: Oh, such a lot of smoke.

(They hear muffled shouts from the chimney.)

Queenie, there's a choke-choking sound in the chimney. Listen to that sput-sputter.

ELIZABETH: But what is it?

BIG MAMA *(Imitates the sounds)*: Choke-choke, sputter-sputter . . . It's the voice of the chimney!

ELIZABETH: Don't be silly. No, it's nothing.

BIG MAMA: It must be the wind, the wind, the wind . . .

THOMAS: Yes, it's the wind.

BIG MAMA: In England they even torture the wind.

ELIZABETH: Quiet. *(Turns back to Thomas; she is enjoying the show)* You're adorable. Have you ever played a woman on stage?

THOMAS: No, never.

ELIZABETH: You know, I subsidize a company of boys.

THOMAS: Yes, Your Majesty. "The Queen's Boys." I've seen them.

ELIZABETH: And none of them play women as believably as you.

THOMAS: You're making fun of me.

ELIZABETH: No, in fact I'll invite them to play *Hamlet* here at Court . . . to better understand what's between the lines . . . and you can play Ophelia, and Big Mama can play the Queen.

BIG MAMA: That whore. No thanks.

(The Assassin comes out of the chimney suppressing his coughs. He hides behind Elizabeth's bed. More shots are heard in the distance.)

MARTHA: What's going on now?

ELIZABETH *(Looking out into the audience)*: Cannon shots . . . or muskets . . . Oh God . . . they're coming from the castle of Essex . . . they've broken the truce. Quick, give me the eye-tube. No, I want to talk to Egerton. *(Goes toward the door. To Martha)* Come, let's go look for him.

(Elizabeth and Martha leave.)

THOMAS *(Holding up the telescope and looking out toward the audience)*: Incredible . . . everything is so big.

BIG MAMA *(Discovers the flute left behind by the Assassin)*: Oh look, a piccolo-piccolo. *(Blows on it and makes a few sounds)*

THOMAS: What are you doing. Christ. No. That's the signal. Give it to me.

(At this point there begins an ongoing gag between Big Mama and the sound technician. As Big Mama plays, a flute recording is heard. Big Mama makes a sign to the technician to stop, but the music does not stop.)

BIG MAMA: A magic flute. It plays the piccolo-piccolo all by itself. All you do is move your fingers.

THOMAS: Give me that flute.

BIG MAMA: Only if you kiss me first. Pooch-pooch.

THOMAS: No.

BIG MAMA: Kiss-kiss.

THOMAS: Get away from me, you hag.

BIG MAMA: "Hag"! You called me a "hag." Be you struck down by lightning. Tach-tach. And shrunk into a dwarf. Nano-nano. A little dwarf. Tach-tach. Nano-nano. *(Exits)*

THOMAS *(Going to the fireplace)*: Father? He's not there. I hope he didn't choke to death. *(Returns to looking through the telescope)* This is fantastic. It's witchcraft.

(The Assassin comes out of his hiding place and approaches Thomas, who is still wearing the dress. Seeing him only from the back, the Assassin mistakes him for the Queen and stabs him with a dagger.)

ASSASSIN: This time I've got you, bitch. Die and go to hell.

(Thomas falls almost without a sound. The Assassin looks around.)

Thomas, where are you? Where is that imbecile hiding . . . Thomas?

THOMAS *(In a frail voice)*: I'm here.

ASSASSIN *(Surprised)*: You! Christ. What are you doing in the queen's clothes?

THOMAS: But it was you . . . who . . . ordered me to wear the clothes . . . of a woman.

ASSASSIN: What a disaster.

THOMAS: And then you murder me. Who is the biggest prick?

(Big Mama enters.)

BIG MAMA: I heard someone shout. I'm sure.

(Big Mama sees Thomas on the ground. The Assassin moves toward her.)

Who are you! Help! A man! The assassin is a priest!

ELIZABETH *(From outside)*: What is it Big Mama? . . . Why are you shouting?

(The Assassin moves toward the door to ambush her.)

BIG MAMA: Don't move, Queenie, and close the door. There's an assassin after you.

ASSASSIN: Damned hag. Shut up or I'll kill you.

(The Assassin threatens Big Mama with the pistol. She escapes behind the bed and returns with her basket, from which she takes two jars. She points them at him as if they were pistols. She screams:)

BIG MAMA: Hornets. Help me, hornets. Buzz-buzz. Bang-bang.

(The Assassin shoots at her, but she avoids the shot and shakes up her jars to incite the hornets to attack the Assassin. The Assassin reacts as if he has been stung by an entire swarm of hornets. He drops his pistol and runs about, jumping and gesticulating like crazy.)

You asked for it, pig. A duel of pistols and wasps! Bang-bang, buzz-buzz!

ELIZABETH *(From outside)*: Open up, Big Mama. That's an order.

BIG MAMA: Don't come in, Queenie. The hornets are loose and they're biting. Buzz-buzz. Tzing-tzing.

(To avoid being seen, the Assassin, half-hidden by the curtain, opens the secret door in the horse and climbs in.)

Careful . . . cover your face with a noseblower.

(Elizabeth enters followed by Martha. They are holding handkerchiefs over their faces.)

(Shouting toward the door) Guards!!!

(Two guards enter defending themselves from the wasps. They hit themselves all over. Following Big Mama's instructions they run to look for the Assassin behind the bed of the Queen.)

ELIZABETH: Where is he hiding?

BIG MAMA: He was just here . . . maybe he's hiding up in the chimney. Choke-choke.

ELIZABETH: You said he was dressed up like a priest.

BIG MAMA: No, he was a real priest, he was, one of those fanatics who gives you a cross to kiss with one hand, smooch-smooch, while he has his other hand on a rope to hang you with, gag-gag, and with the other hand he's lighting a fire under your feet, sizzle-sizzle, while another hand gives you a blessing, amen. Smooch-smooch, gag-gag, sizzle-sizzle, amen. These priests sure have a lot of hands.

ELIZABETH: Do something with these beasts. Open the window.

BIG MAMA: No, wait. I have the hornet queen. If we give them a sniff of her, all the hornets into the basket will fly . . . Hey, hornies, your queen is calling. Buzz-buzz, pant-pant . . . Here they come . . . tzing-tzing . . . Oh, no the queen flew away . . . where is she . . . whizz-whizz . . . ah, she flew into the horse's nostril . . . and all the others are going in after her. Buzz-buzz. Tzing-tzing, whizz-whizz. All clear. The danger's over.

(Elizabeth and Martha take off the handkerchiefs they had used to veil their faces, and only now does Elizabeth notice the wounded Thomas on the floor.)

ELIZABETH: Thomas, Oh, my God. They stabbed you instead of me. *(Gets down on her knees and holds him)*

THOMAS *(Speaking with great difficulty)*: He mistook me . . .

ELIZABETH: Yes, yes . . . I understand . . . darling, you saved my life.

THOMAS: I didn't . . . do it . . . on purpose . . . I'm sorry.

ELIZABETH: What are you sorry about?

THOMAS: This knife . . . was for . . . you.

ELIZABETH: Oh, my God. Quick, Martha. A doctor . . . so much blood.

THOMAS: He didn't even . . . look me . . . in the face . . . that bastard priest . . . the dagger . . . went away . . . ". . . be a woman . . ." he said, ". . . with a candle in your ass . . ."

BIG MAMA: Oh!

MARTHA: He's raving, poor thing . . . he's losing touch . . .

BIG MAMA: He's out of his mind . . . the things he says . . .

THOMAS: And then he goes inside . . . in the horse's belly . . . like it was the one from Troy . . . and now the hornets are eating him alive. *(Laughs)* Ah.

ELIZABETH: Don't laugh, Thomas. You have a dagger in your stomach . . . it hurts you . . . you'll see . . . you'll make it . . . *(Thomas dies in Elizabeth's arms)*

BIG MAMA: He didn't make it. He's dead. Happy though. He was laughing.

ELIZABETH: Oh God. God. It was me. It's my fault. *(Gets up)* My life is full of corpses. I'm a murderer. *(She leaves)*

MARTHA *(Follows Elizabeth)*: It's not true. It was by chance. An accident.

BIG MAMA: Yes, a chance accident. Queens have all the luck. They bring home a boy to warm up their bed, and the kid does her the extra service of taking a knife in his back. That's above and beyond all the kiss-kissing, hug-hugging, lick-licking and hump-humping they do. Meanwhile all I do is ask a boy for a kiss, and he answers, "Shut up, you slut!"

(Enter Egerton followed by the guards.)

EGERTON: Excuse me . . . what's happened? . . .

BIG MAMA: An assassinating priest gave him a stab and it murdered him.

(Elizabeth and Martha return.)

EGERTON: One of your maids?

ELIZABETH: Yes, one of my male maids. I dressed him up to entertain us a little . . .

MARTHA *(In a whisper)*: Don't be silly. *(To Egerton)* Try to understand. It's the shock. *(Quietly to Elizabeth)* Please, the guards. *(Points to the corpse)*

(The guards carry it off. Egerton follows them.)

ELIZABETH: Take him away. He's no use anymore . . .

BIG MAMA: Look. The horse shakes, rattles and rolls.

(The horse moves around as if it is having convulsions.)

MARTHA: Yes, and it's screaming too.

(The cries of the Assassin being attacked inside by the wasps sound like the neighing of a horse.)

BIG MAMA: Look, he's possessed . . . it must be all the hornets buzz-buzzing, tzing-tzinging and hump-humping inside.

ELIZABETH: Stop. It's making me crazy. I'm having nightmares. Who's responsible for this witchcraft? . . . You, Big Mama? . . . You cast a spell? . . . It was you . . . of course . . . you're part of the conspiracy . . . They sent you here . . . *(Shouts offstage)* Egerton. Guards. *(To Big Mama)* Who sent you. Speak. *(Big Mama is frozen with fear)* I'll hang you from your feet by a butcher's hook until you confess.

BIG MAMA: No, don't torture me.

ELIZABETH: Guards. Egerton. Take her.

(Egerton enters followed by the guards, who grab Big Mama.)

BIG MAMA: No, Your Majesty, forgive me.

MARTHA: Stop it, Elizabeth. This woman saved your life a few minutes ago, and look how you're treating her.

ELIZABETH: Let her go . . . I'm sorry, Big Mama . . . forgive me . . . I got carried away by the fear . . .

BIG MAMA: That's all right, Your Majesty. I understand. It's normal: when a queen has a fit of shake-shake, terror-terror, what does she do to get over it? She hangs one of her servants by a hook until it passes. It's only natural. Me, when I'm scared, I just pee on myself, but that's natural too. *(Lifts up her skirt and runs offstage)*

ELIZABETH *(Regaining her composure)*: Egerton, a few hours ago I asked you a question: Why haven't I heard from the Lords who went to the castle of Essex?

EGERTON: There's a problem, Your Majesty.

ELIZABETH: What kind of problem?

EGERTON: Essex and his men have not kept their word. As soon as the Lords entered the castle, they were attacked and locked up.

ELIZABETH: Essex is losing his mind . . . I send the Lords to make an agreement with him and he locks them up!

EGERTON: Unfortunately, that's what happened.

ELIZABETH: But, when?

EGERTON: Late last night.

ELIZABETH: Last night? Wait a minute . . . a few hours ago you told me that the meeting had been postponed.

EGERTON: Yes, Your Majesty, so you wouldn't get upset. I was hoping the matter would be resolved by morning.

ELIZABETH *(Ironically)*: You were worried about me, Egerton. How touching. *(Seriously)* Was anyone killed in the skirmish?

EGERTON: Yes, the entire escort . . . massacred.

ELIZABETH: All of them? . . . and the Lords?

EGERTON: Saved.

ELIZABETH: Are you sure?

EGERTON: The letters were signed by all four of them.

ELIZABETH: What letters?

(Big Mama returns.)

EGERTON: The ones written in the handwriting of the Lords in which they ask you to give more weapons to Essex in exchange for their freedom.

ELIZABETH: Weapons for hostages? Why?

EGERTON: Essex wants to give the weapons to discontented sailors in the Spanish Armada. He's instigating a mutiny.

ELIZABETH: You mean Essex has been secretly plotting to overthrow the Spanish Armada from within. Why wasn't I told about this?

EGERTON: We didn't want you to be held accountable if anything went wrong.

ELIZABETH: Splendid. You concoct these harebrained plots without consulting me. And then you make me out to be an hallucinating idiot. So it was only a nightmare. The screams. The shouts. It was the skirmish with Essex, but you all conspired to keep it from me. Even you, Big Mama.

BIG MAMA *(Embarrassed, caught as she was trying to slip out)*: Yes, true it be. I heard the shots, but he told me . . . Sir Egerton . . . help . . . I be caught in the trap of my tongue . . .

EGERTON: Yes, Your Majesty. I ordered them to cover it up so as not to disturb you. We never imagined that things would get out of hand like this.

BIG MAMA: Your Highness, should we call in the guards? Should I get ready the hook to hang him up by his feet. Schlup-schlup, ow-ow. *(Laughs)*

ELIZABETH: You never imagined? Who are you kidding? You, Cecil and Bacon expected just this. It's clear. You organized the whole trap to screw Essex.

(Big Mama takes a stick and some cloth from her basket and begins to take Egerton's measurements, as if for a coffin.)

BIG MAMA: What a clever schemer.

EGERTON *(Angry at Big Mama)*: Shut up and keep your nose out of this.

ELIZABETH: No, let her speak. You're always talking about listening to the voice of the people, but if the people ever say anything you tell them to shut up. No, let her speak.

BIG MAMA: I speak, I measure and I bury.

ELIZABETH: Of course you wanted to execute your plans without interference. So why didn't you just put my crown on your head, and kick me out of the palace on my ass?

MARTHA: Elizabeth, excuse me . . .

ELIZABETH: Quiet, you pimp . . . you're as bad as the rest of them . . . out . . . out!

MARTHA: Oh, no . . . You can't treat me like that . . . I'm not one of your ministers . . . or your servants . . . understand? And I'd like to remind you, since your memory seems to be slipping, that when that rotten sister of yours locked you in the tower with the rats and the bats, and all the court fops and flatterers abandoned you as if you had the plague, I was the only one—fool that I am—who stayed to comfort you.

ELIZABETH: Yes, I'm sorry . . .

MARTHA: No apologies. You can take your apologies and stuff them . . .

BIG MAMA: The girl's got guts.

MARTHA: Now you're going to listen to me . . . and since what I'm going to say is not very pretty, please ask your police chief to leave for a moment.

ELIZABETH: Excuse us, Egerton. We'll call for you later.

BIG MAMA: Yes, call you we will, and then we'll measure you again . . . six-by-two, two-by-six . . . with head in hands . . . two-by-five . . .

EGERTON: Of course, Your Majesty . . . by your leave . . . *(Exits)*

MARTHA: Now then, first of all . . .

BIG MAMA: Ciao-ciao. Now you can talk.

MARTHA: Look at yourself. Love is dulling your senses. You can't think about anything but him, making yourself beautiful for him, finding a way to meet with him. You're out of your mind, ready for the booby-hatch.

BIG MAMA: Martha, you'd be safer pulling on a tiger's testicles.

MARTHA: That's enough from you. Get out of here.

ELIZABETH: No. She stays. All right, all right, I'm losing my mind, reduced to the state of a headless chicken. But part of the blame is yours, Martha. You were the one who pushed me to try Big Mama's beauty treatments . . . bees on my breast and worms in my ear!

MARTHA: Yes, because I felt sorry for you . . . love-sick . . . teary-eyed . . . I tried to put myself in your place . . . and I knew I'd do the same . . . but that was my mistake . . . I'm not supposed to be the queen.

ELIZABETH: And I'm not supposed to have any feelings . . . no passions of my own . . . nothing!

MARTHA: I'm not moved. No one forces you to do anything. If you want to live the life of a normal woman, throw away your crown. Abdicate! I only know that if you could have seen yourself last year . . . in the state you were in . . .

ELIZABETH: I would have spit in my own face . . . say it!

BIG MAMA: It seems that your beloved Lordship reduced you to a blub-blubbering jellyfish, and took up the habit of sitting on your noggin, making sure, of course, to first put a pillow under him, to protect his delicate bottom from the sting-stinging spikes of your crown. Kiss-kiss, plop-plop, ahhhhh! *(To Martha)* Isn't that right?

MARTHA: Yes.

BIG MAMA: Precisely?

MARTHA: Exactly.

BIG MAMA: Sold.

ELIZABETH: But I can break him, when and how I choose . . . If he goes too far.

MARTHA *(To Big Mama)*: Do you hear that? If he goes too far!

BIG MAMA: Love makes drunkards of us all. He starts a revolution, bang-bang, locks up your advisers, murders their escorts and makes a mockery of your love . . . so you think he hasn't yet gone too far?

MARTHA: And for a finish he calls you "old prune-puss."

BIG MAMA: Old prune-puss? Unpardonable. You can let a man call you a fool, a chicken, even a whore . . . *(She acts out a scene)* "You whore!" "I forgive you. I even like it a little."

But if he calls you "old" . . . cut him down to size . . . zum-zum, zum-zum . . . like that . . .

ELIZABETH: Certainly he shouldn't have called me that . . . it was naughty of him . . .

MARTHA: Elizabeth, stop it. It's time to quit cooing and cuddling and making excuses for him.

ELIZABETH: And why? Don't I have the right to be foolish every once in a while . . . to be languid and lovesick and sleep-walk my way through romantic fantasies like every other woman in the world.

MARTHA: No, not you. I'll say it again, you're the queen. You can't play the part like some character from a second-rate melodrama.

(A moment of silence.)

ELIZABETH *(Changes tone completely)*: All right. Thank you for the brushing down. Tell Egerton to come in. Do you see, Big Mama, the fun is over. Look at my life. Until a few hours ago I was happy, preparing myself for love. *(She is moved)* I was waiting for my Robert. And now, instead, I am preparing myself for a trial in which he will be condemned to death.

BIG MAMA *(Crying)*: That's why I never let myself be talked into being a queen. Never!

(Egerton enters.)

ELIZABETH: Egerton, please excuse the third-rate theatrics you were forced to witness a few moments ago.

EGERTON: But, Your Majesty . . . what are you saying?.

ELIZABETH: Let me continue. It won't happen again. First of all, please convey my congratulations to Cecil and Bacon . . . It was a brilliant idea to send the Lords, knowing that they would be taken hostage. I wish I had thought of it myself. My compliments.

EGERTON: Thank you, Your Majesty. I'll tell them. I'm sure they'll be pleased.

ELIZABETH: You said that Count Robert of Essex persuaded the four Lords to write some letters.

EGERTON: Yes, Your Majesty, I have copies here . . . they've managed to have them read in churches all over the city, during the sermons . . . even in the Cathedral of St. James . . . Would you like to take a look?

ELIZABETH: No, no, I can imagine what they've written. The Lords are indignant. They say they themselves are victims of a conspiracy. They call themselves national heroes.

EGERTON: Exactly.

(Big Mama moves close to Egerton and reads the letters in silence.)

ELIZABETH: And they propose a plan in which we buy their freedom by giving Essex more weapons to arm the mutineers in the Spanish Armada. They say that since they were acting as patriotic citizens, it is the duty of the State to save them.

EGERTON: That's incredible. You guessed it all. As if you were reading from the same script.

ELIZABETH: Then they add: "The funds to support the mutineers can easily be raised by selling spare weapons to James of Scotland, with whom it would be wise to develop stronger ties."

EGERTON: Yes, that's it. Perfect.

BIG MAMA: Word for Word.

ELIZABETH: What else did they write?

EGERTON: They threaten: *(Reading)* "If you allow us to be sacrificed, Elizabeth, it will reveal your weakness and mark the beginning of public dissatisfaction with your policies and the end of your credibility."

ELIZABETH: What arrogance.

MARTHA: You have to take action immediately to show everyone that you're still in charge.

ELIZABETH: Did you say that these bastards had copies of the letters distributed all over the city?

EGERTON: Yes, and someone has even succeeded in having them published and sold in the marketplace . . . like the words of a song.

ELIZABETH: Great sense of propaganda.

EGERTON: I've already given the order to make arrests, close down the printing presses and prohibit all further sales.

ELIZABETH: No. That will only increase the public's curiosity.

EGERTON: I didn't think of that. All right, I'll countermand my orders.

ELIZABETH: Organize your own sermons around the city. Publish counter-leaflets and have them passed out everywhere.

EGERTON: It will be done. *(Starts to leave)*

ELIZABETH: Just a minute. What are you going to write in your leaflets? Be sure to refer to Bacon. Rule number one, in war and peace: If they capture one of your own men and ask for a ransom, the first thing you do is lower the value of the merchandise in your enemy's hands. Devalue them, Egerton. Devalue them.

BIG MAMA: What a devious mind. She thinks like a man.

EGERTON: This will be difficult because the chief justice and the parliamentary president are highly esteemed by the people.

ELIZABETH: We can say that they are great statesmen, but that the poor fellows can't be held accountable for themselves anymore. Maybe they've been tortured, drugged . . . they can't think straight anymore . . . one of them tried to kill himself . . . another one lost his memory . . . another spends hours ripping papers into tiny shreds . . . maybe they've all gone mad.

BIG MAMA: There's something familiar about this story. Where have I heard it all before?

MARTHA: Wonderful, Elizabeth. You're acting like your old self again.

EGERTON: The problem is that these bastards haven't given us much time. They want an answer tonight. At sundown they're going to start throwing the hostages off of the tower one by one.

BIG MAMA: No, not from the tower . . . *(Mimes a succession of men thrown off a tower and squashed by the fall)* Allllllll Squit-squit . . . Allllllllll Squit-squit . . . Coffins keep getting shorter all the time.

ELIZABETH: Then there's no time to lose. Call the two Chambers into session. I'll speak to them myself . . . from the cathedral. I already have a speech in mind . . . and I know how to deliver it. I'll say that I am shocked . . . that's logical . . . and troubled . . . that I knew about the conspiracy, but that I can't remember exactly when I was told . . . that it's possible to forget . . . then I'll lower my voice . . . and give a moving eulogy to the four ministers . . . but then I'll be firm and say, "We cannot give in to their demands. This is a moment that calls for strength. We cannot lower ourselves to compromise with criminals."

BIG MAMA: It breaks our hearts. Boo-hoo. It tortures our souls. ARGH-ARGH. But our dear brothers must be sacrificed. A kiss for the widow. A kiss for the orphans. And a kick for the dog. Awieoooooooooooooo.

ELIZABETH: The State cannot give in to the demands of criminals!

EGERTON: Then we won't let them escape.

ELIZABETH: No.

EGERTON: It's as if we're telling them: Go ahead and murder them . . . you'll be doing us a favor.

ELIZABETH: Yes . . . as things stand now . . . with what they've written and made public . . . our eyes are flooded with tears . . . but . . .

BIG MAMA: State funerals for all.

ELIZABETH: Call for me as soon as the two Houses have assembled. Good-bye, Egerton.

EGERTON: It will all be done as you say, Your Majesty. *(He leaves)*

MARTHA: Bravo.

BIG MAMA: Bravo. Bravo.

ELIZABETH *(Desperate but holding herself together)*: Leave me alone. I'm dying. With four more corpses to account for, Essex is finished . . . he might as well be dead already, and I am dying with him.

MARTHA: No, maybe he still has time to save himself.

ELIZABETH: No, Martha. He will not save himself. Give me something strong to drink.

MARTHA: No. Alcohol's no good for you.

ELIZABETH: Give me my leaves.

MARTHA: No. You know they give you hallucinations.

ELIZABETH: We've reached the final act . . . the massacre . . . just like *Hamlet*.

BIG MAMA: Back to this obsession with *Hamlet* . . . *Hamlet*.

ELIZABETH: I'm sick. Robert, don't leave your palace . . . they'll take you to the tower . . . and I'll have to seal the wax on your death sentence . . . Oh, Robert . . . Robert . . . I'm a madwoman . . . I'm hysterical. I can't control myself. Help me. I'm bursting. I'm having an attack . . . like the one three years ago.

BIG MAMA: Put her feet in this basin of warm water.

ELIZABETH: I'm bursting.

BIG MAMA: Come on, unlace her in back.

ELIZABETH: My feet are going to explode . . . quick, take off my shoes . . . the stockings.

BIG MAMA: The shoes . . . off the shoes.

ELIZABETH: My legs. Look how they're swelling up . . . And my hands. They're starting to swell, too. Take off the rings.

(From this point on, the interventions of Big Mama must be toned down so as not to disturb Elizabeth's dramatic monologue.)

BIG MAMA: Water.

ELIZABETH: God, these damned rings are strangling my fingers. Look closely these rings are tombstones.

(The lights dim slowly.)

Under each ring is buried one of my relatives . . . or my lovers . . . here is my mother . . . *(Each ring is dropped into a basin, making a harsh hollow sound like a funeral bell)* Here is Leicester . . . and now we come to the last one . . . Mary Stuart, Queen of Scots . . . *(Speaks as if she were present)* This is your ring . . . come closer, Mary . . . play with your head as much as you like . . . it doesn't scare me anymore . . . Mary, I hated you . . . It took all the will power I had to keep you prisoner for eighteen years . . . alive! Before I decided to have you butchered. In the tower, your eyes always stared out to the sea. You were waiting for the Spanish Armada. I betrayed you. You came to ask me for protection . . . and I imprisoned you. For eighteen years you asked me to visit you, and for eighteen years I answered no . . . always no. Why? Why? . . . *(Changes tone, shouting, frightened)* Help me. Have pity . . . bandage my wounds. Who's pulling my hair?

MARTHA: Calm yourself. Wake up.

BIG MAMA: Wake up. Wake up.

ELIZABETH: I am awake . . . It's only that I'm dying. *(As if she's just awoken)* Was I only dreaming? Hold my eyes open with your fingers. Don't let me sleep anymore. Bastard conscience, always ready with your mouth on my neck to bite into me. Away. Go away . . . But who am I afraid of? Myself? I'm the only one here. Elizabeth loves Elizabeth. *(Shouting)* Is there a murderess here? Oh! Yes. It's me. Let's run away then. How? From whom? From myself? Yes, certainly, I'm not to be trusted. I could take revenge against myself . . . leap onto my own back . . . and slaughter myself. NOOO! Supported only by the strength I gave to myself, I passed implacably through everything and everyone like a plow . . . Elizabeth loves Elizabeth. Elizabeth loves Elizabeth.

MARTHA: That's enough, Elizabeth. Calm down.

(Shots are heard in the distance.)

BIG MAMA: Look. They're shooting. Robert of Essex has been taken prisoner.

ELIZABETH *(Frightened)*: The Armada. The Spaniards are coming, Mary. You're wild with joy. How many ships? Too many to count. Sails. Sails. A forest of Sails. A hundred. Two hundred ships. Masts towering high. Forty cannons on each.

(Martha and Big Mama retreat slowly until they are offstage.)

And I, what have I to send against them? Pirates! Ships with low masts. Half as many cannons. Half as many men. You're gloating, Mary . . . almost dancing with joy. And if I murdered you now . . . suddenly? What would you say about that, Mary? You're not laughing anymore. The Spaniards are disembarking. My men are running away . . . leaving me alone. It's over. It's over. No. Look, there are my clever pirates. They stayed out at sea to avoid being trapped in the port. Bravo. Bravo. Bravo. The wind is blowing stronger . . . they're raising the mainsails . . . they're getting ready to attack. No. Wait. Come back. I have to talk to the men . . . yes to all of them. Don't be stupid. No heroic speeches. I know it's a risk to allow them to land, but it's a bigger risk to let them attack without having spoken to them. Bring them back . . . Yes, in the dark. Light as many torches as you can . . . I want you to see my face. Come closer. Come closer. Lift up your torches. I want to see your faces, too. No, I'm not giving you the official speech. The one that will be read tomorrow at the House of Commons . . . the one that's written out. The Lords don't have to know about the things I'm going to say to you now. Look at me. Yes, it's me, Elizabeth the Virgin. And you are my army of swashbuckling bastards. But don't worry. You're in good company. My father was the first to call me a bastard. All of Europe spits on you as "an armada of cutthroat buccaneers." And I who have supplied you with ships, I who have always split the spoils with you . . . who am I? Yes, of course, I have exploited you and thrown you into the sea, as would any self-respecting pirate captain. But you, too, have the right to abandon me if I lose.

I won't shout: "Treason!" I won't cry or ask for mercy. But from now on I'll be under your asses with a lighted torch. And woe to anyone who even thinks about deserting. I'll shoot him in the head and howl obscenities filthier than anything you've ever heard from the lips of your mothers. I don't demand that you be heroes . . . that you fight to the death. No. And then, what is a hero? A criminal who finds himself on the right side, at the right time, in the service of the power that wins. So be infamous, be treacherous, be cunning . . . as long as you win. Did you hear that, Mary? Are you disgusted? I'll put an end to your disgust. I'm a skunk. I won't even allow you to watch your own fleet being destroyed. Prepare yourself. I've decided . . . I am signing your death warrant. Robert, what are you doing up on that scaffold? Get away. Maybe you can save yourself. Go away . . . Wait for me . . . I'll come talk to you.

It's your turn, Mary. I've planned a grand spectacle befitting a queen. A distinguished audience . . . dressed in ceremonial gowns, ribbons and silk shoes. Play your part well, Mary. Wear the dress of your choice . . . Yes, black suits you. No, unfortunately, I won't be there. I am not supposed to know anything about it. I should be taken by surprise when they bring me the news. I'm sorry you won't be there to see the despair I wrench up from my stomach when I learn that your head—Zwack! I will cry tears of blood . . . I'll throw myself on the ground . . . Yes, I signed the sentence . . . but I didn't seal it! I still had the right to reconsider. *(Simulates a cry of desperation)* I will pull out my hair: "Damned assassins. My little sister . . . blood of my blood. I loved her." *(Changes tone, becoming frighteningly cold and imperious)* "Who is responsible? Spencer . . . the Keeper of the Seal? Davidson? Lock him up. Cecil . . . my advisor? Him, too . . . no excuses." *(Detached)* People don't believe there is justice in a court where the victim is a woman, and the judge a woman, too. *(Softly the music of "Dies Irae")* And now, Mary. Get up. Be brave. Listen to them singing. What a touching idea it was for me to lend you my choirboys.

How beautiful you are, Mary. How tall. How regal.

Don't move your hands. The executioner will take off your lace. Kneel down and let them tie your hair behind your neck. So much hair. Is it all yours? I've lost a lot of mine, you know. And now . . .

The head . . . yes, on the chopping block. Good-bye. *(Changes tone. Frightened)* No. Who was that? Why is Robert there? *(Imperious)* He hasn't had a trial yet. That's when we'll decide. The trial's over? He's been condemned to death? Only him? Ten? Southampton, too? And Shakespeare? But I haven't sealed the order. Take it away. I'm the queen. I command you. *(She is overwhelmed, barely holding back her tears)* Forgive me, Mary, for having left you so long in such an uncomfortable position, but I'm in such pain that, believe me, at this moment I wish I were in your place . . . and I almost was. But as the people say, "When the tiger and the panther kiss, the one with the smaller mouth is left headless." *(She regains control and becomes her queenly self again)* Look there. All the guests. Cowards. Pigs. They don't have the courage to watch. They're closing their eyes. Turning their heads away. Watch! I command you!

The ax is in the air. It hisses. What a blow. The head's not severed. Incompetent imbecile. Second-rate executioner. Try again. Again. Oh, finally. And now what are you waiting for. Grab the severed head by its hair, lift it high, and shout: "God save the Queen." *(As if the chorus was present)* And you, sing louder. *(A pause)* It's a trap. *(Her voice is almost imperceptible. She takes a few steps backward. The stage is almost black. Only Elizabeth's head is lit)* That's not Mary's head . . . It's my head . . . It's my head . . . It's my head.

(The curtain falls on the singing of "Dies Irae":)

Ille te, Dominus meus
Qui fecit terram et aquam
Laudate Deum.

A peccato mortis servat,
Insuescit confiteor.
Vincere Dies irae.

THE END

ARCHANGELS DON'T PLAY PINBALL

BY **DARIO FO**

EDITED BY **FRANCA RAME**

TRANSLATED BY **RON JENKINS**

WITH ASSISTANCE FROM GLORIA PASTORINO

SONG LYRICS TRANSLATED WITH SALLY SCHWAGER

CADENCES OF COMEDY/ RHYTHMS OF REVOLT

Dario Fo shrieks, laughs, barks, leaps and sings. Franca Rame thinks, smiles, sighs, puts on her glasses and hums. Together they preside over rehearsals for *Archangels Don't Play Pinball* with astonishing theatrical virtuosity. One moment Dario is on his feet acting out the role of a homeless derelict giving advice to Ronald Reagan; then he's howling in a cage, playing the role of a man mistaken for a bloodhound. He rewrites the play as he improvises the roles, inspired by scandals and politicians he reads about in the morning papers. Franca takes his dictation, edits his excesses and inserts the new text into her ever-changing copy of the script. She takes particular interest in the role of Blondie that she performed almost thirty years ago when Dario first wrote it for her. When her husband comes up with yet another gag from the actor playing the role Fo himself performed in the 1959 Italian version, Franca stops him. The invention is hilarious, but she doesn't want laughter to ruin the intimacy of the moment between the two lovers. Their dialogue as they discuss the changes is reminiscent of the banter between the two of them when they perform on stage:

"Basta, Dario." "Ma Franca, è bello." "No, caro. E troppo." "Va bene, vedremo."

It is an intimate dialogue that reflects thirty-five years of living, writing, performing and directing together. No two artists could disagree more knowingly, lovingly, theatrically. Their timing is perfect as they sense each other's rhythms and respond to the scene's needs. Rame's emotional depth and seductive serenity complement the anarchic energy of Fo's comic fury. The scene that emerges from the joint efforts is funny, gentle, ironic, passionate and absurd. Its beauty comes from the contradictions that are embedded in its structure.

Another day Fo is rehearsing the protagonist's climactic monologue, an emotional outburst against the archangels, the fates, the shapers of man's dreams. He speaks the part in cascades of Italian prose poetry as Franca prompts him in soft, steady tones. The two voices reach the ear simultaneously, but remain distinct: Rame's deep soothing alto, Fo's sharp piercing tenor. Fo seems possessed by the sense of outrage that first inspired him to write the monologue. His voice quivers. His limbs tremble. He is pleading a case against injustice before a high court of angels, and the cast watches him in awed silence. The tension is heightened by each of his pauses, but just before Fo reaches the dramatic climax of the scene, Rame breaks out into uncontrollable waves of laughter. Fo stops, momentarily taken aback by her brashness. Then he laughs, too. And the actors laugh with him. No one is sure why they are laughing, but Franca's inexplicable fit of hilarity spreads through the rehearsal hall like an infectious plague of pleasure.

The strangely unsettling moment is representative of the impulses that fuel Fo's play. The seemingly incongruous juxtaposition of rage and laughter sets Fo's plays apart from superficial farce on one hand and didactic political satire on the other. At the heart of *Archangels Don't Play Pinball* is a tortured conflict between cruelty and joy. The human urges to laugh and love are stifled by the human urges to control and possess.

Society's injustices imprison a man in a dog pound. The situation is full of comedic possibilities that Fo exploits to their fullest, but he never loses sight of the grotesque tragedy implicit in his conception of the play. The dogcatcher has a whip, and he uses it. Brutality and humor coexist in Fo's epic comic vision. Fo's protagonist is a slapstick poet fighting to survive. The comic climaxes in the play are orchestrated to coincide with the character's liberation from oppressive conditions. He escapes from the dog cage. He escapes from the illusionist entrepreneur who has bought him from the pound and intends to make a profit by renting out his services as a talking dog.

And he escapes from the degradation forced on him by making his living as the butt of his friends' jokes. There is no explicit polemicizing in *Archangels*, but it is clear that the cadences of the comedy echo the rhythms of revolt.

Fo does not explain his aesthetics or his politics during the rehearsals. He makes no speeches about the multileveled complexity of his play. Without theorizing, without analyzing, without intellectualizing, he brings the play to life through its actions, moment by moment, scene by scene, letting the situations speak for themselves. The American Repertory Theatre cast participated in the collaboration with extraordinary grace, patiently waiting as he rewrote entire passages whenever an inspiration came to him, and gradually intuiting the rhythms of his demanding performance style. The actors were key collaborators in the revitalization of the play, inspiring Fo and Rame to create a completely new work that speaks as urgently to the needs of Americans in the eighties as it did to the needs of Italians almost thirty years ago. The comic hero is still trying to get out of the dog cage that society has locked him into, but now he's barking with a different accent.

—Ron Jenkins

Written for the 1987 production program of *Archangels* at American Repertory Theatre.

PRODUCTION HISTORY

Archangels Don't Play Pinball had its American premiere at the American Repertory Theatre in Cambridge, Massachusetts, in June 1987. It was directed by Dario Fo and Franca Rame. Set and costume design was by Dario Fo, lighting design was by Robert M. Wierzel, music composition was by Fiorenzo Carpi and sound was by Stephen Santomenna. The cast was as follows:

LANKY *(Sunny Weather)*	Geoff Hoyle
FIRST FRIEND *(Clerk, Dog Pound Director, Mayor)*	Peter Gerety
SECOND FRIEND *(Clerk, Dogcatcher)*	Remo Airaldi
THIRD FRIEND *(Clerk, Stationmaster)*	Benjamin Evett
FOURTH FRIEND *(Jules, Bum, Sergeant, Illusionist)*	John Bottoms
FIFTH FRIEND *(Doctor, Clerk, Conductor)*	Dean Norris
PASTRY COOK *(Coptic Priest, Inspector, General)*	Richard Grusin
BLONDIE	Harriet Harris
FIRST GIRLFRIEND *(Clerk, Woman at Dog Pound)*	Sally Schwager
SECOND GIRLFRIEND *(Clerk, Dogcatcher)*	Alison Taylor
THIRD GIRLFRIEND *(Woman at Window)*	Bonnie Zimering
FOURTH GIRLFRIEND *(Second Woman at Window)*	Rima Milla

CHARACTERS

LANKY *(Sunny Weather)*
FIRST FRIEND/CLERK/DOGCATCHER/POLICEMAN/
INAUGURATION PARTICIPANT
SECOND FRIEND/CLERK/DOG POUND DIRECTOR/MAYOR
THIRD FRIEND/POLICEMAN/DETECTIVE/MAGICIAN/
TOWN OFFICIAL
PROPRIETOR/PRIEST/MAN AT CLERK'S WINDOW/
INSPECTOR/SENATOR
FOURTH FRIEND/CLERK/GUARD AT DOG POUND/
STATIONMASTER/INAUGURATION PARTICIPANT
FIFTH FRIEND/CLERK/CONDUCTOR
SIXTH FRIEND/DOCTOR/POLICEMAN AT INAUGURATION
FIRST GIRLFRIEND/WOMAN AT CLERK'S WINDOW/
WOMAN INAUGURATION PARTICIPANT
SECOND GIRLFRIEND/SECOND WOMAN AT CLERK'S WINDOW/
WOMAN INAUGURATION PARTICIPANT
THIRD GIRLFRIEND/WOMAN INAUGURATION PARTICIPANT
BLONDIE/ANGELA/BRIDE

TIME

Now

PLACE

Here

NOTE

All song lyrics were written by Dario Fo. As there is no musical score, it is suggested the lyrics at the top of Act One, Scene 1, be set to modern American rock, pop or rap music; and that all other lyrics be set to American rock or pop music.

ACT ONE

SCENE 1

The curtain is open. The stage is bare.

Seven young men appear upstage against a plain backdrop. They are dressed identically: black pants, striped suspenders, white shirts. Their steps keep time to the music, they walk downstage and sing.

SEVEN MEN:

The night is a big umbrella, full of holes
Somebody's shot it up with lemon drops
The moon looks like a jackpot special
From a giant pinball machine for King Kong.

And my city is one big pinball parlor
With girls who act like replay flippers
As soon as you touch them they scream out: "Tilt."
Don't move. Don't tremble.
  Don't let it tilt.
  Don't let it tilt.
Your eyes are green flashers
Red specials: squeeze me if you want to
  Don't let it tilt.
  Don't let it tilt.
That's the rule of the game
A rule that's little known
  Don't let it tilt.
  Don't let it tilt.

We're a big gang of tough guys
We kidnap wealthy dogs and cats
And when their rich owners start crying
We collect a fat ransom and run.

We steal radios from parked cars
But cars are like flippers too
As soon as you touch them they scream out: "Tilt."
You have to be careful
  Don't let it tilt.
  Don't let it tilt.
Go easy on the flippers
Don't set off the alarm
  Don't let it tilt.
  Don't let it tilt.
There's no need to overdo it
Flip softly if you want to be a crook.

(During the song a fence closes behind the young men. It runs the length of the stage and serves as a half-curtain. At the end of the song, one of the men, the tallest, lets himself go rigid and fall over. Two of his companions grab him under his armpits, and two others lift up his feet. The other two exit stage right.)

LANKY: Oooooooo!

FIRST FRIEND: Dammit, you're heavy.

SECOND FRIEND: Don't overdo it. You only have to look sick. Not dead!

LANKY: And how do I do that?

THIRD FRIEND: Get stiff.

LANKY: Stiff like this? *(Arches his back)*

FOURTH FRIEND: Come off it. Stick in your stomach. *(Flattens him with a chop to the midsection)*

LANKY *(Straightening up quickly)*: Hey. Take it easy. No, that's it. I quit. You can play the part of the stiff. I told you before, I don't like the idea, and I never did.

FIRST: Oh, you don't like it. Did you hear that? He never liked it. We're risking prison so he can get married in style. And this is the thanks we get.

THIRD: Come on. Do you expect gratitude from a wimp like him? You must have your head up your ass.

SECOND: We've all got our heads up our asses. We find him a wife who's a real looker with lots of money . . . a virgin! . . .

FOURTH *(As if reading from a marriage announcement)*: Home owner. Impeccable morals . . . And now we're trying to get him a dowry, and he tells us he doesn't like playing the part of the stiff. What a louse.

THIRD: Aren't you ashamed of yourself?

LANKY *(Teary-eyed)*: Yes, yes. I'm ashamed and disgusted with myself. You're all so good to me. You always help me . . . and what do I do . . . I deserve to have someone spit in my eye. *(Spits in First Friend's eyes)*

FIRST *(Cleaning the spit out of his eye)*: Hey, don't be so hard on yourself . . . my eyesight's bad enough as it is.

(The fence opens to reveal the interior of a pastry shop.)

SECOND: Let's get on with it. Climb up.

LANKY: OK. I'm climbing. I'm climbing. *(Climbs onto Second Friend's back with both arms around his neck)*

SECOND: Not like that . . . on my shoulders.

LANKY: I am on your shoulders: it's not my fault your neck is so low.

SECOND: Stop it.

LANKY: OK. I'm stopping. I'm stopping *(Moaning)* Ohiii Ohiii Ohiii . . .

(The Second Friend carries Lanky on his back. The three others take his feet and they lift him into the shop entrance. The Proprietor greets them. He is worried.)

PROPRIETOR: An accident? Was he run over?

SECOND: If it had only been a car . . . a broken leg . . . a little cast . . . and he'd be back on his feet . . .

PROPRIETOR: Then, what is it? . . .

(Lanky is stretched out on the counter. He moans.)

THIRD: What is it? What is it? Can't you see he's dying?

(Lanky groans.)

PROPRIETOR: And you carried him here to die in the store. On top of my cannolis.

SECOND: You'd rather we let him die in the middle of the street. Have a heart!

PROPRIETOR: All right, then call a doctor.

(Lanky moans.)

THIRD: He's almost gone. Where's the telephone?

PROPRIETOR: Here . . . Wait. I'll get the phone book . . . Maybe it's better to call an ambulance.

FIRST: Give it to me. I think it's on the first page.

PROPRIETOR *(Pointing to Lanky)*: But, what's wrong with him?

(Lanky groans.)

FOURTH: It must be a stomach seizure.

(The Fifth Friend enters, making a path for the Sixth, who is carrying a doctor's bag.)

FIFTH: Here's the doctor. I knew he'd need one. Make room.

DOCTOR: A chair, please.

(Each one passes the Sixth's order down the line with a quick turn of the head.)

FIRST: A chair.

SECOND: A chair.

THIRD: A chair.

FOURTH: A chair.

FIFTH: A chair.

PROPRIETOR: A chair.

(They pass chairs to one another so frantically that in the end all the chairs are back where they started, and no one has succeeded in sitting down.)

DOCTOR *(To Lanky)*: How do you feel?

LANKY *(Asking him)*: How do I feel?

DOCTOR: How should I know? *(In a low voice)* You're supposed to tell me.

LANKY: Oh, I'm supposed to say how I feel. But you told me just to say, "Ohi. Ohi. Ohi . . ."

DOCTOR *(Slaps him)*: Shut up.

LANKY: Shut up. Ohi. Ohi. Ohi.

PROPRIETOR *(Comes from behind the counter pushing aside Lanky's Friends)*: Doctor, what's wrong with him?

DOCTOR *(Checking Lanky's pulse)*: I can't believe he's still alive. He's got no pulse. *(Pushes Lanky into a sitting position)* May I?

LANKY: Yes, you may?

DOCTOR *(Puts his ear to Lanky's back)*: Breathe. *(Lanky takes a deep breath)* Deeper. *(Lanky obeys)* Cough. *(Lanky obeys)* Louder.

(The Friends mimic the phony Doctor by putting their ears against each other's backs, forming a chain starting with the First Friend's ear against the Doctor's back, etc. They react to each cough with successively larger responses as if the sound were getting louder with each person along the chain.)

Stick out your tongue.

(Lanky obeys. The Doctor lifts up his eyelid) Bad. *(Shakes his head)* Let's see your stomach. *(Pokes his stomach. Lanky laughs as if he's being tickled)* I knew it. Third-degree food poisoning.

PROPRIETOR: Food poisoning. No. I'll bet it's just a broken heart.

THIRD: What kind of broken heart. He's getting married tomorrow morning.

PROPRIETOR: Then I was right.

(Lanky listens to his heart with a stethoscope he has slipped out of the Doctor's bag.)

LANKY: It's going beep-beep-beep. *(Pointing to the stethoscope)* The line must be busy. I'll call back later.

DOCTOR *(Pulls it away from him)*: He must have eaten something rancid. Any of you know what it could be?

SECOND: We all had dinner together . . . But he didn't eat anything. He was excited . . . It was his last night as a bachelor.

DOCTOR: Are you sure he didn't eat anything?

FOURTH: Nothing at all. Just five or six cannolis he picked up at some little joint . . .

PROPRIETOR *(Suddenly remembering)*: What do you mean, "some little joint." Now I know why he looks so familiar. He bought the cannolis here.

FIRST: So, he bought them here, did he?

SECOND: He did, did he? *(All surround the Proprietor)* Then you're the assassin.

PROPRIETOR *(Backing up to the counter)*: Let's stop kidding around. You don't think it was my cannolis. We make them fresh every morning . . . poison cannolis . . . never in ten years . . . and if you all ate them, too . . . that proves it!

FIFTH: It doesn't prove anything. Because none of us even tasted them. Fortunately, we didn't have time . . .

ALL *(In chorus)*: We were saved!

DOCTOR *(Taking charge)*: Stop squawking and call an ambulance. Now! We can let the police take care of him.

FIRST: Here's the number. *(Dials, faking a call)* Hello.

PROPRIETOR *(Begging)*: Doctor, please. There must be some mistake. It couldn't have been my cannolis . . .

DOCTOR *(Cold and determined)*: Maybe not, but we'll have to turn it over to the Department of Public Health.

LANKY *(Loudly)*: Ohiohioau!

FIRST *(With the phone in his hand)*: Damn. There's no answer. Where are they when you need them? Lazy bums!

(One of the Friends hits Lanky to get another moan out of him.)

LANKY: Ohi . . . ohi . . . ohi!

SECOND *(As if his heart is breaking)*: Doctor, can't you do something. An injection . . . something. I can't stand seeing him in such pain.

LANKY: Ohi . . . ohi . . . ohi. *(To his Friend)* Pretty convincing, huh? Ohi . . . ohi . . . ohi.

DOCTOR *(Professional tone)*: I'm afraid it's too late for a stomach pump.

FOURTH: Well, if there's no hope . . . maybe we should put hum out of his misery. We could give him a few more of those cannolis and finish him off. *(Picks up a pastry tray)*

DOCTOR: Put down that junk food, and stop joking.

(They all throw the cannoli around the room as if playing ball.)

PROPRIETOR *(Insulted)*: Wait a minute, doctor. Junk food? Let's not exaggerate. You'll see, when the Health Department examines my merchandise . . .

FOURTH: They'll close down your shop. They'll suspend your license. And maybe they'll lock you up for life, dear mister baby-killer.

PROPRIETOR: Take it easy, and don't make any insinuations, because . . .

FIRST: Because? . . . Because why? You call them insinuations, but everybody knows you make your pastries with . . . artificial additives.

PROPRIETOR *(Defensive)*: So what. Everybody uses them. Even the big chain bakeries.

DOCTOR *(Like a referee)*: In any case, additives or no additives, the store will be closed during the investigation . . . for a long time. So we'd better call the police immediately.

LANKY *(As if hallucinating)*: Yes, yes, the police. *(Picking up the phone)* Hello, police . . . send over a squad car . . . *(Shouts as if he were an emergency siren)*

DOCTOR *(Grabbing the phone away from him)*: I should have called them sooner.

FIRST: Police? *(Thumbs through the pages of the phone book with incredible velocity)* Here's the number. *(Dials)*

LANKY *(Still hallucinating)*: Yes, yes. The police; and Mommy, too.

PROPRIETOR *(Desperate)*: No. Please. Wait. You don't understand . . . If they close my shop, I'm finished. Have pity on me. I swear it's not my fault. Don't ruin me!

LANKY *(Playing the fool)*: Yes, yes. Ruin him. Ohi. Ohi. Ohi. I want my mommy!

DOCTOR *(Understanding)*: You understand that as soon as we take him to the hospital, the doctors treating the poisoning would immediately report it to the police.

FOURTH: They'll take away your license forever.

PROPRIETOR *(Crying)*: There's no hope. What can I do? *(The Fourth Friend takes his hand consolingly)* I put everything

I had into this shop. And just when things were beginning to go well . . . I could eat a . . .

(The Proprietor goes to bite his own hand, but bites the Fourth Friend's hand instead. The Fourth Friend screams.)

FIRST: Finally, the emergency number is ringing. Do you want to talk to them, doctor? *(Hands phone to Doctor)*

FOURTH: Listen guys. *(Pulls out a handkerchief to wipe the sweat from the Proprietor's face. He dries his tears and even blows his nose, then uses the dirty rag again on the Proprietor's face)* I don't know if this man is honest or not, but let's give him the benefit of the doubt. We can't let him be thrown into the street on account of a little bad luck. He's not the one who makes the additives. The big manufacturers are to blame. It's the old story of big fish and little fish.

THIRD: Don't start with politics. Get to the point. What do you have in mind. You want us to throw our friend in the sewer to save this guy's shop?

LANKY: No. Not the sewer. Mommeeeee!

SECOND: You, behave yourself, or we'll feed you another cannoli.

PROPRIETOR *(Grabbing the phone from the hand of the Doctor)*: Please . . . if you could help . . . sometimes a little good will is enough to . . .

FOURTH *(Distracted. Putting the phone to his ear)*: What if we took him to some private clinic? Maybe they'd keep it quiet . . . for a price.

DOCTOR *(Takes the phone as if someone has just answered on the other end)*: Yes. But do you know how much it would take to cover up a case like this. A couple of thousand before you even walk in the door.

PROPRIETOR *(Takes the phone)*: I could take care of that. Let's see how much cash I have. *(Puts down the phone and goes to the cash register)*

FIRST *(Winking)*: No. No. We couldn't do a thing like that. I'm all for helping my fellow man, but I don't want to go to jail for him. And if this one dies . . . who wants that on their conscience?

THIRD *(To Lanky)*: Groan, stupid.

LANKY: Yes, yes, I'm groaning . . . ahiohiohi, how I'm groaning . . . ohiohi . . .

FIRST: Look, he's dying already.

FOURTH: Come on, don't jinx him. Have some compassion for this miserable wretch. *(Grabs a wad of bills from the Proprietor's hand)* Give me that. How much is there? *(Starts to count)*

PROPRIETOR: Around two thousand. If you need more I could give you a check.

THIRD: No checks. The clinic we're taking him to doesn't accept them.

DOCTOR *(Grabbing the money)*: That'll be enough for now. Then, we'll see . . .

SECOND: Should we call a taxi?

DOCTOR: No, I've got my car outside. Let's go.

LANKY *(Begins to get up from the counter)*: Let's go, guys. *(A big slap sends him back down)*

FOURTH: Keep still, you idiot. *(Turning to the others)* Give me a hand.

(They lift Lanky onto their shoulders.)

PROPRIETOR: I don't know how to thank you . . . I hope it all goes well.

DOCTOR: Don't worry. The director of the clinic is a close friend. But I think you better give me some of these cannolis to be analyzed. Once they've discovered the cause, it will be easier to prescribe the cure.

PROPRIETOR: Please, please, take them all. I was just going to throw them away . . .

THIRD: We'll take care of them *(Grabbing armfuls of cannolis and cream puffs)* We'll take these too. You never know.

(One of the Friends takes a pie.)

PROPRIETOR: What do the pies have to do with it?

FOURTH: Pies are crucial. Pies are always crucial. *(Loads them up onto Lanky's belly as if he were a serving tray)*

SECOND: You have no idea how much material is required for a complete analysis. See you later.

(They exit.)

PROPRIETOR: I hope not. *(He lets himself flop down into a chair)* What a day. *(Without thinking he picks up a cannoli and takes a bite)* What a close call. I'll never use artificial additives again . . . You know you'd never guess from the taste of them that they're poisonous at all . . . Poisonous. *(Realizes that he's eaten half a cannoli)* Oh God, what have I done. Oh God, I'm dying. Doctor, wait for me. *(Runs out of the store)* Hey, you, wait for me. I'm coming, too. *(Exits running)* Oh God, what have I done.

(The fence closes hiding the store. The Friends enter. They laugh and slap each other with satisfaction.)

FIRST: Ah. He really fell for it. What a turkey.

DOCTOR: You were all brilliant. I would have fallen for it myself . . .

LANKY: Was I brilliant, too?

PROPRIETOR: Wait for me, stop . . .

FOURTH: Looks like he's had second thoughts.

(They slap Lanky again, lift him up and quickly leave.)

PROPRIETOR: They're gone. Where are you? . . . Wait for me, I don't want to die. *(He follows them, but goes the wrong way)*

LANKY *(From opposite wing)*: Hey, Mr. Cannoli, we're over here. *(Exits chased by Proprietor)*

(The Friends reenter.)

FIRST: What a chase.

LANKY: It was so beautiful.

THIRD: We lost him this take.

FOURTH: Yes, but let's get out of here and go to a bar. It'll be safer.

(The Friends walk. At the same time, from the left, a table and chairs are carried on. On the chair, in the shadow, a man is seated. When the Friends get close, a light reveals him to be a Gentleman who looks exactly like the Proprietor.)

FIRST: Look, there he is again.

LANKY: Let's go, guys.

(Lanky lets himself stiffen and fall backward, but this time there's no one to catch him. He falls with a thud and stays on the ground without moving. The others bump into each other as they run away. One of them trips and falls.)

GENTLEMAN: Hey, you guys. What's got into you? Andy, Bert . . . have you gone crazy?

DOCTOR *(Stopping suddenly)*: Michael, it's you. With that light from the side, I took you for the pastry shop owner. You know if you had an apron, you'd look just like him.

GENTLEMAN: What pastry shop owner?

(One at a time the other Friends reenter.)

FIRST: Hey, Michael, you really threw us for a loop.

THIRD AND FOURTH: But who is it?

DOCTOR: Excuse me, these are my friends: Peter, Mark, Luke and Jules.

FRIENDS *(Introducing themselves)*: Nice to meet you.

GENTLEMAN *(Noticing the pastry tray)*: On your way to a party?

THIRD: We're coming back from one . . .

DOCTOR: We just finished fleecing a pastry shop owner who could pass as your brother.

(Two of the Friends approach Lanky, who has not moved since he fell down.)

GENTLEMAN: Now I see why you were in such a hurry . . .

SECOND *(Poking Lanky with his foot)*: Hey, Lanky, wake up. All clear.

FOURTH: We know you can play a great corpse, but you can stop now. *(Slaps him)* Son of a bitch. He must have hit his head, Andy, come here. You're so good at playing doctor. Take a look at him.

(The Doctor takes Lanky's pulse and heartbeat.)

FIFTH: Acts like a real doctor.

DOCTOR: It's nothing. Throw a little water on his face and see what happens. Waiter, a pitcher of water please.

THIRD: I'll get some.

GENTLEMAN: Let's hope he doesn't have a concussion.

SECOND: Don't worry. Before you can have a concussion, you have to have a brain. He's got a head full of billiard balls.

DOCTOR: We only keep him around for laughs. We play tricks on him, and he falls for them every time. *(He goes to sit down on the only free chair, but one of the Friends pull it out from under him and he falls)*

FOURTH: One time we made him believe he was invisible. *(One after another they pull the chair out from under each other—executed like a violent ballet—until finally the last Friend thinks he has the chair to himself. Then, it gets kicked out from under him, and he makes a theatrical fall. All this happens without interrupting the Fourth Friend's story)* He fell for that one too: he walked down the street behind a woman and goosed her. The best part was that she liked it. But her boyfriend didn't. He was walking behind her and . . . poor invisible man. He got two black eyes and couldn't see anything for days.

FIRST: But the best trick is the one we're playing on him now. We're marrying him to a streetwalker.

GENTLEMAN: To a what?

FOURTH: To a streetwalker, a woman who walks the streets.

SECOND: Well, she's not really a streetwalker, in the sense that she doesn't do it for a living. She's a part-timer.

FOURTH: Yes, she works at home. *(Imitating a female voice)* Hello, honey.

GENTLEMAN: But you're not going to marry them for real, are you?

DOCTOR: Are you crazy? Where would the fun be in that? . . . Listen to what we did . . . *(Turns to the Third Friend, who's just arrived with the water)* Wait. Let me tell him the story before you wake him up . . . Then he can help us, too . . . *(Pointing to the Gentleman)* OK, first we put the idea into his head . . . telling him he had to find a wife, that he couldn't go on living like a bum his whole life . . . like this . . . like that . . . etc. Then we made him take out a classified ad in the paper . . .

FOURTH: Wait. He probably still has it in his pocket . . . *(The First Friend goes through Lanky's pockets and finds a scrap of old newspaper)* There it is. Read it.

FIRST *(Reading)*: "Unemployed youth, nondescript, mediocre appearance, slight physical defects . . ."

FOURTH: We convinced him that it is always best to tell the truth.

FIRST *(Continuing)*: ". . . would marry young, rich, blond but still virgin. Good family background. Own apartment. No physical defects."

GENTLEMAN: And he actually went in person to place the ad? Imagine the clerk's face.

DOCTOR: Yes, but you should have seen his face when he got the letter we had sent, pretending it was from a beautiful, rich Albanian.

GENTLEMAN: Why Albanian?

FOURTH: So that we could invent an Albanian orthodox ritual which prohibited the groom from seeing the bride's face before the wedding.

THIRD: Imagine how much fun the wedding will be. We found a bride, and got the money to pay her and her friends from the pastry shop owner . . . *(Pointing to the stolen goods)* . . . Along with some nuptial pastries and pies.

FOURTH: We even have a holy robe. *(Takes a black tunic from under his jacket)* All we need is a coptic priest.

DOCTOR: But we have one now . . . Look: there he is. *(Pointing to the Gentleman)*

GENTLEMAN: Me? You're crazy. A setup like that. I couldn't do it. I'd burst out laughing.

FOURTH: You can do what you want. He'll never know the difference.

SECOND: Quiet, he's coming to.

(Lanky begins to move his arms, he brings his hands to his neck.)

LANKY: Ahiohi, what a fall!

FIRST: Quick, father, transform yourself.

(From under his jacket the First Friend takes out the hat of an orthodox priest and puts it on the Gentleman's head. Another one helps him on with the black tunic. They lift the Gentleman up onto the table where he sits on a chair as if it were a throne.)

FOURTH *(Slapping Lanky)*: Come on, wake up. It's nothing. You had a nice nap, didn't you?

LANKY: Where am I? . . . Oh, it's you guys. *(Seeing the Gentleman)* Mr. Cannoli. Let's run! *(Starts to leave)*

DOCTOR: No. Calm down. It's not the pastry shop owner. They look alike, but it's not him.

FOURTH: This is a coptic priest. We invited him especially for you.

LANKY: A coptic, for me? *(Gets up slowly and walks over to the phony priest)* A pleasure to meet you.

(The Third Friend signals him to kneel.)

FIRST: Kiss his hand, you pagan.

LANKY *(Kneeling)*: Yes, yes, excuse me and thank you for everything. *(Kisses his hand)*

GENTLEMAN: Don't mention it. Rise my son, rise. *(Turns his head away so as not to laugh in Lanky's face)*

FIRST: Did you hear? Rise. That means pick him up and make him rise.

LANKY: Pick him up? Why should I pick him up.

DOCTOR: It's an orthodox custom. Like here when the groom carries the bride over the threshold. In Albania the groom carries the bride's priest over the threshold . . . Go ahead. Get moving. Lift him up on your shoulders. It's better.

LANKY: The bride's priest on my shoulders? Where should I take him?

FOURTH: To the bride's house. Where else? Come and we'll show you the way.

(The Gentleman jumps off the table. A red tablecloth is placed over the table, which the Friends lift up over the Gentleman's head as if it were a religious canopy.)

LANKY: Good, good. Finally I get to see her.

FOURTH: Now, sing.

(They form a procession as they sing: "The Night Is a Big Umbrella Full of Holes, Someone Has Shot It Up with Lemon Drops."

The fence opens, they leave.

Blackout.)

SCENE 2

Inside the Bride's house. Paper party decorations. The phony Priest ties Lanky's wrists to the wrists of the Bride. Lanky is blindfolded. His Bride is dressed in white, a veil hiding her face. Three Girls and the Friends stand in chorus, each with a candle in hand, singing "Squeeze My Wrists Tightly":

FRIENDS AND GIRLS:

Squeeze my wrists
Tight against yours
Even with my eyes shut
I can see your eyes.
Please take my love
I'll give it for a smile.
Squeeze my wrists
Tight against yours
Even with my eyes shut
I can see you with my heart.

PRIEST *(Steps between the bride and groom)*: Repeat after me, but not out loud: whatever your virtues, whatever your flaws, I will honor and keep you till death do us part.

CHORUS: ". . . till death do us part."

PRIEST: Forever close, now that fate has brought you to me.

CHORUS: ". . . till death do us part."

PRIEST: From now on, my shadow will be your shadow, I will see light through your eyes, and I will speak with your mouth.

CHORUS: ". . . till death do us part."

PRIEST: My blood will flow through your heart, and yours through mine. We will be one till death do us part.

CHORUS: ". . . till death do us part."

PRIEST: You are man and wife . . . You may now see each other.

(Two Friends untie them and remove the blindfolds. First Lanky, then the Bride, a blond bombshell with an incredibly pure face. Everyone applauds. Then there is silence. The Bride smiles. Lanky is dumbfounded and still.)

LANKY: Oheuuu.

DOCTOR: Is that all you can say? How do you like her?

LANKY: Oheuuu.

BRIDE: It's a pleasure to meet you.

LANKY: A pleasure. Oheuuu.

THIRD: Say something. After all, she's your wife.

LANKY: Is she really my wife?

CHORUS: Yes, you just married her.

LANKY: Oheuuuu. A pleasure.

BRIDE *(With simplicity)*: A pleasure.

PRIEST: And you, miss . . . I mean Mrs. . . . I just married you . . . I was saying, how do you like your husband?

BRIDE: He's wonderfully lanky . . . Oheuuu, so lanky. He's the lankiest.

LANKY AND BRIDE *(In chorus)*: Oheuuu. A pleasure.

DOCTOR: Ah, what a beautiful couple. Long live marriage.

ALL: Hallelujah.

THIRD: Come on. Come on. The groom pours the drinks!

LANKY *(Grabbing a bottle while the Girls get trays of food)*: Listen, Jules, you're sure this isn't a joke . . .

JULES: A joke? You must be joking. Do we look like jokers?

LANKY: No, but what if she changes her mind?

JULES: Don't worry, she won't change her mind . . . She never had a mind. How can she change it?

LANKY: No mind? But she's beautiful, oheuuu. Ehiii . . .

(All the Friends kiss the bride and one of her friends.)

Me, too. I want to kiss the bride, she's my bride . . .

(Lanky can't get to her through the crowd. The Friends pass her back and forth to one another as if playing a kissing game, and the girls play along, allowing themselves to be kissed and hugged. There is spinning, shouting and laughter, until gradually they all disappear through the wings. Lanky is left holding the Priest.)

She's my bride . . .

PRIEST: What are you doing? I'm the priest.

LANKY: The priest. It's a pleasure to meet you. *(Kisses his hand)* Excuse me, but I wanted to kiss the bride. Where is she?

PRIEST: Probably in some bedroom with one of your friends.

LANKY: Oh, I see . . . *(As if struck by lightning)* In some bedroom?! In bed?

PRIEST: Yes, it's an old orthodox custom. Here you kiss the bride, but in Albania you go to bed with her. It's the custom.

(Suddenly there are loud voices offstage:)

BLONDIE: Creep! Take it off. Take it off, now!

VOICE: What's the matter? . . . Ohi. Get your hands off me.

BLONDIE: It's not yours. You've no right to ruin it like that.

(Doctor enters wearing Blondie's white dress. Blondie is behind him in her slip.)

DOCTOR: All right, I'll take it off. I was only joking.

BLONDIE: And be careful not to rip it.

(Another Friend enters wearing the dress of one of the Girls. Then another and another. All in drag. The Girls giggle stupidly.)

FIRST TRANSVESTITE: Calm down, girls. This is serious. Let's get on with it.

SECOND TRANSVESTITE *(Turns to Lanky)*: What a beautiful hunk of a man. Too bad he's married, otherwise . . . I'd do something wild.

THIRD TRANSVESTITE *(Pointing to the Friend he has in his arms)*: Please, Mr. Priest, we want to get married.

FOURTH TRANSVESTITE: Yes, we want to legalize our relationship. Until now we've been living in sin.

BLONDIE: You make me sick. Out. All of you.

DOCTOR: But, Blondie, we made a deal.

BLONDIE: We made a deal that you wouldn't wreck the place.

GIRL: But they didn't do anything.

ANOTHER GIRL: What's the big deal. It's only a nightgown.

BLONDIE: But it's a real nightgown. I sleep with that nightgown.

DOCTOR: With just the nightgown?

(All laugh.)

BLONDIE *(Turning to the Girls)*: And if you don't like it, you can leave, too. Get out.

GIRLS: OK, we're going. A little edgy, aren't you . . . what a drag . . . Good-bye . . . Let's go to my house where you can wear all the women's clothes you want.

FOURTH TRANSVESTITE: The only parties you remember are the ones that end badly. Good-bye, dear. *(Exits with Friends)*

FIRST TRANSVESTITE: And to think that this joke cost a thousand bucks. I'm still not sure who the fool is, him or us. *(Exits with rest of Friends)*

BLONDIE *(Turning to the Priest, who is chanting)*: You, too, your holiness, get lost.

PRIEST *(Going toward the door)*: Be happy, my child. *(She blows him a raspberry. He responds to her elegant style)* Oh, a Radcliffe girl! *(He leaves)*

BLONDIE: Drop dead . . . *(Closes the door)* Finally, they're gone. I couldn't have stood another minute.

LANKY *(Has been sitting upstage, away from the action)*: They got a little carried away.

BLONDIE *(Without thinking)*: You call that "little."

LANKY: Once they get started, they don't know when to stop . . . then somebody always gets hurt . . .

BLONDIE *(Stops herself)*: Hey, what are you doing here? I thought you left with the others.

LANKY *(Bluntly)*: But why would I want to? We're newlyweds, and it wouldn't be right for me to leave you on the first night. It just wouldn't be right.

BLONDIE *(Runs to window, leans out and shouts)*: Hey, you forgot something.

VOICE *(From outside)*: Oh, yeah, Lanky. He's a gift from heaven. Enjoy him . . . *(Laughs)* Good night, lovebirds.

BLONDIE: Bastards! . . . And now, what can I say?

LANKY *(Without irony)*: Tell me about yourself: what you were like as a child.

BLONDIE: What?

LANKY *(Still with candid sincerity)*: If we want to get to know each other, it might be best to start with our childhoods. For example, I remember being so mature as a child that at the age of fifteen, people took me for ten.

BLONDIE: And I remember being so mature as a child at the age of fifteen they took me for five.

LANKY: No. So young?

BLONDIE: Five dollars. Cash.

LANKY *(Laughs, then changes attitude)*: Don't act tough with me. I can see through it. I felt you tremble when your wrists touched mine, like that . . . *(Comes close to her and re-assumes the position of the ritual)* Admit it, you were getting emotional.

BLONDIE: Well, a little emotional, sure . . . *(Starts to take down the party decorations, Lanky gives her a hand)* Everybody was singing . . . all those words: ". . . my shadow will be your shadow . . . my blood will flow through your heart . . ." Uhei! That stuff has an effect! . . . And the white dress . . . Dammit, I bet if you put a white dress on an elephant, she'd get goosebumps, too. It was the situation that got me all worked up . . . not you . . . or anybody else.

LANKY: Me or anybody else? But what about when you said: oheuuu, you're so lanky . . .

BLONDIE: I just said you were lanky, that's all. You are lanky, aren't you?

LANKY: Yes, but when you said I was lanky . . . it didn't have anything to do with lankiness . . . nobody ever told me I was lanky like *that* before . . . say it again.

BLONDIE: That you're lanky?

LANKY: Yes, I like the way you say it.

BLONDIE: Now, you're making fun of me? Don't you ever . . . *(Throws some of the decorations at him, which he catches calmly)*

LANKY: Me, make fun of you? Never. You're too beautiful. And pretty lanky yourself . . . And for you I'd like to be even lankier . . . lanky, lanky, lanky . . . So lanky that you'd say, "Oh, you're the lankiest."

BLONDIE *(Angry and flattered at the same time)*: Come on, let's stop. When I hear you talk like that, I feel like I'm in a madhouse. They told me you were a little unbalanced, but I had no idea . . . *(Walks toward him maternally)* Is it possible that after all this, it still hasn't dawned on you that your friends . . . ?

LANKY *(Without taking in what she said, worried)*: Speaking of my friends, that custom about everyone sleeping with the bride . . . does it still go on after the first day? . . .

BLONDIE: What are you talking about? What custom?

LANKY *(Almost talking to himself)*: No, because it might start getting on your nerves, if someone was sitting quietly at home with his wife, and a friend came in and said, "Excuse me, could I borrow her for a while. I want to try out the custom again." *(Firmly to Blondie, who is looking at him with a stunned expression)* I'm sorry to have to say this, but it's better to make things clear from the start . . . call me old-fashioned, call me conservative, but I don't like it at all.

BLONDIE: What did they tell you? *(With angry gestures she picks up glasses from around the room)* How did I ever get myself mixed up in this farce. How the hell could anyone enjoy making fun of someone like you? It's an out and out disgrace. What fun is it to hit someone over the head if they're only going to smile at you and say thanks. Or to spit in someone's face and have them just stand there and look at you, the way you're looking now.

LANKY *(Maintaining an unchanging melancholy smile)*: What's wrong with my face? Is it ugly?

BLONDIE: Of course not. It is a little stupid looking, but at least it's honest.

LANKY: Yours is honest, too.

BLONDIE *(Looks at him; she begins to smile, but suddenly becomes cold)*: Shouldn't you be leaving? I'd like to be left in peace.

LANKY *(Gets up reluctantly, stretching out his words)*: OK, I'm going . . . but calm down. It wasn't a total loss. In fact, you were paid rather well. *(Suddenly evil)* And now your conscience is bothering you, because you earned your money at the expense of a poor idiot who stands there looking at you as if you were Snow White with her seven dwarfs. So you start yelling and raving . . . Calm down, OK. *(Blondie is speechless.)* Calm? . . . Good night. *(Begins to leave)*

BLONDIE: Wait . . . You're not going to tell me that all of a sudden your brain has started working?

(Lanky comes back a few steps, and leans against a chair, looking at her with a melancholy smile.)

LANKY: Don't worry. My brain has been working all along. I know they make fun of me. In fact I'm usually the one who sets up the joke in the first place. They don't have much imagination, and if I didn't help them out, they wouldn't come up with much on their own.

BLONDIE *(Falls into a chair, astonished)*: What kind of fool are you? Not only do they make fun of you, but you help them. Why?

LANKY *(Takes a cigarette out of his pocket)*: For me playing the fool is something of a profession.

BLONDIE: You're a professional fool?

LANKY: Did you ever hear of a court jester. *(Lights his cigarette)*

BLONDIE: Of course I've heard of them. *(Erudite, encyclopedic)* Court jesters were employed to evoke the laughter of kings . . . right?

LANKY *(Laughing)*: Absolutely. It's the same with me. The only difference is that they don't have kings anymore. So I evoke laughter from my friends at the cafe. I'm a poor man's Rigoletto. But the important thing is, that it earns me a living.

BLONDIE *(Incredulous)*: They give you a salary?

LANKY: I earn more than I would if I were a clerk, and I work a lot less. Look. Everything I'm wearing, they've given me. I sleep at their houses. They pay for my food, wine, cigarettes. And if I ask for a loan, they never turn me down. No one refuses to lend money to a fool.

BLONDIE *(Spits on the ground in contempt)*: What kind of a man are you?! Doesn't it disgust you to earn a living that way?

LANKY *(In the same tone as her, provoking her)*: How does it make you feel to earn a living in that other way?

BLONDIE *(After a moment of silence)*: Bull's-eye.

LANKY *(Expecting another defensive reaction, now he's sad for her)*: Excuse me, it slipped out.

BLONDIE *(Melancholy, sighing)*: No, I deserved it. Me, preaching about self-esteem. It's enough to make you die laughing. But the idea of it makes me angry. When a woman's only asset is her looks, there's only one way for her to make a living. But for a man . . .

LANKY *(Gets up, carries his chair close to her and sits down)*: It's the same thing. It all depends on how you begin . . . Someone like you doesn't wake up one day and decide to become a hooker. Either you're born into it, or you ease your way in slowly. Me, I was born into it. It started with my father. His last name was Weather, so for a little joke, he baptized me with three names: Sunny, Cloudy and Stormy. "This way he can choose for himself according to the atmospheric conditions," he said.

BLONDIE *(Laughs, then she stops, embarrassed)*: Ah, what a fool.

LANKY *(Getting louder)*: Yes, what a fool. Imagine what it was like with my friends at school . . . "How are you," "What's the weather forecast today?" . . . For years and years.

BLONDIE *(Without smiling)*: It must have been awful.

LANKY *(Relaxed now, like a storyteller talking about something that happened to someone else)*: Even the war made fun of me . . . Soldiers get wounded everywhere, I know . . . in the arm . . . in the leg . . . even the head . . . But I got shot in the coccyx. A bullet it knocked it clean away. Zac. Trach.

BLONDIE *(Unable to control herself, explodes into laughter)*: Ah. *(Giggles)* Ihp . . . But how is it possible that you got hit right there . . . ihp?

LANKY: You see. "How is it possible?" . . . You're laughing so hard, it's giving you the hiccups. Even fate found it fun to shoot me in precisely that spot.

BLONDIE: Ah. Ah.

LANKY: I was discharged as a partially disabled veteran, and now I'm eligible for special benefits, privileges, and even a pension. One day I was sitting on a bus and a guy asked me to give him my seat. "I'm a disabled veteran," he said. "I'm disabled, too," I answered. He looked at me in disbelief and asked, "Where?" "In the coccyx," I said. Before I could finish speaking, he pulled me up by my tie and shouted, "Listen, I've got nothing against homosexuals, but I can't stand people who go around bragging about it." He was ready to throw me off the bus.

(Blondie laughs.)

BLONDIE *(Affectionately)*: Excuse me for saying so, but you bring it on yourself. Anyone who walks with his head turned 'round to listen for people talking about him behind his back is bound to bump into the nearest lamppost. SHANG . . . IHP! *(Hiccups)* Then he curses fate for planting lampposts on sidewalks.

LANKY: Congratulations. This time you hit the bull's-eye . . . .But may I ask how you can be so accurate in assessing the flaws of others, mine in particular, and still let yourself be trapped in the kind of life you live.

BLONDIE *(Takes a tray and speaks in staccato)*: Because when I began, I was more ignorant than I am now. And ignorance is the worst flaw of all. My father always said . . . IHP . . . *(Hiccups, then repeats the phrase with the cadence of a broken record)* My father always said . . . IHP . . . my father always said . . .

(She wipes a tray, moving her hand as if it were the arm of a gramophone needle. Lanky lifts up her arm, then puts it back on the tray as if he were adjusting the needle on a broken record. Blondie continues speaking as if nothing had happened.)

My father always said that if a man or a woman was afflicted with ignorance, they would turn out like plants without leaves: empty poles. Even as a pole, I'm a twisted specimen.

LANKY *(Smiling sympathetically, without looking at her)*: Well, sometimes you're better off being twisted, if you happen to find another pole who's twisted in the opposite direction . . . If you tie them together at the top . . . *(Takes a breath)* . . . the two of them would stand up stronger than if they were straight.

BLONDIE *(Takes a step to observe him better)*: Is there a double meaning to that? *(Hiccups)* Are you talking about us?

LANKY *(Stands up slowly, speaking erratically)*: Why don't we pretend, that we don't know: me, who you are; you, who I am . . . Tell me . . . would you want to, be with me?

BLONDIE *(Speeding up the rhythm. Slowing down at the end)*: Be with you? How? . . . Just for tonight, or for as long as it works? No, because if it was only a night, I'd tell you who I am, and you'd have to pay my fee.

LANKY *(Sits down again, rubbing his hands together)*: We're not laughing anymore.

BLONDIE *(With intensity, almost falsetto)*: What did you expect? . . . Don't you see that I'm telling you all this because I think I understand you, and because, God knows, I never get a chance to be honest like this with anyone?

(Knock at the door.)

FRIEND *(From outside)*: Anybody home?

BLONDIE: IHP . . . *(Hiccups)* Go away. I'm busy.

FRIEND: Let me in. I brought back your clothes.

BLONDIE: OK. *(Opens the door)* Come in. Let's see . . . You've made a mess of them.

FRIEND *(Noticing Lanky)*: Oh. So he's still here? *(Swaggers)* I'll get rid of him for you? *(Speaks to Lanky with undisguised irony)* Excuse us, Lanky. I have to speak to the lady about a delicate subject. Would you please get your ass out of here?

(Lanky doesn't move. Blondie throws the clothes violently down on a chair.)

BLONDIE: His ass is staying right here. If anybody's ass is leaving, it's yours. *(Advances threateningly)*

FRIEND *(Trying to avoid her)*: You don't understand . . . I'm not here to waste your time . . . I'm a paying customer . . . Cash in advance . . . Look . . . *(Shows her a roll of bills)* Just like a bunch of roses. Come on. Throw him out. Tonight, there's poetry in my soul.

BLONDIE *(Looks for a moment at Lanky who is still sitting, distracted)*: You throw him out while I go to put away these clothes. *(Whispers to Lanky as she leaves)* Come on, let's see if you're really interested in a twisted pole.

FRIEND *(Takes off his jacket, turns to Lanky with firm resolve)*: Now, listen . . . and try to get it into your fat head . . . *(Throws his jacket on a chair)*

LANKY *(As if he's just waking up, he stands)* OK. I get it. I'm leaving . . .

FRIEND *(Surprised)*: You're leaving?

LANKY *(Turning back)*: Why, don't you want me to?

FRIEND: No . . . no . . .

LANKY *(Sits down again)*: Then I'll stay.

FRIEND: No . . . no! I meant: yes, yes . . .

LANKY *(Gets up again, perturbed)*: Yes, yes or no, no? You seem to be a little mixed-up. *(Sits down again)* In any case, you'll have to lend me fifty dollars for a taxi . . .

FRIEND *(Automatically reaches into his jacket on the chair and pulls out some money)*: Fifty dollars? . . . Where are you going?

LANKY: To the central police station. It's the only one that's still open.

FRIEND *(Turns around suddenly)*: Police station? . . . What for?

LANKY *(Casually crossing his legs)*: To report a few minor incidents: like fraud and blackmail at the pastry shop . . . my conscience is bothering me . . . the more I think about it the more I'm convinced I should turn myself in . . . Now that I'm married, I've decided to reform.

FRIEND *(Shocked, then becoming aggressive)*: What's gotten into your head? . . . Do you want to get us all locked up? . . . I'll strangle you. You ungrateful, miserable, stinking skunk. And after all we've done for you.

LANKY *(Feigning shock)*: Only for me? . . . And who is this for? *(Pointing to Friend's money)*

FRIEND: What do you care? That's for our trouble. We have to eat, too, pal.

LANKY *(Bored, stretches out his legs)*: Of course, you have to eat. On second thought, maybe I shouldn't turn myself in. I'd end up in jail, too . . .

FRIEND *(Relieved)*: And they'd keep you in longer than all the rest of us put together.

LANKY *(Casual again, smiling)*: No longer than you. No. I'm a fool . . . everyone knows I'm a fool . . . I could always say you forced me into it . . . that I really believed I was poisoned. If you can make someone believe he's invisible and married to a hooker, you can make him believe anything. In fact, the judge might even give you a few extra months for taking advantage of a helpless fool.

FRIEND *(After a pause, he approaches Lanky in amazement)*: What's going on? . . . Is that you talking, or some brother of yours with a Harvard degree that you've been hiding in the closet? So you were only playing the fool to get a free ride at our expense. Son of a bitch. And we thought you were just a clown.

LANKY *(With an insolent smile)*: Yeah. Life is strange that way. You think one thing, and on the contrary . . . This money for example *(Points to Friend's money)* You thought it was yours, and now . . . it's mine. *(Takes it)*

FRIEND: Give me that money . . . or I'll break your face. *(Grabs Lanky and lifts him to his feet)*

LANKY: There's something else I forgot to tell you . . . I have a mean right hook. *(Punches him and kicks him out the door)* Out. Out.

FRIEND: You'll pay for this, Lanky. You won't be talking so big when the rest of the gang finds out about this.

(Blondie returns.)

BLONDIE: IHP. *(Hiccups)* He's right. They won't let you get away with that. Good-bye, court jester . . .

LANKY: If I were worried about that, I would never have made the mistake of telling you about myself.

BLONDIE: IHP. *(Hiccups)*

LANKY: Why don't you try drinking from the wrong side of the glass. Maybe it will cure your hiccups.

BLONDIE: What?

LANKY: Like this, look. *(Takes a glass of water, bends over and tries to drink from the opposite side of it. The water spills all over him and he coughs)* I was saying that maybe it was a mistake to start telling you all about me. Maybe I should have left things as they were.

BLONDIE *(Tries the trick with the glass. Takes a deep breath)*: Ah. I'm cured.

LANKY: That's great . . . IHP . . . *(Hiccups)* Now I've got them.

BLONDIE: I'm sorry . . . what were you saying about leaving things as they were.

LANKY: I was saying that if I'd left things as they were, maybe I wouldn't be leaving empty-handed.

BLONDIE: You're leaving? *(Lanky nods his head)* But where will you go?

LANKY: I've got enough here for a hotel. *(Indicates the money he took from the Friend)* And maybe enough to get to Washington. *(Hiccups)*

BLONDIE: Washington?

LANKY: Yes. I want to see if I can get some of my pension money. Then it'll be easier to walk down the street without turning my head around, as you put it. *(Hiccups)* 'Bye. It's been a pleasure. *(Holds out his hand)*

BLONDIE *(Slowly, almost embarrassed, she gives him her hand)*: 'Bye. A pleasure.

LANKY: "A pleasure," what?

BLONDIE: What do you mean, "A pleasure what?"

LANKY *(Lecturing)*: When you say, "It's been a pleasure," you're supposed to give your name. What's your name?

BLONDIE: Angela.

LANKY: IHP. *(Hiccups)* Angela?

BLONDIE *(Taking his hand tenderly)*: Yes . . . well, my real name is Angelica . . . But you know, in my profession . . . being called angelic would be a little silly. I guess when they baptized me, they never imagined . . .

LANKY: No . . . anyway, Angela's more beautiful. *(Smiles. Tilts his head)* Good-bye, Angela. We'll meet again. *(Hiccups)*

BLONDIE: Good-bye . . . we'll meet again, eh? Be careful. There's no light on the stairs.

LANKY: Don't worry. I can see fine. *(Exits)*

BLONDIE: Good-bye.

(A crashing sound offstage.)

What happened?

LANKY *(From offstage, trying to restrain himself from cursing)*: Dammit. You were right. I really do have this problem of walking around with my head turned backwards. I didn't see the steps.

BLONDIE: Did you hurt yourself?

LANKY *(Offstage)*: No. It's nothing.

BLONDIE: Did it cure your hiccups?

LANKY *(Offstage)*: Let's hope so.

BLONDIE: Good-bye.

LANKY *(Offstage)*: Good-bye, Angela. We'll meet again.

BLONDIE: Wait. Wait.

LANKY *(Offstage; a note of hope in his voice)*: Yes?!

BLONDIE: I have to tell you something. Uh . . . what should I call you? I mean, which of your names do you prefer?

(A brief pause.)

LANKY *(Offstage; disappointment, then euphorically)*: Call me Sunny . . . because after tonight, I can be happy my father gave me that name.

BLONDIE: Good-bye, Sunny.

LANKY *(Offstage)*: Good-bye, Angela.

(Prolonged sound of someone falling down the steps.)

BLONDIE: If that doesn't cure your hiccups, nothing will.

(She laughs. Then she takes out a transistor radio and turns it on. She hangs it around the neck of a tailor's mannequin that's in the center of the room. We faintly hear the song, "Squeeze My Wrists Tightly.")

Sunny . . . Lanky Sunnyweather . . . He's right: it brings on the urge to make puns . . .

(She sings along with the music from the radio. She looks out through the window curtains. Slowly she starts to get undressed, kicking one shoe up in the air.)

"Squeeze my wrists tight."

(She picks up a jacket that was forgotten on the chair. Without thinking, she puts it on the mannequin. She lifts up the mannequin and mimes a passionate embrace. Only now does she realize the jacket belongs to Lanky.)

This belongs to Sunny . . . What do you know . . . I sent him out in the cold with no jacket . . . now he has to come back . . . he can't go to Washington without his jacket . . . he'll be back for sure . . . and when he comes in I'll say, "Sunny, dear, if you want to wear your jacket, you'll have to wear me, too." *(Tries to imitate Lanky's voice)* "But, you said no." "And now I say yes . . . I changed my mind. I think I could be very happy with a twisted pole like you . . ." *(Embraces the mannequin again)* Come here, come here close to me. Come on, don't tremble like that . . . Oheuuu, my heart's beating like crazy . . . And yours? *(Puts her ear to the mannequin's chest. Someone starts knocking at the door)* Don't get carried away. *(Realizes sound is the knocking at the door)* Is it you? You came back to get your jacket. Come in. *(Realizes she's undressed)* . . . No, wait. Don't come in. *(Hides behind a screen)* OK. You can come in now.

(The First Friend enters.)

But don't come here. Excuse me if I made you wait, but I was undressed . . . I know it's silly of me to want to hide myself . . . I'm not usually so squirmish . . . I don't know why . . . When I'm with you, I get shy . . . It's stupid, but that's how I feel . . . I've already said and done a lot of stupid things today . . .

FIRST FRIEND *(Flattered)*: Well . . .

BLONDIE: No . . . don't say anything . . . otherwise I won't have the heart to tell you the things I've got to tell you . . . if not I'll just burst . . . I've got a crush on you . . . Don't laugh . . . I've really got a crush on you.

(The First Friend is feeling like a king.)

I didn't realize it until you had gone, and I found myself talking to your jacket: "I hope he comes back to get you, then he'll have to take me, too." There, I've said it! . . . *(Laughs)* Aren't you going to say something? . . . I knew you'd be surprised . . . It wasn't easy for me either, to tell you that, but now I'm glad I said it. *(Comes out from behind the screen)* Here I am . . .

(Blondie is shocked to see the Friend. He smiles happily. He comes toward her on his toes, walking like a horny rooster.)

FIRST: Damn. I'm a wizard. I put a spell on you. And I thought you didn't even like me. Funny how you get it all wrong sometimes. *(Caresses her)* And now you'll see that you made the right choice. *(Blondie doesn't move)* What's the matter, did the look in my eyes turn you to stone? Come on, beautiful. *(Slaps her gently)* Wake up, and I'll take you to bed.

(Blondie slaps him.)

BLONDIE: Out. *(Throws everything she can find at him)* Out. Out. Out.

FIRST: OK, I'm going. I'm going. You don't have to . . . Take it easy.

(The First Friend exits. There is the sound of another big crash on the stairs. Crying, Blondie goes to the mannequin, looks at it for a moment, then kicks it over onto the ground. The radio that was around its neck also falls down. Concerned, Blondie picks it up, turns it on and shakes it, hoping it isn't broken. The radio still works. An Announcer's voice is heard saying:)

RADIO ANNOUNCER: . . . Most of the region will enjoy sunny weather. This has been a report on atmospheric conditions. Our next broadcast will be at one o'clock tomorrow.

(Blondie bursts into tears and smashes the radio onto the ground.

Blackout.)

ACT TWO

SCENE 1

City Hall. Washington. Enter five Clerks in black tailcoats, wearing clown wigs adorned with bright clumps of hair, which make a semicircle from one temple to the other. The Clerks wear rubber stamps around their necks. They parade in front of a partition made up of window stations. They march toward the audience singing:

To give glory to Cheops they made him a pyramid
An altar to Leonidas, and Caesar got an arch,
For Vercingetorix a monolithic obelisk,
In memory of a sailor, they baptized America, the continent discovered by Christopher.
They christen microbes with the names of doctors and scientists.
Those who want to be immortalized,
Short of pyramids, have given their names to organs
There's Berio's bone, and the Eustachian tube
There's Bario's nerve, and Scipio's helmet
There's Dario's chariot, and a monument for each
But nobody remembers who thought of it all.

Who was the great bureaucrat who invented forms in triplicate?

Transit papers, and verification stamps
Endless applications, and additional taxation

Invalidated signatures, certificates of discharge
Honorary discharges, obligatory gratuities, common protocol, certified bonds?
No stone records his date of birth
Perhaps his file's labeled: "Anonymous." "Anonymous."

Brothers of the office. Let us raise our heads
Let's sing to the spirit of reusable rubber stamps
Open up our windows and praise the Lord
Who loves us enough to help us keep in stock:
Official seals and bonded paper
Postage stamps and preaddressed stationery
The doorkeeper, the pen and pencil holder,
And circular files for department supervisors.

(The five Clerks take their places behind their service windows. During the song all windows were open. Now they're all closed except one. A Woman enters, goes to the first window, and quickly takes care of some business. Lanky enters. He's carrying a heavy suitcase and a package. He gets in line behind the woman. When his turn comes the window shuts, as another window opens. Lanky, weighed down by his suitcase and package, but above all distracted by the strange resemblance between the Woman and one of Blondie's friends, is late getting to the open window. Consequently he arrives at the window just after a Gentleman, who has just walked in.)

LANKY: Excuse me, but I was here first . . . If it were just a matter of running, there'd be no need for lines.

GENTLEMAN: I wasn't running.

LANKY *(Noticing a strange resemblance between the man and one of his Friends)*: It's the coptic priest . . . What are you doing here in Washington?

GENTLEMAN: I beg your pardon?

LANKY: Come on. Stop joking. I recognize you, even with the mustache.

GENTLEMAN: It's you who should stop joking . . . especially with those who have neither time nor desire.

LANKY: Excuse me, but I mistook you for one of my friends who doesn't have a mustache . . . In any case, since you do have a mustache, I'd advise you to hold onto it . . . OK? . . . Still friends?

(Another window opens.)

GENTLEMAN: Listen, my mustache is not to be laughed at . . . That window is free. Go about your business . . . And thank your lucky stars that I'm in a hurry. Otherwise . . . *(Goes to the other window)*

LANKY: What are you so mad about? OK, so I talked about your mustache. It's not against the law to criticize mustaches, especially now that priests don't wear them anymore.

(At this moment the window closes in front of him. Lanky is annoyed, but he has no choice but to get in line behind the Gentleman with the mustache, who looks at him suspiciously. A Woman gets in line behind Lanky. She also looks a lot like one of Blondie's friends. Lanky looks at her and then says:)

Excuse me, but you're the spitting image of a friend of a friend of mine who makes her living as a . . .

WOMAN *(Annoyed, she looks at him coldly and interrupts)*: I beg your pardon?

LANKY: Makes her living as a . . . Oh . . . I mistook you for one of my relatives who works for the Red Cross in Switzerland.

(Meanwhile another window opens. The Woman walks over to the window with her suitcase. The Gentleman is talking a long time, but the Woman finishes her business quickly and prepares to leave. So Lanky picks up his things and moves to her window. But then the Woman changes her mind and comes back to the window.)

WOMAN: I forgot . . . could you make me a list of the forms I have to get from City Hall? Thank you . . .

(Lanky is perplexed, as if losing a game of musical chairs. The Gentleman's window becomes free, so Lanky rushes over to it, and in his haste takes the Woman's suitcase with him.)

Young man. Enough of your joking. That's my suitcase.

LANKY: Excuse me . . . I wasn't thinking.

WOMAN: That's a fine excuse. First you confuse me with someone else, then you take my suitcase . . .

LANKY: Please don't think . . . our suitcases really do look alike. And then . . . you're so suspicious . . . Do you think I'm some kid of psychotic suitcase snatcher . . . besides, it's cardboard. *(Goes to the window)* Could you please—

(With a loud crash the window closes.)

It's all your fault. Why didn't I leave you at home. *(Kicks the Woman's suitcase)*

WOMAN: What!! Are you insane?

LANKY: Oh. I'm sorry. I thought it was mine . . .

WOMAN: Sorry. Sorry. You should thank heaven that I'm not a man. *(Exits)*

LANKY: I do. Thank heaven! *(Makes a gesture to clean off the suitcase where he kicked it, and then moves to another window, which shuts in his face)* It's like going to confession at the automat.

(The Woman leaves in a huff. Lanky turns and trips over his own suitcase. He is about to punish the offending suitcase by kicking it, but stops himself with leg in midair. A Waiter enters with a tray, cups and a coffee pot. He looks like one of his Friends.)

Jules! . . .

WAITER: My name is Harry, not Jules . . . in any case, if you want to order something you have to go to the bar. I serve only the clerks.

(The Waiter taps a spoon against a cup. As if by magic the sound of the spoon results in the immediate opening of the first window. The Waiter holds out the coffee cup. The Clerk takes it and smashes the window down again as Lanky approaches holding out his form.)

LANKY: If I may, I'd like . . .

(Meanwhile the Waiter has moved to another window. He taps a cup, the window opens, and Lanky rushes over.)

Excuse me, if I may . . .

(Same result. Lanky gets smart. He ignores the third window and moves to the fourth in anticipation of the Waiter's arrival, ready to thrust his document at the Clerk as soon as he appears. The cup sounds and a window opens, but it is the fifth window. Lanky rushes over to it, but he is too late. The Clerk has already taken his coffee cup and disappeared.)

Doesn't this one drink coffee? *(Pointing to the fourth window)*

WAITER: No. He takes tea with lemon.

(The Waiter takes a larger cup and places it in front of the fourth window, which opens just long enough for the Clerk to grab his tea before it slams shut.)

LANKY: That's it. I leave my friends because they make too much fun of me, and here I find their doubles mocking me even more.

(Lanky kicks the suitcase in a rage. He shouts and jumps around in pain. Meanwhile the Waiter swiftly takes back the empty cups from each of the Clerks, the windows opening and closing like an assembly line. Lanky arrives at each one too late, and gets his finger caught as the last one bangs shut.)

Ahi! My finger!!

WAITER *(Snickering)*: Ha. Ha. He smashed his finger. Ha. He has a smashed finger . . .

(The Waiter laughs so hard he doesn't notice the arrival of the Gentleman from earlier in the scene. They bump into each other and the cups fall to the ground. All the windows open and the Clerks laugh in unison. The windows shut. The Waiter, with the help of the Gentleman, picks up the cups, then tries to clean the Gentleman's stained jacket. They keep apologizing to one another. The Waiter gets carried away with the cleaning, and begins polishing the Gentleman's nails as if he were giving him a manicure.)

Excuse me, I didn't see you . . .

GENTLEMAN: No, it was my fault. I was looking at my documents . . . I've made a mess for you.

WAITER: No, it's nothing. But your jacket . . . look at the stains on the sleeves.

GENTLEMAN: A little water will wash it away . . .

WAITER: Let's hope so . . . *(Spits on the jacket and tries to clean it off with his own sleeve)* I'm so sorry.

(The Waiter starts to walk away but Lanky intentionally trips him with the suitcase. This time the Waiter's fall is catastrophic. Broken dishes everywhere. Loud crashing sounds. The Gentleman goes to help the Waiter, but Lanky slides a package under his feet and trips him, too. The Clerks open their windows and stick their heads out to get a better view of the fall. They laugh. Lanky closes the windows in a way that traps each of their heads on the counter, like a guillotine. Then he kicks the Waiter, who has just finished picking up everything. The kick sends the Waiter flying out the door, and the Gentleman runs out, fearing that Lanky will kick him, too. All the Clerks shout for help.)

LANKY: Enough! Silence! . . . I said that's enough! Silence! Enough! Shut up! *(Locks the door with a key)* Now that I finally have the honor of your full attention . . . listen to me!!!! I've come here on very important business: my pension. I brought everything with me . . . *(Opens the suitcase. Takes out a large packet of documents, and deposits a pile under each one of the Clerks' heads)* Birth certificate . . . residence papers . . . unemployment papers . . . discharge papers . . . military discharge . . . declaration of permanent disability . . . authorization forms . . . duplicates of the authorization forms . . . triplicates of the authorization forms . . . carbon copy originals of the authorization forms. I don't understand any of them, but I did my duty, now you do yours: verify them, sign them, stamp them. Put on the seals, the counter-seals, the stamps, and the counter-stamps. Sign. Initial . . . All I want to do is to leave here with the proper papers to get my pension. *(Grabs the rubber stamps hanging from elastic cords around the necks of each of the Clerks, and attaches them to their foreheads. Then he moves to the side of the windows and grabs a lever, which is attached to the counter on which he has placed all his papers to be stamped)* I've got no time to lose . . . And to make my intentions clear, I brought a little something with me from Africa, that I swear I'll set off if any of you tries to get smart with me. Take a look: a model-38 hand grenade. *(He takes the grenade out of his suitcase. He begins shouting commands)* Round rubber stamps. *(Two Clerks respond by lowering their heads to stamp his papers)* Square stamps. *(Two other Clerks obey)* All stamps. Stamp. Stamp. Stamp. Stamp, stamp, stamp. All stamps. *(The Clerks do not obey)* All stamps. *(They still don't obey)* Damn. It's stuck.

(Lanky pulls on the lever, trying to force it down. When he succeeds the counter begins to shake rhythmically, up and down, under the noses of the Clerks, whose foreheads, equipped with rubber stamps, bob up and down, in alternating rhythms as they stamp the bouncing documents. It all gives the impression of an extraordinary futuristic machine.)

Stamp, stamp, stamp, stamp.

(As the rhythm builds, the action transforms itself into a steam engine that chugs along with a final "toot-toot" as it grinds to a stop.)

Toot-toot . . . ding-ding. We made it. And now all we need is my registration card, which we'll find in my personal file. *(One wall is covered with filing drawers. He pulls out the drawer that interests him)* The A's are here. S's over there. This must be the W's. Here it is. *(Puts the drawer under the face of the First Clerk)* Go on, find the file for Mr. Weather. First name: Sunny, Cloudy, Stormy, and anyone who laughs gets a bomb up his nose. *(The Clerk picks out the file with his teeth. Lanky narrates the search as if he were a game show host)* It's the wheel of fortune. 'Round and 'round the clerk's mouth goes, but where it stops, nobody knows. Can he do it? Yes, that's it. He's hit the jackpot. It's me. Weather, Sunny, date of birth, distinguishing features . . . race: Labrador retriever . . . No?!!! Yes, that's what it says—race: Labrador retriever . Profession: hunter of birds. Stunted tail, floppy ears, small teeth, apparently a mongrel . . . Ha ha. *(Laughs hysterically)* Apparently a mongrel?! *(The Clerks laugh. Lanky grabs the grenade and removes the safety pin. The Clerks stop laughing)* Whose idea was it to play this stinking trick on me? Come on, who was it? I warned you not to make fun of me. Not to play around. I don't even let my friends make a fool of me anymore, and they used to pay me for it . . . A Labrador retriever, eh? *(Lifts up his arm to throw the grenade)* This will teach you. Go on, laugh. Laugh for the last time. Laugh. Ha ha ha. *(The Clerks would like to shout for help, but are struck mute with terror. Lanky spins around, playing with the grenade as if it were on a wheel of fortune)* Place your bets, folks. 'Round and 'round the little bomb goes and where it lands, nobody knows . . . ha . . . ha . . . ha.

(Sounds of banging and knocking at the door.)

VOICE: Open up. What's going on . . . Open up!

LANKY: Look at their long faces . . . ha . . . ha . . . ha . . .

(Blackout. During the blackout there are shouts and sounds of the door being broken down.)

VOICES: Stop him. —Wait he has a bomb! Grab it!

LANKY'S VOICE: Step right up. Grab it if you can. First prize is a shiny medal. A little monkey for the gentleman. A balloon on a string. *(Laughs like a madman)*

(The lights come up. Lanky is handcuffed to a chair. Sitting in front of him is a Police Inspector. A plainclothes Detective stands nearby.)

LANKY *(Looking them over)*: A balloon with a string. *(He seems to recognize them)* Get a load of that. Two more doubles. *(Turns to the Inspector)* Excuse me, but you wouldn't happen to have a twin brother . . . an orthodox priest who runs a pastry shop on the side.

INSPECTOR: A priest in a pastry shop?

LANKY *(All in one breath)*: Yeah . . . well, he's not really orthodox . . . he just pretends to be an orthodox priest . . . anyway he married me . . . not in the sense that I married a priest . . . not in the biblical sense . . . but the fact is you look a lot like the man who owns the pastry shop . . . so much so that I said to myself right away: he's the spitting image of the man in the pastry shop! *(As he speaks he moves his handcuffed arms in a way that suggests the unwinding of a skein of wool)*

INSPECTOR: Enough of that, for heaven's sake. Listen, it's useless to keep ranting on like this. *(Without realizing it the Inspector has got caught up in the game and moves his hands as if he were winding up the wool into a ball of yarn)* Trying to pass yourself off as a madman is the oldest trick in the book, and it's not going to fool me. *(He realizes the absurdity of the game and throws away the imaginary ball of yarn. The Detective catches it and puts it in his pocket)* Come on. Be good. What's your name?

LANKY: What's yours?

INSPECTOR: What do you mean, "What's yours?" I'm the one asking questions around here.

LANKY: Only you? No. That's not fair. Come on. Maybe your friend has a question, too. Give somebody else a chance. Be a sport. Let's play for it. OK. *(Moves his arms as if playing a child's game)* One potato, two potato . . . tell me when to stop . . . three potato, four . . .

INSPECTOR: Stop!

LANKY: OK. Stop on "four potato." Good. *(Starts the count again)* Four potato, five potato, six potato, seven . . . *(Points to the Inspector)* Your turn . . . He's not playing. *(Points to the Detective who slaps him. Lanky blocks the slap with the palm of his hand. Another slap. Another block. There is a mechanical progression, and they end up playing a game of patty cake that finishes with the Detective getting a big slap)*

DETECTIVE: Stop clowning around, and answer the inspector's questions.

LANKY: Oh, he's an inspector. Why didn't you tell me sooner. I was wondering why a priest with a pastry shop would want to put me in handcuffs . . . Well, inspector, you know what I think. I think you're a hell of a nice guy.

DETECTIVE *(Losing his patience, gives Lanky a backhanded slap on the neck)*: Don't try to get personal.

LANKY: Well, he's getting pretty personal with me. Is there some article in the penal code that says an inspector's allowed to get personal with a citizen, but the citizen can't reciprocate.

DETECTIVE: Insolent dog. Who do you think you are? *(Slaps him in the face)*

LANKY: That's it. This brutality is getting out of hand. I'm leaving. *(Moves to leave)*

INSPECTOR *(Holding him down)*: Calm down. Come over here and sit down. And I'll try to address you more politely, OK?

LANKY: You know, inspector, I've thought it over, and I think we might as well get personal. It's more intimate. And we were just beginning to break the ice.

INSPECTOR: You're starting to bust my balls! . . . *(Gets control of himself after a sign from the Detective)* OK. Name. Last name first.

LANKY: Weather. Sunny, Cloudy, Stormy.

DETECTIVE *(Losing his composure)*: Stop screwing around. The inspector may be a patient man, but I'm not. *(Slaps Lanky with the back of his hand)*

LANKY: Come on, this is like beating up a slave with his hands tied. It's not fair. *(Sees another slap coming and ducks)*

INSPECTOR: Why you . . . *(The slap hits the Inspector)* That will be enough, detective. *(Turns back to Lanky gritting his teeth)* How much longer do I have to wait?

LANKY: Just tell your slaphappy assistant to control himself and we can get on with it . . . Now Sunny, Cloudy, Stormy Weather really is my name. And if you don't believe me, just look at these papers. That one for instance. *(Points to a paper sticking out of his suitcase)* You'll see . . .

DETECTIVE *(Takes the paper and reads it)*: Rehtaew Ynnus.

LANKY: It's upside down.

DETECTIVE: Of course. *(Turns paper over)* Sunny Weather. That's what it says. *(Gives the document to the Inspector)*

LANKY: Cloudy and Stormy are my middle names. I told you . . .

INSPECTOR *(Reading the rest of the paper)*: Veteran's Administration, Declaration of Permanent Disability . . . What's this? Are you disabled?

LANKY: Certainly: second degree. *(To the Detective, who has gone white)* I don't know where it was that I read about severe penalties for the use of violence against the disabled . . . especially when they are in a position from which it is impossible to defend themselves. Sergeant, you're in big trouble this time. *(Slaps him)*

INSPECTOR: Unlock the cuffs, sergeant.

(The Detective removes the handcuffs.)

LANKY: Isn't life funny. A person works his whole life to build up a career, and one day, a silly little thing knocks it all to pieces. All because of the bad habit of slapping people around. Bad hands. Shame on them. *(Slaps the hands of the Detective, who wants to retaliate, but Lanky stops him)* No . . . no. Disabled vet, remember. You know the saying, "Don't touch the disabled, even with a flower." Do you want some advice. Put those handcuffs on yourself.

(Mechanically, the Detective starts to obey, but then stops himself.)

INSPECTOR: All right, can we continue? Sergeant, take notes, please. *(The Detective takes out a notebook)* From the top. First name: Sunny. Last name: Weather. Got it? *(The mortified Detective nods his head yes)* Profession?

LANKY: Hunting dog; race: Labrador . . .

INSPECTOR *(Distracted)*: Hunting dog . . . *(Stands up suddenly)* Now you're going too far. *(Losing control, he closes in on Lanky)* No punk like you is going to make fun of me like that.

LANKY: Be careful, inspector . . . disabled veteran. Think of your family.

INSPECTOR: All right. *(Sits down again)* But I warn you. Disabled veteran, or not, you better stop fooling around . . . Now let's get to the bottom of this . . . *(Pulls the grenade out of his pocket)* Where did you get this bomb?

LANKY: That's not a real bomb. It's only a shell. Allow me. *(He takes it in his hand, unscrews it and pretends to throw it at the Detective)* Hey, sergeant, you're dead.

(The Detective jumps backward and ends up sitting on the Inspector's lap.)

INSPECTOR AND DETECTIVE *(With their arms raised)*: Stop joking around.

LANKY: I'm not joking. I want you two to read what it says on this card . . . out loud. *(Hands them the registration card)* Two-part harmony. Let's go. *(Threatens them with the grenade)*

INSPECTOR AND DETECTIVE *(In unison with one sitting on the other, their four arms moving synchronously like Hindu dancers)*: Sunny Weather, born March 24, 1954, in Sangiano; race: Labrador retriever . . .

LANKY: With a stunted tail, apparently a mongrel!

INSPECTOR: Unbelievable!

LANKY: Yes, it's unbelievable. And you wanted to smash my face in because you thought I was making fun of you . . . What am I supposed to do when I come here to collect my pension and discover instead that I have to pay a dog tax, wear a muzzle, and walk around on a leash. Can you blame me for wanting to throw a few hand grenades? *(Makes a gesture as if about to throw the grenade)*

INSPECTOR: OK. OK. We'll straighten out this ugly joke as soon as possible; but now calm down, and put that thing away.

LANKY: Don't worry, there's no danger . . . it's a cigarette lighter . . . *(Opens it, flips a switch, makes a flame and lights a cigarette with it)* You see, this is a joke too . . . I'm playing a joke on you . . . *(Throws the grenade-lighter to them while it is still lit)*

(The Inspector and Detective are barely able to catch it.)

INSPECTOR AND DETECTIVE: No. *(Throwing it back to him)*

LANKY *(Catching it on the fly)*: . . . And you're playing a joke on me . . . That way the whole world becomes a joke. But don't worry . . . I'm used to it. It doesn't bother me.

INSPECTOR: Well, it bothers me. I can't stand jokes.

(The Inspector and Detective continue the pantomime of synchronized gestures, building it to a frenzy.)

Especially when they're perpetrated by public officials who have been entrusted with the protection of our citizens' rights and welfare. *(Turns to the Detective who is still in his lap)* Sergeant, I know you're very attached to your superiors, but I must ask you to get up.

DETECTIVE: Yes, of course. *(Gets up)*

INSPECTOR *(Still to the Detective)*: I want to talk to all the clerks in this office . . . Get to it. They'll find out what happens to people who joke around with serious business.

(The Detective opens the door. All the Clerks, who were listening at the keyhole, fall into the room.)

DETECTIVE: So you were listening through the keyhole?

INSPECTOR: Good. Now I won't have to waste time explaining things. Make yourselves comfortable.

(The Clerks line up in front of him.)

What kind of farce is this? *(He waves Lanky's papers under their noses, pacing back and forth like a drill sergeant)*

LANKY *(Marching behind the Inspector with evident satisfaction)*: Yeah, what is this?

INSPECTOR: Nobody knows anything about it, right? All right then, I'll tell you what it is. It's a bad joke. It's an insult to our citizens.

LANKY *(Prompting him)*: Who pay the taxes.

INSPECTOR: Who pay the taxes . . .

LANKY: That pay your inflated salaries.

INSPECTOR: That pay your . . . hey, let's take it easy.

LANKY: Yes, yes, we'll take it easy, but you'll see. We'll get to that.

INSPECTOR: I want to know who's responsible for this deplorable act which dishonors not only your department, but public servants everywhere.

LANKY *(Still prompting)*: Including me.

INSPECTOR: . . . including me . . . and in defense of the honor and the dignity of . . . of . . .

LANKY: . . . the above-mentioned.

INSPECTOR: . . . of the above-mentioned—thank you—that I demand to know which one of you is guilty. I'll give you three minutes. Then . . .

LANKY: I'll put you all up against the wall.

INSPECTOR: I'll put you all up against the wall.

(Lanky performs a firing-squad pantomime. He mimes that the machine gun is jammed. He takes it apart and puts it back together as a violin. He plays a brief fugue on the transformed machine gun.)

LANKY: Maybe shooting all of you would be a bit excessive. Maybe just a few: one, two, three. *(Starts to count the Clerks)*

FIRST CLERK *(Taking a step forward)*: Can I speak?

LANKY: No.

INSPECTOR *(Stupified)*: No.

DETECTIVE *(Parroting)*: No.

INSPECTOR: You have one minute left.

DETECTIVE: One minute.

FIRST CLERK: On behalf of my colleagues, I think I can give you an explanation.

LANKY: See that, inspector? Mass murder gets results . . . Take this down, sergeant.

FIRST CLERK: The whole thing began fifteen years ago.

SECOND CLERK: We were still at war.

FIRST CLERK: One of the older workers here was forced into early retirement.

THIRD CLERK: A few months before he would have been entitled to a promotion.

(Each Clerk takes a few steps forward before speaking, and steps back into line afterward.)

LANKY: Another good joke to add to my collection.

FIRST CLERK: As I was saying, the clerk, on whom fate had played this miserable trick . . .

LANKY: I didn't know you called your supervisors Fate. Commissioner Fate. Undersecretary of Fate. Assistant Department Manager Fate . . .

INSPECTOR: Please let him finish.

LANKY: I'm sorry. So what did he do, this victim of Fate?

FIRST CLERK: He almost went insane . . .

FOURTH CLERK: And as a desperate act of revenge against the injustice he had suffered, the clerk began making random changes in the registration files . . .

SECOND CLERK: Since he had been in charge of those files for thirty years, he knew just what to do to create total chaos.

THIRD CLERK: For example, he rearranged things so that we had a priest married to a forest ranger.

FIRST CLERK: One man died before he was born.

FIFTH CLERK: And there was a general who had never spent a day in the military.

SECOND CLERK: Another was resurrected twenty years after his death, went to Argentina for a sex-change operation and married . . .

THIRD CLERK: . . . a mulatto from Martinique.

(The forward and back movements of the Clerks begin to look like a traditional folk dance, with spins and changes.)

But all those changes were directed against the families of the people he blamed for his predicament.

LANKY *(Interrupting)*: OK, but what do I have to do with it? What did I do to deserve being transformed into a dog . . . a mutt!

FIRST CLERk: Do you have any relatives who worked in the department?

LANKY: No.

FIRST CLERK: Maybe there was someone with a similar name?

LANKY: A similar name? Not many people have a father as crazy as mine.

SECOND CLERK: I guess he just let things get out of hand.

LANKY *(Almost hysterical)*: Out of hand?!! I'll teach him to get out of hand with me. I'll put him out of hand, out of arm, and out of feet! I'll tear him to pieces!!! *(He grabs one of the Clerks by the collar)* Where is he? I'll give him a promotion . . . to the moon. Where does he live?

SECOND CLERK: In the cemetery.

LANKY: He's dead?

THIRD CLERK: Yes. About two months later. They say he did nothing but laugh . . . and that his laughter was so contagious that his friends and relatives couldn't stop themselves from giggling at his deathbed . . . they were still laughing at the funeral.

FIRST CLERK: I was there. It was the funniest funeral I've ever been to.

ALL CLERKS *(In chorus)*: What a load of laughs.

LANKY: Come on, let's forget about happy funerals and get back to our story. How did you dig yourselves out of this mountain of falsification?

(The Clerks begin to move in all directions. Lanky sits down to watch the show.)

FIRST CLERK: At first everyone was desperate. Especially our superiors: the alterations were executed with such perfection, that it was impossible to restore order without personally contacting every individual concerned.

SECOND CLERK: Not to mention the dead ones.

THIRD CLERK: Or the ones who hadn't been born yet.

FIRST CLERK: There would have been a scandal . . . an investigation and, inevitably, a special prosecutor.

(The Clerks move more and more frantically. The Detective puts on white gloves to direct traffic.)

Not to mention a trial, and all the embarrassment it would cause for everyone involved, including some high-placed government officials.

(The Inspector gets caught up in the game, but crosses the stage just as the Detective/Traffic Cop signals stop. The Detective repeatedly blows his whistle at the Inspector, and is about to give him a ticket for jaywalking when the Inspector pulls out his badge, and sticks it in the Detective's face.)

DETECTIVE *(Stopping)*: Enough said . . . *(Turns to the others)* Move along. *(Then to the Third Clerk)* You, keep going.

THIRD CLERK: We were saved by chance when a wing of the building was destroyed by fire. We collected all the incriminating documents and shredded them, blaming the loss on the fire.

ALL CLERKS *(In chorus)*: Hallelujah!

LANKY: All the documents, except mine.

THIRD CLERK: Yes, all but yours. I don't understand how we missed it.

LANKY *(Gets slowly to his feet, looks them all over, and begins aggressively)*: So you don't understand, huh? I'll tell you why? Because the name on the card wasn't one of yours . . . so none of you gave a damn . . . Last time you were saved by a fire, but this time the fire's going to burn your asses till they're cooked. *(To the Inspector and the Detective)* Not yours of course. Nothing's going to save you . . . *(Turns back to the Clerks)* I'm going to put each one of you in a filing drawer and roast you alive . . . with an apple in your mouth. *(To the Inspector and the Detective)* We'll think of something for you later. *(Back to the Clerks)* Now I understand why your colleague included me in his revenge. I was the backup fuse, the emergency reserve plan, in case the first one sizzled out. Ha. Ha. *(Laughs and turns to someone in the audience, as if he has found the dead Clerk resurrected)* Insane? No, you were shrewd . . . Ha. Ha. You had a wild card up your sleeve. A joker. You were right to laugh with your dying breath . . . Ha. Ha. Listen, he's still laughing. What a . . .

DETECTIVE *(Seriously worried)*: He's really losing his mind.

INSPECTOR: Calm down. Don't get excited. It's bad for your health. Everything is going to be all right, you'll see. But first you have to sit down and relax.

(Everyone runs to get chairs for Lanky. The Inspector ends up sitting on nothing and falls to the ground with a thud.)

LANKY: That's easy for him to say.

INSPECTOR *(Paternalistically)*: Now let's get this straight. You came here to speed up your pension payments. But how many months, days, years, will it take to clear all this up. Don't forget, you'll have to wait till the investigation is over before you can retrieve your true identity. The first step is to correct your registration status. For the rest, just relax, and I assure you that those who are responsible will not go unpunished. *(Turns to the Clerks)* And since you are the ones responsible for this mess, it would be in your own interest to give this case top priority. Is that clear?

FIRST CLERK: As far as the registration is concerned, there might be a solution, but it all depends on the gentleman's willingness to collaborate . . .

INSPECTOR *(Turning again to the Clerks)*: Hold on! I'm trying to meet you half way on this, but I can only go so far. I don't want to hear about the details, but if everything's not straightened out in three days, I'm going to write out arrest warrants for everybody in the department. And I'll make sure you spend the investigation period in jail. Get it? Good-bye.

DETECTIVE *(To the Inspector as he leaves)*: So long, chief.

INSPECTOR: See you later, pal. *(Leaves, but comes back immediately, walking backward as if in a movie being run backward)* Get it? Good-bye. *(Signals the Detective)*

DETECTIVE: Oh, yeah . . .

(Lines up behind the Inspector. They leave with synchronous steps, in rhythms dictated by the blowing of the Detective's whistle.)

LANKY: All right, let's hear it. What's the plan?

CLERKS: Excuse us?

(They huddle together like a team of football players.)

FIRST CLERK *(Coming out of the huddle)*: If you would be kind enough to remain a Labrador retriever for just a few more days, then . . .

LANKY *(Threateningly)*: Then?

SECOND CLERK *(Hesitantly)*: Everything would be resolved: it would only take three days. *(Consults with his colleagues in a whisper. They agree)* Naturally we'd need your help.

LANKY *(Ironic, unconvinced)*: All right. What do I have to do?

FIRST CLERK *(All in one breath)*: Turn yourself in, without a license or a muzzle, to the city dogcatcher.

LANKY *(Almost shouting)*: What?

THIRD CLERK *(Moving backward, ready to run)*: Naturally, the dogcatcher would be informed about our plan. The director of the pound is one of our former colleagues, and he wouldn't deny us a small favor.

LANKY *(Calm, chewing each word)*: In other words, you want me to pass myself off as a lost pooch. And then what happens?

FIRST CLERK *(Only slightly reassured)*: You know, under the law, after three days in the pound, if no one comes to claim them, stray dogs are put to sleep in a gas chamber.

LANKY *(Distracted)*: Yes, I know that stray dogs . . . *(Suddenly shouting)* What? A gas chamber? I don't know if I like this plan; I'll have to think it over.

FOURTH CLERK *(With a smile)*: No, you've misunderstood. We weren't planning to send you to the gas chamber. *(As if he were recounting the most banal story in the world)* After three days, the records will show that you are dead, as a dog. Then, once that problem is eliminated, you can present yourself to us with two witnesses to get back your real identity.

THIRD CLERK *(In the same tone)*: Then, on the same day, you'll be able to collect the back payments on your pension, which I've roughly calculated to amount to something like . . .

(All the Clerks lift up their fingers. Lanky is obliged to do the same. The Clerk finishes his calculations by pulling on their fingers as if he were operating an adding machine.)

If you don't mind . . . A hundred thousand dollars.

LANKY *(Enthusiastically)*: A hundred thousand dollars! That's a great price for a used coccyx. Dogcatcher, here I come. I'd rather spend three days as a poor dog, than a hundred as a poor man. Long live bureaucracy!!!

(All the Clerks come downstage to sing the "Song of the Bureaucrats." The fence/curtain is drawn behind them.)

CLERKS:

Who was the great bureaucrat who invented forms in triplicate?

Transit papers, and verifications stamps
Unpermissable practices, and additional taxation
Invalidated signatures, certificates of discharge
Honorary discharges, obligatory gratuities, common protocol, certified bonds?
No stone records his date of birth
Perhaps his file's labeled: "Anonymous." "Anonymous."

(Blackout.)

SCENE 2

Lights up. Fence/curtain opens. We are in the city dog pound. There are several cages. The one in the center has a sign that reads: BEWARE OF THE MAN. *Lanky, muzzle on his face and a dog collar around his neck, is reluctantly dragged in by a Dogcatcher. The Dogcatcher guarding the kennel opens the central cage and tries to push him in. Another Dogcatcher pulls Lanky forcefully by his leash.*

LANKY: Hey, take it easy with that leash . . . a little respect for your fellow man.

FIRST DOGCATCHER: Get moving then . . . If all the mutts were like you, I'd be pushing up daisies. Come on, take off your clothes. *(Keeps trying to force Lanky into the central cage)*

LANKY *(Breaks free and shouts with a high-pitched voice)*: What!!?

SECOND DOGCATCHER: That's the rule.

DOGCATCHERS *(In unison, reciting a lesson)*: The captured animal must be stripped of all accessories being worn at the moment of capture: flea collar, leash, doggie blankets, etc.

(Lanky gestures like an orchestra conductor signaling his musicians to finish.)

LANKY: OK. OK. I get it. You've learned your lessons well. An A for effort. *(Nasty)* But as far as accessories go, all I've got is this collar, leash and muzzle. And I'll give them to you with pleasure. *(Takes them off and throws them violently at the Dogcatchers)* And stop trying to push me around. I only went along with this charade to help out your friends. So if you don't start behaving more politely, I'm going to blow the whistle on everyone and you'll all be looking for new jobs. You'll be out catching cats. Is that clear? *(Approaches the Second Dogcatcher)*

SECOND DOGCATCHER: It's clear. It's clear. But the regulations require . . .

(Lanky enters the cage, but comes out immediately holding his nose.)

LANKY: Speaking of regulations, that cage stinks. Is that a regulation smell? *(With air of a drill sergeant)* Come on. Scrub brush. Soap. Hot water. Clean it out. Get moving . . . Now.

(Unthinkingly the two Dogcatchers stand at attention. They turn on their heels and leave.)

VOICE FROM THE LOUD SPEAKER: Attention please. In a few minutes the pound will be opened to visitors interested in adopting our animal guests. We ask the visitors to refrain from molesting or feeding the guests in their cages. Stay away from cages marked: DANGEROUS SPECIMEN. And remember that the gas chamber, especially during operating hours, is reserved for the exclusive use of our resident guests.

(Lanky listens with interest. Meanwhile the First Dogcatcher, having returned with a brush and a bucket of water, begins to clean up. The visitors begin to appear. Lanky browses around the cages, and stops in front of one of the cages, removing the sign from its bars. A Woman stops in front of the cage to the right.)

WOMAN *(As if speaking to a baby)*: Pretty, pretty, pretty. Oh what a pretty pointer.

LANKY *(Coming up behind her)*: That's not a pointer. It's a retriever.

WOMAN *(Without turning around)*: How can you be so sure.

LANKY: Because I'm a retriever, too.

(The Woman turns with an amused smile, but when she sees Lanky, who has put on his muzzle again, she screams and runs away.)

FIRST DOGCATCHER *(Running up to Lanky)*: What are you doing? You can't go around scaring the ladies like that. The director will have my head. *(Grabs him by the collar)* Come on. Your cage is clean now.

LANKY *(Entertaining himself by making puppy sounds)*: OK. But leave me alone so I can get a little reading done. *(Pulls a newspaper out of his pocket)* Would you mind shutting the door? Thank you. And please tell the doorman that I don't wish to be disturbed. You're very kind.

(Lanky opens the newspaper in front of his face while one of the keepers puts a sign on the bars of his cage. A strange Man in old-fashioned clothes and a bowler hat approaches the cage, grabs the sign and gets up on his toes in an effort to see what's behind the newspaper. Lanky barks, looks out over the newspaper, then disappears again. Annoyed by the Man's insistent curiosity, he jumps aggressively towards the bars, barking and growling like a mad dog. The Man jumps back, speechless. Then he very politely turns to the First Dogcatcher.)

MAN: Excuse me. Are you sure that's a retriever?

FIRST DOGCATCHER *(Mocking him openly)*: I don't know. They pay me to catch them, not to identify their breeds. But if the sign says so, then it's a retriever.

MAN *(Convinced, without irony)*: Good. Then, I'll take him.

FIRST DOGCATCHER *(Convinced the Man is making fun of him)*: What?

MAN *(Still serious. Holding out some bills)*: Here's the money for the license and the fine . . . and here are my identification papers. I'd like to take him with me now.

FIRST DOGCATCHER: Are you joking?

MAN *(Hurt; with the air of a lucid madman)*: I don't see how you could suspect me of such a thing. Am I or am I not within my rights to take home the dog of my choice? This is the animal that interests me. I demand that you turn him over to me . . .

(Lanky, listening with great interest, suddenly sticks his arm out of the cage and grabs the man with the bowler by the collar.)

LANKY: Listen, you second-hand Victorian relic . . . *(Alluding to the Man's nineteenth-century clothing)* If I hear you expressing any more "interest" in this "animal" that happens to be me, you're going to get a kick in the head that'll send you into emergency surgery.

MAN *(Amazed, turning to the First Dogcatcher)*: Excuse me, was that him talking or are you a ventriloquist?

SECOND DOGCATCHER *(Just arrived)*: I'll explain everything, sir. *(Then whispers aside to the First Dogcatcher)* Quiet, I know this one. He's crazy. *(Kindly taking the Man's arm and leading him away from the cage. He speaks softly and sadly)* You see, it's a sad story. In all outward appearances, he looks like a dog. But he is actually a man . . .

MAN *(Turning his head to verify Lanky's identity)*: No?!!!!!!!!

SECOND DOGCATCHER *(Sighing sadly)*: Yes, a man. Poor thing. He's lost his mind.

MAN *(Sad)*: You mean he's insane? What happened?

SECOND DOGCATCHER: It's a pathetic story. He had a dog who ran away and ended up in that cage . . . but by the time the man arrived to retrieve him, the poor dog was dead.

MAN *(With a lump in his throat)*: In the gas chamber?

SECOND DOGCATCHER *(After a short pause)*: No, suicide. Maybe he thought his master had abandoned him . . . *(Sighs)* and in a moment of despair . . . *(Mimes the cutting of a throat)*

MAN: Suicide? How?

SECOND DOGCATCHER *(Begins to mime a pistol shot, but has second thoughts)*: With a piece of broken glass. He slit his wrists. The wife of the master died that way, and you know how dogs pick things up.

MAN *(Staring into space, remembering)*: I know. My dog was alcoholic. *(Tips his hat, turns back the cage)* Poor man. He's mad with grief. But how did he end up in there?

SECOND DOGCATCHER *(Taking the Man by the arm. They walk downstage together)*: Every day, during visiting hours, he comes and asks us to let him into the cage where his faithful friend had died. We don't have the heart to say no. He's in such pain. Poor beast.

MAN *(Stops. Turns to look into space)*: I understand . . . yes, I understand. I, too, grieved deeply when Lincoln died.

SECOND DOGCATCHER: You were an abolitionist?

MAN: No. I was an illusionist. A Republican, but an illusionist. And Lincoln was a black poodle. *(Happily traces the dog's figure in the air)* And when the pom-poms on his ears flopped down under his chin, he was the spitting image of Honest Abe. *(Short pause. He looks directly at the*

Second Dogcatcher) He was an intelligent beast, you know. He even learned how to perform sleight of hand. *(Raises his voice to grand eloquent tones)* Can you imagine the effect on the audience of a canine magician!

SECOND DOGCATCHER *(Leading him on)*: Amazing. A canine magician.

MAN *(Almost in tears)*: Yes, but he died a few days before his theatrical debut. *(Sighing, very sad)* When he died, I thought I'd go mad.

SECOND DOGCATCHER: It shows. *(Trying to hold back his laughter)*

MAN *(Suspiciously)*: What did you say?

SECOND DOGCATCHER: I said "One never knows."

MAN *(Toying with the sign on Lanky's cage. Suddenly angry with the Second Dogcatcher)*: And I almost fell for it. Why have you been telling me these lies?

SECOND DOGCATCHER *(Taken aback)*: What lies?

MAN: Don't play dumb with me. The description on this card fits him to a T: Labrador retriever, stunted tail, floppy ears, unmarked coat, thick dark hair on his head, short teeth. There's no doubt about it. It's him.

(Lanky aggressively slaps the Man on the top of his bowler hat, grabs him around the neck and pulls him back against the bars)

LANKY: You guessed it. Yes, I am a Labrador retriever. And since I'm also a mongrel bastard mutt, you better got out of here before I bite off your ear. *(Loosening his hold)* I warn you that I have rabies, distemper and fleas. And when I'm done with your ear, I'll skin you alive.

MAN *(Terrorized, adjusting his damaged hat. To the First Dogcatcher)*: Is it true what he says?

FIRST DOGCATCHER *(Trying to keep from laughing in his face)*: Very true. Don't you see how he's beginning to foam at the mouth.

MAN *(Hysterical)*: How irresponsible of you. What does he have to do before you label him: DANGEROUS?. . . Bite someone? *(Nervously moves back and forth as Lanky jumps up and down howling in his cage)*

LANKY: Uhuuuuuuuu. Uhuuuuuuuu. Grrrr . . . Uhuuuuuuuu!!!

(As the Man leaves, another gentleman arrives running. He grabs a whip from the guard and begins lashing Lanky severely.)

DIRECTOR: Good. Down, dog, down.

LANKY: Ehi. Ahi. Uhuuuu. Uhuuuu. *(Wounded in the leg, he hops in pain)*

DIRECTOR: Down, dog. *(Lanky sits down immediately. The man turns authoritatively to the Dogcatchers)* What's the matter with you? Can't you keep this animal muzzled? What kind of dogcatchers are you?

FIRST DOGCATCHER *(Trying to take the whip out of his hand)*: Today is the day of the madmen. Who are you?

DIRECTOR: I'm the director.

(He takes a step forward and puts his foot in the cleaning bucket.)

SECOND DOGCATCHER: Stop playing games. I know the director. It's Dr. Campbell.

DIRECTOR: It was Dr. Campbell, but this morning he was transferred to another department. *(Frees himself from the bucket)* And since I am the director now, I'm going to institute a few changes. So listen up, or I'll use this on you, too.

(Another step forward lands him in another bucket. While trying to get out of it, he leans back against Lanky's cage)

LANKY *(Grabs the whip quickly. Ties up the Director's legs and immobilizes him)*: Listen, boss, you've already got a strike against you because you look just like a friend of mine that I can't stand. So I'm warning you. If you ever try to brand me again with the mark of Zorro, I'm going to come out and pluck you like a daisy, till there's nothing left of you but the little yellow lump in the middle. *(Pushes him away with such force that the Director turns pirouettes across the stage)*

DIRECTOR *(Staggering, dizzy)*: What's that man doing in a cage?

FIRST DOGCATCHER *(Supporting him)*: Excuse me, but didn't the other director tell you about the favor we were doing for the registration office?

DIRECTOR: Oh, yes, he told me. *(Moves toward Lanky, but stops at a respectful distance)* In any case you'd better conduct yourself in a manner befitting an animal of your breed. *(Takes the bucket off his foot)* A race noted for its meek and quiet behavior. Otherwise I won't even wait for the three days to pass. *(His voice is transformed)* I'll throw you into the gas chamber and be rid of you right away. Is that understood?

LANKY *(Pushing his head through the bars, shouting)*: Do I understand? What's this about not waiting three days for the gas chamber and getting rid of me right away? We made a deal that you'd only pretend to put me to sleep after three days. It's supposed to be a fake. *(Turning to the two Dogcatchers)* Let's not joke around with gas.

DIRECTOR *(Gesturing like the conductor of a military band)*: I didn't make any deals with anybody. And I've never faked anything in my life. I've always believed in serious respect for the law. If three days go by and nobody picks you up, we'll finish you off. In a county plagued by favoritism and special interests, the least we can do is keep corruption out of the dog pound. And now get out of my way. I want to meet the rest of the staff.

(The Director puts his foot in another bucket, and marches off, followed by the two Dogcatchers. Lanky is stunned. He shakes the cage, but it doesn't open.)

LANKY *(Crying)*: Mama. Mama. Murder. Murder. *(Shouts to the other cages)* Spaniels, terriers, mongrels, unite. Let's organize an escape. I don't want to end up in a gas chamber. It's not fair. Do I look like a man's best friend? Wake up. Rebel . . . Do something. *(He waits, hoping that something will happen)* Not even a bark. You bastards. You know what I have to say to you? You disgust me. Good riddance. Anyone who lets themselves be muzzled, clipped and beaten without even a whimper of protest deserves to end up in a gas chamber. It makes me happy. Look how happy I am.

(Lanky breaks down into sobs that sound like dog whimpers. Just then the Man reappears. Lanky shouts:)

I don't want to die.

MAN *(Jumps from fright)*: Oh, you ugly beast. *(He leaves)*

LANKY: Wait, sir. Please listen . . .

(Barks, speaks, barks. This has no effect on the Man, so Lanky begins meowing. The Man returns to the cage.)

I'd like to tell you something . . .

(The Man watches him for a moment, then leaves. Lanky meows again, and the Man returns.)

MAN: What's wrong?

LANKY *(Begging)*: Sir, get me out of here. Save me. They've trapped me . . . they're really going to put me in the gas chamber . . . they're all nasty, especially the daisy . . . Please take me away . . . be kind.

MAN *(Moved, fatherly)*: My dear pooch, I'd love to take you home. I've been looking all my life for an animal like you to take the place of my poor Lincoln. But try to understand. How could I keep you in the house? You'll get over the fleas and distemper, but you can't fool around with rabies. If you bit me . . .

LANKY *(Passionately begging)*: No, no. I don't have anything. I'm in perfect health. That was just a story I made up to try to be funny.

(Enter one of the Dogcatchers.)

Look, there's the guard. Ask him to tell you what's happened, and then, when you hear the truth, you'll take me away from here. And you won't be sorry. I'll be good. I'll do everything you tell me. I'll eat my dog food and biscuits. I'll fetch your paper, your slippers, your pipe. If you want I'll even pee against a tree. Just get me out of here. *(Barks and yelps)*

(All the other dogs join him.)

MAN *(Turning to the Dogcatcher)*: Listen, about this retriever . . .

(The dialog of the two men is lost in the barking of the dogs. It's feeding time. The Dogcatcher distributes food to the

cages as he talks, nodding in agreement as he moves from cage to cage. He takes the money, signs a card and goes over to open Lanky's cage. He puts a collar and muzzle on him. The Man takes the leash.)

It's done. From this moment on, you are no longer a stray dog. You have a master. But I'm warning you that if you don't behave yourself like you promised, if you do anything nasty, I'm going to take you back to the pound. OK?

LANKY: Yes, yes, OK. But before we leave, will you let me be nasty one more time? Just a little?

MAN: OK, as long as it's the last time.

LANKY: Thank you.

(Lanky grabs the whip from the hand of the Dogcatcher, disappears to the right, and reappears a moment later, chasing the Director with the whip.)

Jump, boss, jump. Be strong. We have to eliminate favoritism and special interest. Every one should have a chance to be whipped. The law demands equal opportunity for all: dogs, men, cats and bosses, too!!

(Like a circus animal trainer, Lanky makes the two Dogcatchers and the Director line up. Then with a crack of the whip, he makes them step forward, jumping as if they were horses in the circus ring. They spin, pirouette and gallop. The routine is accompanied by a crescendo of circus music.

Blackout.)

SCENE 3

The lights go up. In front of the fence/curtain, the Man rolls across stage in a wheelchair.

MAN *(Shouting at full voice)*: Sunny. Sunny. Come here Sunny. Look how he ignores me and he promised to be faithful and obedient. He's going to give me another stroke . . . That's what I get for taking the word of a dog . . . a mongrel retriever. Who ever said that mongrels were the most affectionate, who? *(Raising his eyes to heaven)* Lincoln. My Lincoln. You were a real dog. *(Makes a fist with his left hand and caresses it with his right hand as if it were a dog's head)* You were the only one who really loved me. Ah, the way you wagged your tail for me . . . this one never does. Not only is he tail-less, he doesn't even have a stump. And besides that, he's lazy! He never pays attention when I try to teach him the tricks of the trade. The few magic tricks I've taught him have cost me my health. A stroke put me in this wheelchair. And to think that I saved that mongrel's life. He wants me dead. I sent him out a half-hour ago to get a newspaper, and he's still not back. Sunny. Sunny.

(The sounds of Lanky barking are heard from outside.)

I told you a thousand times that I don't want you reading my newspaper. A dog that reads the newspaper! And on the street! Who knows what people will think! Come over here and present yourself properly.

(Lanky enters on all fours, still barking. He holds the paper between his teeth. He wears a Scotch plaid blanket on his trunk and ragged, wool long underwear on the rest of his body. He comes up to the Man and gives him his newspaper.)

LANKY: Here. Enjoy your newspaper.

MAN: And the bread and eggs and other things I asked you to buy? . . . Where are they?

LANKY: Inside the newspaper.

MAN *(Unfolding the newspaper)*: There's nothing in here.

LANKY: Impossible. I'm sure they're in there. I remember opening up the newspaper . . . *(He takes the newspaper in his hand, holds it out in front of his master, and imitates his gestures)* . . . and saying, "Could you please give me two eggs?" And they gave me two eggs. *(Mimes the action)* I took the two eggs and folded them up inside the newspaper. Are they there or not? Should we look and see?

MAN *(Holding his breath)*: Yes.

LANKY *(From behind the newspaper)*: Oop. There's the two eggs. Then I said, "Could I have some bread?" They gave me bread, and I put it under the newspaper. Should we see if there's any bread in there?

MAN: Yes.

LANKY: Oop. There's the bread. Then I said, "Listen, I'm tired of waiting around. Just give me the rest of the stuff and we'll get it over with." They gave me everything else, and I put it all in the newspaper. Should we see if it's there? Oop. There's the rest of it. *(Pulls out a tray overflowing with fruits, vegetables, cold cuts and other produce. He rests the tray on the palm of his master's hand, and makes him lift up his other hand to imitate a grocer's scale. As he presses on one hand, the other lowers and raises)* See. The exact weight. To the gram. You thought I was a failure, that I couldn't learn your tricks. Watch: One, two, three. Now you see it. Now you don't. *(Everything disappears)*

MAN *(With childlike enthusiasm)*: Wonderful. You deserve a treat. I'll give you . . .

LANKY *(All in one breath)*: Give me back my trousers.

MAN *(Shrewdly)*: Why? So you can run away? No. No pants. But since you've learned your lessons so well, I'm going to take you to see an old friend of mine who runs a circus. Ha. Ha. And when he sees you performing the tricks I've taught you . . . Ha. Ha . . . I can't wait to see his face. *(Imitating his voice)* "What? A canine magician? I never saw anything like it. How much do you want for him?" *(Taking the attitude of the king of all clowns)* "He's not for sale." "OK, then I'll rent him: a thousand dollars a month." "No." "A week." "No." "A day." "Yes." A thousand dollars a day, and zam, balooey. Jackpot. *(Insanely pleased)* And do you know what I'm going to do with all that money?

LANKY: Give it to a hospital for underprivileged dogs?

MAN *(Dismissing him with a cynical chuckle)*: Let the dogs die. I never did like dogs, anyway. I'm much more fond of cats. I'll use the money to buy hundreds and hundreds of cats. Cats of all colors, sizes and breeds. Because I love cats. *(Caresses the back of his left hand as if it were a cat)* Meow. Meow. Prrr. Prrr. Too bad you're not a cat.

LANKY *(Playing the orphan)*: But I can be a cat, really I can. Don't you remember how I meowed at the pound? Meow

. . . purr. *(The meow finishes with Lanky spitting in the master's face. Then he makes his hands into cat paws and claws at the master)* Pfuuuu. Pfuuuu.

MAN: What's got into you. You spit in my face.

LANKY *(Kicks the wheelchair and knocks it over)*: Sure I spit in your face, because you're a stinker and a madman. So it was all a lie. That you loved dogs. That you needed my protection.

MAN *(Terrorized, cowardly)*: Don't be jealous. Come here and I'll tell you the truth. I only buy cats to sell them again at a profit. You have no idea how much money there is in cats . . . When you think that half of the furs sold as leopard are actually dyed cat skins.

LANKY *(Meows and spits)*: Double stinker. Not only are you making a profit off my skin, but off the cats' skin, too. Damn you. Frrsptu . . .

(The Man stands up and gets out of the wheelchair.)

MAN: Get down, you mutt!

LANKY: And you can walk too. You were just pretending to be a cripple to make me feel sorry for you. You were taking advantage of my tender heart to keep me from leaving you . . . Bastard. *(Kicks the wheelchair again)*

MAN *(Grabbing him by the collar)*: Down, dog, down. *(Forces Lanky to his knees)* I'll show you what happens to dogs who disobey their masters . . . I'll chain you up and beat you to a pulp.

LANKY: And I'll bite you. Take that. *(Bites Man on the hand. The Man screams and lets him go)* And now I've got a surprise for you. I do have rabies.

MAN: No?!! *(Looks at his hand in shock)*

LANKY: Yes . . . I've got the most poisonous form of rabies known to man or dog. Republican rabies. And now that I've attacked you, you've got them, too. Good-bye.

MAN *(Crying in desperation)*: No. Sunny. Sunny . . .

LANKY: Down, dog, down.

(Lanky exits barking.
Blackout.)

SCENE 4

A section of a first-class corridor railroad car. We see only a passenger compartment and a bathroom on the extreme right. There is another bathroom on the left. As the curtain/fence opens, we see a gentleman in pajamas sleeping in the compartment. Lanky, still in his long underwear, crawls down the corridor. He sees a folded pair of pants in the compartment, grabs them and locks himself in the bathroom. The Conductor arrives and wakes up the gentleman delicately.

CONDUCTOR: Senator, we'll be there in fifteen minutes . . . *(Shakes him)* Senator.

POLITICIAN *(Stretching)*: Oh, my back is all cramped.

CONDUCTOR: Of course, the bed . . . could have been better.

POLITICIAN: Yes, but the express train doesn't stop in this one-horse town. Why do they always send me out in the middle of nowhere. *(Rummages through his bag of toiletries.)*

CONDUCTOR: Excuse me . . .

(The Conductor goes out to the corridor where he sees Lanky, who is now wearing the Politician's pants. He jumps back into the bathroom when he sees the Conductor coming. The Conductor becomes suspicious and knocks on the door.)

Sir, may I see your ticket please. Sir. Are you sick? Don't try any tricks with me. I'm warning you, if you don't come out right away, I'll open the door with my key.

(He takes a key out of his pocket and puts it in the lock, but Lanky pulls on the handle, and a cracking noise is heard. The Conductor pulls out his key and looks at it.)

Dammit. It's broken. You're going to pay for this too if you don't get out of there now. *(Short pause)* OK. I'll wait. And at the next stop, I'll call the police.

(Lanky is inside with the doorknob in his hand. Meanwhile the Politician in the compartment is looking for his pants.)

POLITICIAN: I'm sure I put them in this luggage rack. *(Leans his head out of the compartment)* Conductor. My pants!

CONDUCTOR: What's wrong?

POLITICIAN: I can't find my pants. They're gone.

CONDUCTOR *(Looking in the corridor)*: Impossible.

POLITICIAN: I remember putting them there. Someone must have stolen them while I was asleep. Fortunately, I put my wallet in the suitcase.

CONDUCTOR: Lucky for you.

POLITICIAN: Lucky my ass. How can I get off the train without my pants?

CONDUCTOR: Don't you have another pair in your suitcase?

POLITICIAN: Yes, I have two pair, but they're not dressy enough. I can't go to the inauguration in a tailcoat and Scotch plaid trousers.

CONDUCTOR: That's a problem. But what can you do?

POLITICIAN *(Looking at the Conductor's black pants)*: You can give me yours. They're not exactly elegant, but they're black and they look like they're about my size.

CONDUCTOR: And I'm supposed to go around in my underwear?

POLITICIAN: No. You can have a pair of my pants. Pick the ones you like best, and try them on. Meanwhile I'll go to the bathroom.

CONDUCTOR: Well, OK.

POLITICIAN: Thank you. You're very kind. I'll remember you.

CONDUCTOR: Oh, thank you, senator.

(The Politician goes out into the corridor and comes across Lanky, who has come out of the bathroom with the doorknob still in his hand. He doesn't know what to do with it, so he puts it in his pocket. He goes quickly past the compartment where the Conductor is standing with his pants off. He has taken tools out of his pants' pockets and is trying to open the Politician's suitcase, but it won't open.)

Damn. It's locked. *(Goes cautiously out into the corridor, afraid of being seen in his underwear. He knocks on the door of the bathroom at the left, in which Lanky is hiding)* Senator . . . He must be in that one, over there. The other character must have slipped away. *(Goes outside the door of the bathroom on the right, where the Politician is brushing his teeth.)* Senator.

POLITICIAN: Who is it?

CONDUCTOR: The suitcase is locked. I didn't want to look through your jacket for the key without asking you first.

POLITICIAN *(Gargling, distracted)*: No, it's not in the jacket. It's in the back pocket of my pants . . .

CONDUCTOR: In your pants?

POLITICIAN *(Realizing what he's said, as he gargles and almost chokes)*: Pffui . . . It was in my pants. *(Coughs)* No what? . . . Wait, if you have a pocketknife, we can force open the lock. *(Tries to open the door to the bathroom, which has an inside knob)*

CONDUCTOR: Yes, I've got a penknife. *(Takes one out of his jacket pocket)*

(Lanky has returned to the Politician's compartment. He takes a dress shirt from the luggage net and puts it on. He also takes the jacket that is hanging from the window. Only after he puts it on does he realize it's a tailcoat with very long tails. Lanky grabs the tails with curiosity and flaps them as if they were wings, almost hoping to take off and fly.)

POLITICIAN: There's no doorknob in here. Could you open it from out there with your key?

CONDUCTOR: I'd be happy to, but my key's broken.

POLITICIAN: Well, do something. I can't stay here locked in the toilet. When do we get into the station?

CONDUCTOR: We're almost there. *(Pulls all kinds of things out of his jacket pocket that might help him open the door)* I don't know what to do.

POLITICIAN: Hurry. Call the other conductor. He'll have a key.

CONDUCTOR: He has one, but he's at the other end of the train, and to open the door to the next car I need the same key that's broken. We'll just have to wait till the next stop.

POLITICIAN: Not a chance. I have to get off at the next stop . . . with my pants. Sound the alarm. Stop the train. You've got to get me out of here now!

CONDUCTOR: It's no use. The train's already stopping on its own. Excuse me, but I have to go and put my pants back on.

POLITICIAN: No you don't. You gave me those pants, and I'm not going to let anybody take them away.

(Meanwhile Lanky has finished dressing himself. He's fixing his tie and putting on a top hat.)

CONDUCTOR: But I can't do my job if I don't get off the train. And if I don't get off, how can I get the key from my colleague?

(The train stops.)

POLITICIAN: Shout out to him through the window.

(Lanky gets ready to leave. The Stationmaster appears. Lanky gets off and finds himself between two policemen in formal uniforms. Resigned, he offers them his arms to be handcuffed. A gentleman with an official government sash around his waist welcomes him. One of the policemen takes a suitcase, grabs the Conductor's pants, puts them in the suitcase, and passes the suitcase to the other policeman.)

CONDUCTOR *(Still pressed against the bathroom door)*: But he won't be getting off the train. It's not his station.

POLITICIAN: Then do what you want, but I warn you, if you don't get me out of here in time, I'll report you. I'll have you fired. I'll ruin you.

CONDUCTOR *(Runs to the compartment and finds it empty)*: My pants. Where are my pants?

(The group has gone, accompanied by the sounds of a fanfare. The Stationmaster looks for the Conductor.)

STATIONMASTER: Hey, conductor. Where are you?

CONDUCTOR *(Leaning out)*: I'm in here.

STATIONMASTER: Well, aren't you getting off? Who's going to signal for departure?

CONDUCTOR: I was just looking for my pants . . . They've disappeared, and I can't very well go out looking like this. *(Shows himself in his underwear)*

STATIONMASTER: You've gone mad.

CONDUCTOR: I took them off for the senator. He was insistent. He wanted them at any cost.

STATIONMASTER: The senator wanted your pants. But which senator are you talking about?

CONDUCTOR: The one who's locked in the toilet.

STATIONMASTER: But the senator we were expecting has already left the train. Look, he's over there with the mayor and the other town officials.

CONDUCTOR: Then who have I got in there?

STATIONMASTER: Beats me. But I don't know why you'd take off your pants for him if he doesn't even work for the government.

CONDUCTOR: Now I know who it is . . . It's the same character that locked himself in there before. That's why he's pretending he can't get out. He's passing himself off as the senator while the real senator left with my pants, thinking I'd already taken a pair of his. As soon as I get him out of there, I'll murder him. No. First I'll take his pants, then I'll murder him.

STATIONMASTER: Murder whoever you want, but let's get this train out of the station. We're already late.

(He raises the flag. We hear the noise of the locomotive building up steam, and we have the impression that the train is leaving the station, as the Stationmaster slides off sideways across the proscenium until he disappears into the wings.)

POLITICIAN *(Shouting)*: Stop! Stop! Don't let the train leave. I have to get off. Conductor. Open the door!

CONDUCTOR *(Taking off his jacket)*: Don't worry, I'll open it. I'll break the whole door down. Then I'll teach you to play tricks on people who work for a living. Your career in government is over, you fraud.

POLITICIAN: My career's over? What are you saying? Oh, no. Tell the congressional investigators I didn't know anything about it. I swear. I'm innocent. Trust me. Trust me.

(Blackout. Military band music plays and continues into the next scene.)

SCENE 5

The lights go up, revealing the fence/curtain. Lanky stands in front in a tailcoat, and is flanked by the town officials and their wives. They raise their glasses in a toast.

ALL: Cheers.

(The Mayor listens to one of the officials who's whispering in his ear. He then turns to Lanky with a wide malicious smile.)

MAYOR: Senator, we have a wonderful surprise for you . . . Your wife is here.

LANKY *(Spitting out the wine that was in his mouth)*: My wife? *(Coughs)*

MAYOR: Ah. I knew you'd be pleased. An unexpected treat, isn't it?

LANKY: Yes, it is unexpected. *(Continues coughing as he slaps the Mayor on the back)*

OFFICIAL: She told me you'd be surprised.

LANKY: More than surprised. Surprised is not the word.

MAYOR *(Friendly, man of the world)*: She arrived last night, but asked me to keep it a secret until the toast. Guess why?

LANKY: Why? See how well I guessed? Why?

OFFICIAL: Because today is your wedding anniversary.

LANKY: That's it. You guessed it.

OFFICIAL: She told us you'd probably forgotten.

LANKY *(Laughing stiffly)*: She told you, yes. Ha, ha, ha.

(The Mayor moves toward the wings, and extends his arm as if he were introducing a singer.)

MAYOR: You can come out now.

(Lanky closes his eyes, and when he opens them he finds Angela standing in front of him.)

Senator, your wife.

LANKY *(Takes a step back)*: Angela.

ANGELA *(Takes two steps forward)*: Sunny.

LANKY AND ANGELA *(In unison)*: What are you doing here?

MAYOR *(Paternal matchmaker)*: Come on. Don't stand there looking at her like that. She came all this way to celebrate your anniversary. That means she loves you, doesn't it? I'll leave you two alone, but only for five minutes, no more. They'll be waiting for us to lay down the first stone. *(He moves away and joins the other officials)*

LANKY *(Holding his breath)*: Are you married to the senator?

ANGELA *(Dismissing the idea)*: No, I'm his mistress. I needed to see him, so I passed myself off as his wife. Lucky he never arrived. Who knows what kind of fuss he'd raise. He's so boring, and he's a prude besides. Do you believe he forces me to wear this dress backwards because it has a low neckline. Look. *(She turns around and shows him her back, which is bare to the waist)* Don't you think he's a prude?

LANKY *(Teases her, emphasizes "hard-core")*: Yes, he's a *hard-core* prude.

ANGELA *(Not following his tone)*: It's a good thing he never showed up. *(As if seeing him now for the first time)* Oh, Sunny. I'm so happy we found each other again. *(Notices the tailcoat)* Looks like you've moved up in the world. What a career! How did it happen?

LANKY: Well, I started out as a dog.

ANGELA *(Understanding)*: Yeah, it's always tough at the beginning. *(Returning to a loving tone)* Oh, Sunny. I'm so happy we found each other again. I hope the senator doesn't come and ruin everything.

LANKY *(Sure of himself)*: Don't worry, he won't be coming.

(Every so often a waiter passes by to refill the glasses. Lanky takes several refills.)

ANGELA: How can you be so sure? Do you know him?

LANKY: Of course I know him. How else would I be here?

ANGELA: He sent you to take his place?

LANKY: No. He doesn't know anything about it.

ANGELA: He's in trouble, huh?

LANKY: Well . . . *(Laughs)*

ANGELA: I knew he'd end up like this. He thought he was smarter than all the rest of them, but you'll see. They'll steal the pants off him.

LANKY: They already did . . . *(Laughs in a high voice, then suddenly becomes lucid and melancholy)* But how did you get mixed up with him?

ANGELA *(Turning away)*: Because of you.

LANKY *(Surprised, forcing her to look him in the face)*: Because of me?

ANGELA: Well, if you promise not to laugh, I'll tell you.

LANKY *(Reassuring)*: I won't laugh.

ANGELA *(Speaks without pausing, without expression)*: When you left you said, "We'll meet again," and I said it, too. "We'll meet again." *(The waiter comes back with a tray of glasses. Lanky empties his, passes his glass to Angela, and takes another)* But days and days went by and we didn't see each other again. And since I had such a strong desire to see you . . . You're not laughing?

LANKY *(Moved)*: You wanted to see me?

ANGELA *(Continuing in the same tone)*: Yes, I even went looking for you at the bar. Nobody knew where you were, so I went to Washington to look for you.

LANKY *(Short pause)*: To Washington, to look for me?

ANGELA *(Looking away)*: To Washington. I went to all the government offices. I walked all over town. I saw so many people. *(Pause. She looks him in the eyes)* But I didn't see you.

LANKY *(Punching the fence)*: Damn. If you'd only gone to the dog pound . . . ZAC! *(Makes a gesture that means, "I was there.")*

ANGELA: The dog pound?

LANKY *(Quickly, making light of the story)*: Yes, the municipal dog pound. Cage number twelve . . . But it's a long story. Go on, so how did you meet the senator?

ANGELA: I was just getting to that: so one day I met a man who was the spitting image of the orthodox priest . . .

LANKY *(Happy, he stops her and continues the story in the same tone)*: . . . who was actually a police inspector without his mustache.

ANGELA *(In a hurry, spitting out her words)*: No. It was the senator. I said, "How ya doin', priest?" He laughed. We joked about the coincidence, and we became friends. *(Pause. Takes his hands)* And it was a good thing we did, because now you and I have found each other again.

LANKY: Speaking of coincidences, don't the people here look familiar?

ANGELA: Yes, they look a lot like the guys in your gang, and the women look a little bit like my friends.

LANKY *(Sighing with relief)*: I'm glad you think so, too. I was beginning to think there was something wrong with me.

For the longest time I've been seeing the same faces over and over again. The only one I didn't see was yours.

ANGELA: Me, too. But I'm so happy to have found you again, Sunny.

(The waiter passes by again. Lanky drinks another glass.)

ANGELA: You look wonderful dressed as a senator. It makes you seem even . . . lankier.

LANKY: I feel wonderful. *(Swaying, already a little tipsy)* I never felt so wonderful in my life.

ANGELA: I believe it. With the career you've made for yourself. I see you've even learned to walk without looking back over your shoulder. You remember?

LANKY: I remember. I remember. The only thing I don't remember is what I'm supposed to be doing here.

MAYOR *(Arriving at their side)*: Come now, senator: the ground-breaking ceremony for our new school.

LANKY: Ah, yes. The school of hard rocks.

MAYOR *(Laughs obsequiously)*: Your husband has such a great sense of humor. This way please.

(The fence/curtain slides open revealing a construction site full of flags. Some pillars. Some poles. A red, white and blue ribbon the width of the stage is held on each end by two women. Lanky, staggering, is taken to the front of the ribbon. Scissors are offered to him on a pillow. Lanky grabs them with ease and shows them to the spectators. After having proven their effectiveness by snipping off part of a feather on the hat of a woman standing nearby. Then he grabs the ribbon, and cuts it without letting the parts fall. With elegant gestures he folds the ribbon and cuts it into many tiny pieces and puts them into the top hat of one of the spectators. He passes his hand over the hat with a magician's gesture, and pulls out of the hat dozens of tiny American flags on tiny flagpoles, which he hands out to the spectators. They are amused and applaud.)

MAYOR *(Speaking through a microphone)*: And now ladies and gentlemen, and now before we begin the ground-breaking ceremony for our new school, we would like the good senator, who honors us with his presence, to present our teachers with outstanding achievement awards for everything they have done . . . *(The microphone malfunctions and we only hear fragments of the speech as we watch the Mayor's mouth move)* . . . justice . . . liberty for all . . . our great country . . . the glory . . . love . . . America . . .

(Everyone applauds. Some medals are brought out on a pillow. Lanky grabs one and pins it on the chest of the first gentleman who steps up to him. He embraces him and goes on to the next. He finds himself in front of a large-breasted woman. He is embarrassed and doesn't know where to pin the medal. Finally he decides: he turns her around and pins it onto her back. Then, feeling even more embarrassed, he embraces her.

The spectators applaud each time an award is given. When Lanky gets to Angela, there are no more medals left on the pillow, so he approaches one of the previous prize winners and, excusing himself with a smile, plucks off the medal, so that he can put it onto Angela and embrace her. But he gets another idea: he gestures for the pillow-bearer to approach. The pillow is empty, but with two fingers Lanky squeezes the nose of the bearer and pulls out a medal as if by magic. He returns to Angela, pins it on her and embraces her. He looks at her happily. He wants to embrace her again, but without another medal, he can't. He goes to the pillow-bearer and repeats everything: extracting the medal from his nose, pinning it on, they embrace. Lanky returns to the pillow-bearer again, who this time stops him with a gesture, and pulls a medal out of his nose by himself. The bearer gives the medal to Lanky who pins it on Angela. Everyone applauds. The Mayor approaches Lanky and taps him on the shoulder. Lanky pins a medal on him and embraces him.)

MAYOR: Thank you, senator, and now would you do us the honor of placing this parchment in the cornerstone of the school?

LANKY *(After embracing Angela still another time)*: The honor is all mine.

(Lanky grabs the parchment, unrolls it, shows it to the audience, rolls it up again, puts it in the cornerstone, lights a match, puts it into the hole and sets off a lively display of fireworks. Explosions and lights everywhere. A mad fanfare of music. Everyone runs away in terror. Lanky and Angela remain alone, continuing their embrace.)

ANGELA: Oh, how beautiful . . . it's really you, Sunny.

OFFSTAGE VOICE: You can't run away from me . . . I'll get you yet.

(The Conductor runs onstage, still in his underwear, followed by the Senator, still in his pajamas. They both disappear backstage.)

ANGELA *(Leaving Lanky and following them)*: Hey, senator, wait for me.

(The Conductor runs on again, recognizes Lanky and chases him offstage.)

ACT THREE

SCENE 1

Colonial-styled bedroom, with a four-poster canopy bed. There is a double-doored main entrance and a door that goes to the bathroom. A sofa and two armchairs are on the right. On the left is a screen and a small desk. There is a table with three suitcases on it.

The entrance door opens. The Mayor leads Lanky into the room, handing him the key.

MAYOR: Please, make yourself comfortable. Here's the key . . . *(Lanky puts it in his pocket.)* How do you like it?

LANKY *(Looks around)*: Not bad. And you were saying that George Washington slept in this bed?

MAYOR: Yes, he did. Before it became a hotel, this place was a colonial plantation.

LANKY: It's extraordinary how many beds Washington slept in. Same with Napoleon. If you believe all the stories, you'd think they never had time to do anything but sleep.

MAYOR *(Openly admiring)*: Ha. Ha. I never thought of that . . . You know you're the funniest senator I ever met.

LANKY *(Pointedly, but without dwelling on the issue)*: Maybe that's because I'm less of a senator than you think . . . *(Lets himself fall onto the couch)* Excuse me if I sit down, but after all that running . . . I haven't run so much since I was a retriever . . .

MAYOR: What?

LANKY *(Almost whispering)*: Nothing, nothing . . . just reminiscing about the early days of my political career.

MAYOR *(Full of adulation)*: I understand. In any case, excuse me for repeating myself, but you were magnificent today: the fireworks, the magic tricks. A politician and an illusionist, all in one. I never could have imagined it.

LANKY *(Nonchalant)*: Well, nowadays, you never know what to expect from politicians: you've got acrobats, tightrope walkers, contortionists, jugglers, actors, ventriloquists, snipers and escape artists. The illusionists are the most common. They can do a little of everything.

MAYOR: Ha. Ha. If they were only listening now.

LANKY *(Pointing to the three suitcases on the table)*: Whose are they? I only stole . . . I mean, brought one.

MAYOR: They're your wife's. She slept here last night.

LANKY: In Washington's bed? It's a good thing the father of our country's been out of action for a while, or I'd be jealous. Well, I hope she at least got rid of the guy in the pajamas.

MAYOR: Pardon me?

LANKY: Uh, no, I was just saying that I lost track of my wife Angela in the confusion and now I can't find my pajamas. *(Pretends to rummage through a suitcase)*

MAYOR: Don't worry, I'll give you a pair of mine. My room's just down the hall.

LANKY *(Grabs the suitcase and puts it on the desk)*: No. Don't bother. It's only a pair of pajamas.

MAYOR: Exactly. It's only a pair of pajamas. After everything you've done for us, it's the least I could . . . That reminds me. I almost forgot the most important thing. For you. *(Hands him an envelope)*

LANKY: What's this? Ah, I understand. You know I never believed any of those stories about political payoffs . . . *(Chuckles, and the Mayor chuckles with him)*

MAYOR: And you shouldn't start believing them now, because this is not a bribe.

LANKY: No. Too bad.

MAYOR: What a character. Always ready for a good laugh.

LANKY *(Bitter)*: Yep. That's me.

MAYOR *(Still admiring)*: Do you think we'd insult a man of your reputation by offering you a payoff?

LANKY *(Disappointed)*: No, of course not.

MAYOR *(Continuing)*: This is the money that we've raised for the Monument to Man's Best Friend.

LANKY *(In falsetto)*: What? *(Jumps to his feet)* I think I've heard that name before.

MAYOR: Of course you have. The Monument to Man's Best Friend, his faithful dog. Don't you remember we wrote to you because of your special interest in animal rights?

LANKY: Yes, yes. Now I remember. The Monument to the Faithful Dog, man's best friend. Uhhuuuu . . . *(Barks)*

MAYOR: That's a damn good imitation. Sounds like a real dog.

LANKY *(Not amused)*: That's enough, please. *(Points to the envelope)* How much is there?

MAYOR: A hundred thousand. Five thousand for the monument and the rest for the new dog pound.

LANKY *(Feigning sincere interest)*: Why, do you want to build a dog pound?

MAYOR: Yes. Unfortunately, the old one burnt down and you have no idea how many strays there are in town.

LANKY *(Rhetorical)*: Yes. So all you need is a little gas chamber, and . . . Uhuuuu . . . *(Makes a gesture of exterminating dogs)* Zac . . . Death to the strays, and a monument to the faithful. *(Puts his hand on the Mayor's shoulder)* Bravo. I'm glad you thought of coming to me.

MAYOR *(With pride)*: There's no need to sign for it. We know our money's in good hands.

LANKY: How right you are.

MAYOR *(Leading him out)*: After you.

LANKY: Where are we going?

MAYOR: To get the pajamas.

LANKY *(Taking big steps out the door)*: Yes, I might as well take the pajamas too.

(They go out and lock the door. After a few seconds a key is heard in the lock.)

ANGELA *(Coming in, followed by the Senator)*: Here we are . . . See what a beautiful room it is. Look at that big, soft, wonderful bed. *(She caresses it)* You know I didn't close my eyes all night. Every time I was about to fall asleep, I'd remember how good it felt to be in such a luxurious bed, and I wanted to make the night last longer. So I turned on the light, splashed a little water on my face, and kept myself awake. I was as happy as a clam.

SENATOR *(Feeling sorry for her)*: You know, I've met some real looney-tunes in my line of work, but you are . . .

ANGELA: Look who's talking. A guy who runs around in his pajamas chasing a train conductor in his underwear. I wish I had a picture of the doorman's face when he saw you.

SENATOR *(Angry, hysterical)*: Stop it.

ANGELA *(Mortified)*: OK, I'll stop it. That's the thanks I get for pulling you out of this mess . . . if the senator who took your place hadn't been a friend of mine, you'd still be . . .

SENATOR *(Sarcastic)*: Don't make me laugh. Your friend . . . Don't think that just because I'm fool enough to trust you, everyone else will, too. If he was nice to you, it's probably only because of that stupid idea of passing yourself off as my wife. *(Notices his suitcase)* My suitcase. They found it. *(Takes the suitcase and puts it on the bed)* And since he believed you, who knows what he thought of me.

ANGELA *(Sits on the sofa, gets up, sits on the armchair, gets up, goes to sit on the table where she finally feels comfortable)*: Don't worry. I didn't tell him that I was your wife. And as for being nice to me, he was always nice . . . even before he became successful . . . because he isn't all wrapped up in himself the way you are . . . and if you want to know the truth, he even asked me to marry him.

SENATOR *(Rummaging through the suitcase)*: The bum! *(Pulls out a bathrobe)*

ANGELA: Well, not exactly to marry him, but he asked me to try and stay with him. But like an idiot I said no . . . and ended up saying yes to you. What an idiot!

SENATOR *(Sure of himself)*: There's still time to change your mind, if you want.

ANGELA *(Melancholy)*: But who knows if he's still interested. *(With a hopeful smile)* When he gave me the medals, it seemed like he was. *(Sinking back into melancholy)* But with a position like he has now . . .

SENATOR *(Mocking her)*: He's probably thought it over, and . . .

ANGELA *(Missing the irony; speaking as before)*: No. As long as he was playing Rigoletto, we might have been able to . . . but now that he's come so far . . .

SENATOR *(Cutting)*: What. You never told me you worked in the opera.

ANGELA *(Lashing back at him in the same tone)*: No? That's where I learned to play *La Traviata*.

SENATOR *(Surprised for a moment by her sarcasm; resuming his cutting tone)*: Now that we've established your illustrious origin, I'm going to go and take a bath . . . And to prove that you're not entirely useless, would you be kind enough to sing something for me. If nothing else it will keep me from falling asleep in the tub.

(The Senator's words leave Angela cold. He goes into the bathroom. She makes faces at him through the door like an angry child. The Senator keeps talking from inside the bathroom.)

Well? Did you lose your voice? Come on. Say something. Tell me about this true love of yours. Ha. Ha. You know what I think: that your imagination is getting the best of you: a senator from Washington comes to take my place and his name is Sunny Weather, and ex-baritone who's madly in love with you . . . what a whopper . . . Ha. Ha. Senator Sunny Weather . . . I'd like to meet him.

(The sound of running water is heard. Angela stays quiet for a moment, and then gets an idea. She goes to the door and knocks on it. Then she starts acting out a scene in a loud voice with the pauses and sing-song intonations of an amateur actress.)

ANGELA: Who's there? . . . What? . . . Oh, it's you, Sunny . . . No, dear, don't come in. I'm not alone. Go away, he's in the bathroom . . . You want to talk to me? OK, come in, but only for a minute. *(Opens and shuts the door, slamming it several times to be sure it is heard. She walks across the room, stamping her feet heavily on the floor)* Don't make such a racket, dear. He'll hear you. What are you doing? *(Mimes a passionate embrace)* What's got into you, hugging me like that? Let me go, Sunny, let me go. You want a kiss? No, I can't. He might hear us. *(Kisses her hand)* Oh no . . . *(Slaps her hand)* Excuse me for slapping you, but I had to do it. No, no, no . . . *(Imitating the voice of a man)* "Yes." *(Begins kissing and slapping her arm and hand repeatedly until she gets confused and slaps herself in the face)* Oh, no. That's enough. Sunny, please . . . No go. *(Imitating the voice)* "Come away with me . . ." I can't . . . *(Turns toward the bathroom hoping to see the senator lean out)* Let me go. You're tearing my dress *(Imitates with her mouth, the sound of cloth ripping)* Ripppp. Look, you've ripped it. What? You'll buy me another one? All in white? *(Goes toward the bathroom door. Raises her male voice)* "Yes." . . . A wedding gown? . . . "Yes." . . . You want to marry me? *(Gets the voices confused)* "Yes." Then I'll come with you . . . Wait for me downstairs. *(Realizes her mistake from before and tries to make up for it)* I'll get my things and come down right away. Good-bye my love . . . "Ciao, sweetie pie." *(Kisses her hand and slaps it again)* Oh, excuse me. Force of habit . . . Good-bye. *(Opens the door, then closes it again. In the meantime the Senator has appeared. He watches her, amused, as he dries his hair. She feigns surprise)* Oh, it's you.

SENATOR *(Mocking her)*: Yes, it's me.

ANGELA *(Feigns embarrassment)*: It was, uh . . . room service . . . the waiter . . . wrong room . . .

SENATOR: The waiter? A waiter named Sunny?

ANGELA *(Still acting)*: Oh my God. You heard everything? But I swear I didn't mean to . . . the door was open . . . I couldn't stop him from coming in. *(Opens the door, behind which is revealed another door, the second of the double doors)*

SENATOR: Yes, that one was open, but the other one?

(Angela tries the door, but it won't open.)

ANGELA: It's locked?

SENATOR *(Bursts out laughing)*: Ha. Ha. Yes, it's locked, and it's always been locked. I locked it myself . . . and here's the key. So how did your beloved get in. Through the keyhole? Ha. Ha. What people won't do for love. In any case you have my compliments. It was a nice performance. My compliments and my thanks for the entertainment. But now calm down and be good while I write a few letters that I have to send out tomorrow. You can go to bed and turn off the light if you want. I'll sit here.

(The Senator goes behind the screen, sits at the desk, lights a small lamp. His silhouette is partially visible. A shoe thrown by Angela hits one of the screen's panels. The Senator snickers.)

I think I heard someone knocking, dear. Why don't you open the door?

ANGELA: Very funny.

(A key is heard turning in the keyhole. The door to the room opens and Lanky enters. Angela is leaning over the bed retrieving her shoe, and doesn't see him at first. When she realizes it's him she whispers:)

Sunny, how did you get in?

LANKY *(Happy)*: Angela, I'm so happy you came back. I thought you'd run off with the senator.

ANGELA *(Pushing him)*: Quiet. He's behind there.

LANKY: He's sleeping here?

(The Senator snorts and tilts his head, convinced that Angela is playacting again.)

ANGELA *(Still whispering)*: No. He's writing letters, but you should leave before he hears you.

LANKY *(Also whispering)*: No way. I'm not leaving unless you come with me.

(The Senator stops writing, listens for a moment, then begins writing again with a self-satisfied smile.)

ANGELA *(Moved, embraces Lanky)*: With you? . . . Oh, Lanky, do you really mean it? *(Kisses him on the cheek)*

LANKY *(Touches his cheek in shock)*: Angela, a kiss? *(Kisses her. She slaps him)*

ANGELA: Oh. I'm sorry . . . it's just a reflex . . . It's all the excitement. *(Lanky hugs her so hard, he almost suffocates her)* No. No. Don't squeeze me so hard. You'll tear my dress . . . Look you've torn it . . .

LANKY: I'll buy you a new one.

SENATOR *(Without stopping his writing, he imitates Lanky's voice, convinced it is still Angela acting out the two voices)*: All in white.

ANGELA: Did you say, "All in white"?

LANKY: No, I didn't say, "All in white," but if you want a white one, I'll buy you a white one.

ANGELA: But how can we get out?

LANKY: The same way I came in. I have the key. *(Shows it to her)* Let's go.

(Angela grabs her suitcase, Lanky helps her. Then he takes the Senator's, which is on the bed.)

ANGELA: It's too bad we can't take that beautiful bed with us too.

LANKY: We'll come back for it later. Now, its enough just to be able to take you . . .

(They exit.)

SENATOR *(Happily singing the "Wedding March")*: dum-dum-de-dum . . . dum-dum-de-dum. *(Applauds)* Bravo. Bravo. Have you finished your heartwarming melodrama? . . . Ha. Ha. But that's enough for now. You're starting to get carried away. *(Folds his letter and puts it into an envelope)* The first act was almost believable, but the second time, you really overdid it. The male voice was so phony . . . strictly amateur . . . and then after I'd just finished telling you that I had the key, you made the same mistake again . . . how were you supposed to get out: under the doormat? Ha. Ha. *(Leans out from behind the screen)* Angela, where are you? Come on, stop playing around, come out . . . I know, you're in the bathroom. Come on, don't tell me you're angry . . . After all, you were joking, too. Weren't you? *(Opens the door to the bathroom)* No, not in there. Where are you hiding? *(Looks under the bed)* Stop kidding around, Angela.

(The door opens and the Mayor walks in.)

MAYOR *(Not seeing the Senator, who is looking under the bed)*: Senator, here's the pajamas. Senator.

SENATOR *(Standing up, distracted)*: Yes?

MAYOR *(Surprised, in an accusing tone)*: Excuse me, who are you?

SENATOR *(Angry, arrogant)*: What do you mean, who am I? I am . . . *(Looks around)* But, how did you get in here?

MAYOR *(Obviously)*: Through the door. It was open . . .

SENATOR: It was open? *(Goes toward the door and opens it)* It's open!

MAYOR *(Looking suspiciously)*: Would you mind telling me what you're doing in the senator's bedroom?

SENATOR *(Becoming crazed)*: But if it was open, and you didn't open it . . .

MAYOR *(Challenging him, coming closer)*: Will you answer my question? Who opened the door?

SENATOR *(Letting himself fall into an armchair)*: That's what I'd like to know.

MAYOR *(Slapping the back of the armchair)*: That's enough. Where is the senator?

SENATOR *(Without moving)*: Here I am. What do you want?

MAYOR *(Slaps the chair again)*: Stop playing the clown. Where is the senator?

SENATOR *(Jumps to his feet. Points his finger at the Mayor)*: Leaving aside the clown remark, which is worthy of a libel suit in itself, what senator are you talking about?

MAYOR: The Honorable Senator Sunny Weather.

SENATOR *(In a choked voice)*: Sunny Weather?

MAYOR *(Rapidly, annoyed)*: Yes, the one who's staying here with his wife (who seems to me to be more like his lover), but what does it all have to do with you?

SENATOR *(Flabbergasted; without moving his lips, speaking like a ventriloquist)*: Senator Sunny Weather? . . . Then he really exists?

MAYOR *(Opens his arms)*: And why shouldn't he exist? Thank heaven he exists. He's the best senator there is. *(Changes tone)* But where is he?

SENATOR *(Feeling the loss)*: He's run off with my girlfriend. *(Notices that his suitcase is gone)* . . . and my suitcase too.

MAYOR *(Amused)*: Aha. It was your lover. I get it.

SENATOR *(High-pitched voice, tearful)*: Left again without my pants!

MAYOR *(Snickering)*: I can't say I'm sorry, because I do find you a bit unpleasant.

(The Senator looks at the Mayor and gets an idea. He grabs a letter opener from the desk and points it at the Mayor.)

SENATOR : I want those pants!

MAYOR *(Flustered)*: But . . . why . . . What are you doing?

(The Senator grabs the Mayor from behind with a shoulder lock, still threatening him with the letter opener.)

SENATOR: Take off those pants or else . . .

MAYOR: OK, OK. I'll take them off. But, please, don't ruin my political career.

SENATOR: Your political career is a joke. Ha. Just give me those pants.

(The Mayor takes off his pants, and gives them to the Senator. Suddenly the Conductor runs in, still in his underwear, sees the pants, grabs them and runs out.

Blackout. Music plays.)

SCENE 2

Lights. The fence/curtain is closed. The actors are positioned as they were in Act One, in the scene that preceded the wedding. The action resumes exactly at the point when the Friends notice that Lanky has fainted. Lanky is still on the ground. One of his Friends is slapping him. The Gentleman, whom we also know as the Priest, is sitting at the table, just as he was in that moment in the scene. The lights come up slowly. A series of muffled sounds accompany Lanky's awakening.

VOICE OF ANGELA *(Coming from the void, as if it were suspended in the air)*: Did you see, did you see the look on their faces?

LANKY *(Speaking in his dream)*: Ha. Ha. And look at that conductor run!

VOICE OF ANGELA *(As before)*: Come on, we can run, too. Come on.

LANKY *(Still in the dream, moving his arms slightly, his eyes still closed)*: Wait for me, Angela. Angela, wait for me.

FIRST: He's still dreaming.

DOCTOR: Throw a little water on him. That'll wake him up.

(One of his Friends sprays him in the face with a seltzer bottle. Lanky gasps, opens his eyes and looks around.)

LANKY: Angela . . . Angela . . . Where's Angela? *(Sits up and looks at his Friends in disbelief)*

FIRST *(Slapping him)*: It's about time. You had quite a snooze.

SECOND *(Passing his hand in front of Lanky's eyes)*: Hey, wake up. You had us scared for a while . . . You were delirious, you kept talking and talking . . .

THIRD: And not only talking. You were barking too . . . Uhuuu . . .

(They all laugh.)

LANKY *(Very sad)*: So it was only a dream?

DOCTOR *(Holds out a hand to help him up)*: Yes, and you were babbling about it for a full fifteen minutes. We were on the verge of calling an ambulance . . . for real . . .

LANKY *(Violently pushing away his Friend's hand)*: Goddammit son of a bitch! It was a dream . . . But it's not fair . . . It's too easy to end a story that way . . . When you don't know what to do next, you stop everything and say it was only a dream. *(Kicks the Doctor)* Goddamn bastard, son of a bitch . . . *(Short pause)* I should have guessed. Just the fact that everyone had your faces should have made me realize it was a dream. Goddammit to hell . . . *(Another pause)* And son of a bitch.

(All laugh.)

DOCTOR: Come on, Lanky. Stop cursing, and give us a chance to cheer you up. While you were taking your nap, we prepared a little surprise for you: guess who this is.

(They all move away to reveal the new arrival.)

LANKY *(Jumping to his feet)*: Impossible. No. It can't be him.
FIRST: Calm down. It's not the pastry shop owner.
LANKY: I know, it's the orthodox priest.

(They all look around at one another.)

DOCTOR: Yes, but how did you know?
SECOND: Maybe he heard us while he was sleeping . . .
THIRD: Don't be silly.

(As if in a spell, Lanky walks toward the phony Priest, touches him, and then almost screams:)

LANKY: You're alive?
PRIEST: Why, do you wish I weren't?
LANKY *(Ecstatic)*: Dear priest, did my friends bring you here for my wedding?
PRIEST *(Going into his character)*: Yes, my son . . . but calm thyself and be good.
LANKY *(As if he's gone mad)*: Kind priest, you're wonderful. Good priest, you're spectacular. Dear, dear, priest. *(Kisses his hands and slaps him vigorously on the back)*
FOURTH *(Grabs him by the arm and tries to calm him down)*: He's gone mad? Lanky, what's wrong with you?
SECOND: He's flipping out. His head has gone into permanent "tilt."
LANKY *(Breaks free and lifts up his arms ecstatically)*: Quiet, guys. It's a replay.
THIRD: What do you mean, "a replay"?
LANKY *(Whispering, as if he is afraid to break the spell)*: Don't you understand. We're going back to the beginning . . . It's like in the movies. After the coming attractions, they show you the whole film again from the start. It's a continuous showing.

(The Friends look at one another with worried expressions.)

FIRST: He's over the edge.

LANKY *(Embracing the Priest again)*: Only this time the show is for real. *(Stops suddenly)* Wait. I didn't fall asleep again, did I? *(Hits the First Friend, who is standing nearby)*

FIRST *(Surprised)*: Hey . . . Oh!!

LANKY *(Takes First Friend's hand and shakes it warmly)*: Thank you. That means I'm awake. And if I'm awake and he's the priest, pretty soon we'll get to the part of the show where Angela comes in . . .

DOCTOR: Who told you her name was Angela?

LANKY: Her name is Angela. It's true! . . . *(In a high-pitched voice)* Great . . . Come on, priest, let's get rolling . . .

(Lanky lifts the Priest up onto his shoulders.)

PRIEST: Hey, what's got into you?

LANKY: What's got into me? Tradition! I'm supposed to carry my wife's priest in my arms. Isn't that what you said? Forward march, men. Carry me to my blond . . . I swear that if she's the one I've been dreaming about, I'm going to hold her in my arms and never let go.

(They march in formation as before.)

Come on. Let's sing!

(They exit singing in chorus: "Squeeze My Wrists Tightly.")

SCENE 3

Blondie's room. As in Act One, Lanky and Blondie stand, with their wrists bound, in the center of the room. His eyes are blindfolded. Her face is completely covered by a veil. The Friends and Girls are there. The Priest has come to the end of the ceremony.

PRIEST *(In a nasal chant)*: My blood will flow through your heart and yours will flow through mine, and we will be one, till death do us part.

ALL *(In a chorus, including Blondie)*: "Till death do us part."

LANKY *(Euphoric)*: Yes, yes . . . that's her voice . . . she's the one . . . oh, I'm shaking all over . . . I can't take it anymore.

PRIEST: You are now man and wife. Untie them, and let them see each other.

LANKY *(Electrified)*: Yes, yes . . . let us see each other . . . take this blindfold off . . . *(Two Friends help to untie them)* Come on. Hurry up . . . Wait. Let me take off her veil myself . . . *(Rips the blindfold from his eyes and begins to take off Blondie's veil, but stops with his hands in midair)* It's you . . . Just as beautiful and tall as the one I dreamt about . . . Even the same dress, the same veil . . . *(His hands tremble)* No I can't do it . . . My fingers are jumping as if they were playing an accordion . . . Somebody else take it off. *(Points to the veil, which is still on Blondie's face)*

(Two Friends reach out their hands. Blondie moves away.)

BLONDIE: No. Don't move. I'll take it off myself. I don't want to ruin my hairdo.

LANKY: Come on. Hurry up. My eyes are going to pop out of my head.

(Blondie takes off her veil and reveals herself to look something like a marionette: a long and ugly nose, a thin masculine mouth, eyes hidden behind thick glasses, and bushy eyebrows that join together over her nose. Unable to hold themselves back, everyone laughs.)

Nooooo!

(Lanky stands petrified.)

DOCTOR *(Pushing himself toward the ugly creature)*: Is that all you have to say? What do you think of your new wife? We picked you a winner, didn't we?

LANKY *(Shouting)*: Quiet, you shit-faced bastards! *(Grabs the first one he can reach by the collar, and almost strangles him)*

DOCTOR *(Trying to get out of his grip)*: No . . . Let go . . . let go . . . you dimwit . . .

(The First Friend tries with the others to free the Doctor.)

FIRST: Take it easy.

(The Second Friend punches Lanky, who doubles over in pain.)

SECOND: What a spoilsport. And after we fix him up with a beautiful girl like that.

(The Third Friend throws Lanky across the table. Lanky responds by kicking him in the stomach.)

THIRD: You're already married, pal. It's too late to kick up a fuss now.

(The Fourth Friend jumps on Lanky's back, grabs him by the neck and slams him violently against the left wall.)

FOURTH: Are you going to calm down now? Come on. Don't act like this in front of your new bride. Go ahead, apologize . . .

LANKY *(Panting, trying to compose himself)*: Excuse me, but I've got nothing against you. If you're not beautiful, it's certainly not your fault. It's just that these sons of . . . *(Short pause)* You're a professional, so I'm sure you understand. *(Walks downstage)* But most of all, I'm fed up with whomever's in charge of manufacturing dreams. *(Almost speaking to the balcony)* I want to know who's got that job. Which one of you archangels is it? Gabriel? . . . Michael? . . . Raphael? . . . Who is it? . . . *(Speaks as if he sees each one of them in the theatre)* Speak up, you archangels. If it's true what they told me when I was a child, that the Lord put you in charge of dream-making, why did you have to come and pick on me? . . . Giving me two-timing dreams . . . Why? . . . Now I'm going to start screaming such filthy curses that you'll have to plug up your ears with corks . . . Because if we can't even believe in our dreams anymore . . . *(Shouting)* . . . then there's nothing left . . . it's the pits . . . it's the god-awful shit in the hole pits . . . *(Tense)* What the hell do you think I am? A goddamn pinball machine that you can put your money in and bang around as long as you feel like it?

(They all laugh, but without much conviction.)

PRIEST *(Trying to break the tension)*: Come on, guys. We're missing our chance to kiss the bride.

FIRST *(Shouting euphorically)*: Yes. Yes. Let's kiss the bride. Me first . . .

BLONDIE *(Freeing herself violently from the Priest who has been holding her by her shoulders)*: That's enough. Stop it. *(Takes off her glasses, fake nose and false eyebrows, revealing the beautiful face of Angela)* A joke is a joke, but he's right. This is the pits and I think it's disgusting . . . You're not better than a bunch of wild baboons. Look what you've done to him. He's shaking like he's got the d.t.'s.

(Lanky, who has had his back to Blondie, turns suddenly, sticks his neck out in shock, swallows.)

LANKY: Angela.

DOCTOR *(Goes to sit down lazily at the table)*: Now she's ruined everything. And now the pea-brained idiot wants to pontificate about it.

LANKY *(Feeling his face with his hands)*: Angela, I'm dreaming again. *(Goes toward the Doctor)* May I? *(Hits the Doctor. The Doctor responds by hitting him back harder)*

DOCTOR: Hey. What are you mad at me for?

LANKY: Ahi. *(Dazed, he supports himself on a chair)* No, I guess I'm really awake . . . *(Goes back to the Doctor and gives him a blow that sends him flying across the ground)* That's for the "pea-brained idiot . . ."

ANGELA *(Coming to him)*: Thank you . . .

LANKY *(With great tenderness)*: Thank you . . .

ANGELA: That will teach them to respect you. Do you know what I think? That even though they make fun of you, you're better than all those creeps put together . . . Excuse me for playing along with them, but if I'd known that you were so . . .

LANKY: So . . . what?

ANGELA: Well . . . what can I say? I feel like I already know you . . .

LANKY *(Lost in his vision of her)*: Of course you know me already. This is a continuous showing. Haven't you figured that out yet?

SECOND *(With real affection, putting his hand on Lanky's shoulder)*: Hey, Lanky, now that you've seen what she really looks like, you're not cursing anymore.

THIRD: How could he? He looks like he's been mummified.

(Suddenly Lanky is in the center of the group, turning around, looking at them like Samson among the Philistines.)

LANKY: Stop it . . . or I'll throw you all out of here . . . *(Plays the conquering hero to Angela)* See how I shut them up? *(They all blow him a big raspberry in a chorus. He pays no attention)* Listen, I don't have to watch the whole film again from the beginning . . . Let's skip the slow parts and get to the good stuff . . . I already know how it's going to end. I know that your name is Angela, that your father knew all about plants and poles . . . I'm your pole. Say yes, so we can run the credits and say good night.

ANGELA *(After a long silence)*: Yes.

LANKY *(Surprised)*: What?

ANGELA: I said yes.

LANKY: Yes, that we'll be together? Nooooo.

ANGELA: Yes.

LANKY: Oheuuu.

PRIEST: Come on gang, it's time for the violins.

(All of them make a circle, miming an entire gypsy orchestra, playing "Squeeze My Wrists Tightly." Lanky and Angela don't notice them. They continue to talk and look at each other as if they were the only ones in the room. The Friends and the Girls continue to imitate in subdued tones the sounds and the gestures of violin players.)

LANKY: Well, if you can say yes that quickly with no second thoughts, then . . . *(Looks up)* Hey, archangels, I'd like to apologize for what I just said. I should have guessed that you wouldn't joke around like that . . . How could I imagine guys like you making fun of people? . . . I always knew that archangels don't play pinball . . . I should have trusted you . . . You do a hell of a good job making those beautiful dreams. Better than Hollywood.

ANGELA *(Sweetly)*: Hey, Lanky, come down to earth. What should we do? We can't very well spend the night in this gypsy camp.

LANKY: You're right. We should throw them out, or leave ourselves. Let's get on a train and go . . . go . . . go. All we need is some money.

ANGELA: Oh, I have some . . . *(Goes toward the dresser on the right)*

LANKY *(Stopping her)*: No . . . No . . . I've got a whole envelope of . . . *(Reaching into his jacket)* How stupid. That was in the dream. *(Stops with his hand at the level of his inside jacket pocket)* Eh. Is it possible? . . . *(Puts his hand inside his jacket and pulls out an envelope. Rolls of hundred dollar bills are sticking out of it)* It's here!

(Everyone is dumbfounded.)

FIRST: Holy cow. There must be hundreds of thousands in there.

LANKY *(Again looking up at the roof of the theatre)*: Eh, no, archangels. Now you're going too far. You're trying to embarrass me, humiliate me. First you help me to find her, and now all this money . . . No, I can't accept it.

(By now all of the Friends are also looking up at the ceiling in shock.)

DOCTOR *(Whispering, panting)*: Take it, you idiot . . . the bills are real . . .

THIRD *(Touching the bills that are sticking out of the envelope)*: Hey, Lanky, remember that I've always liked you, and that I've always been your friend . . .

ALL FRIENDS *(Reaching out their hands)*: Me, too. Me, too.

PRIEST *(Clearing them away)*: Me, too.

LANKY *(Nose to nose with the Priest)*: I beg your pardon. I don't even know you . . . And with all this business about the gas chamber . . . you're really starting to get on my nerves.

(Everyone looks at the false Priest with scorn.)

Nothing. Nothing for anyone. *(Opens his arms, parting them all, to get some breathing room)* Before I'd give any of you a single dollar, I'd throw it all out the window. *(With three leaping steps he moves to the window, opens it, and throws out the envelope)*

ALL FRIENDS *(Desperate, they catch up to him)*: What are you doing, you fool . . .

DOCTOR *(Leaning out the window)*: The idiot really did it. He threw all the money out into the street . . .

PRIEST *(Opens the door to the stairway and rushes out)*: Come on down. Maybe we can get some of it before it blows away.

(The Friends trample each other in a mad rush to the exit.)

ANGELA *(Making her way to Lanky)*: Let me by.

FIRST: Hurry.

(All Friends and Girls run downstairs. Only Angela and Lanky remain.)

LANKY: Aren't you going down with them?

ANGELA *(Quietly)*: No.

LANKY *(Slightly anxious)*: And now that I don't have any more of that bankroll, do you still want to stay with me?

ANGELA: Well, I'm sorry you did it, and I think you're crazy . . . but since I said yes before . . . *(She offers him her hand)*

LANKY: Ha. Now I can pull out that bankroll. Again. *(Pulls out a packet of money from his pants' pocket)* Oopla . . . Count it please.

ANGELA: Ehou . . . But how did you do it?!

LANKY: It's a trick I learned from them. *(He points to the ceiling, and shouts at the top of his lungs)* Archangels, you're the greatest.

(Lanky takes Angela by the hand and runs away with her. Music. Curtain.)

THE END

RON JENKINS has investigated comic traditions in Italy, Indonesia, Lithuania, Israel, South Africa and Japan with the support of fellowships from the Watson Foundation, the Danforth Foundation, Harvard University's Sheldon Fund and the Asian Cultural Council of the Rockefeller Brothers Foundation. He holds a doctorate from Harvard and a masters in buffoonery from the Ringling Brothers Clown College. His translations of plays by Dario Fo and Joshua Sobol have been staged at the American Repertory Theatre, the Yale Repertory Theatre, the New York Theater Workshop and the Royal Shakespeare Company. He is the author *Acrobats of the Soul* and *Subversive Laughter*, as well as numerous articles on comedy and culture for the *Drama Review*, *Kyoto Review*, *American Theatre*, the *Village Voice*, the *New York Times* and other publications. A former circus clown and juggler, Jenkins is currently professor, chair and artistic director of the theatre department at Wesleyan University in Connecticut. His latest book, *Dario Fo and Franca Rame: Artful Laughter* (Aperture, New York, 2001), was written with the support of a fellowship from the John Simon Guggenheim Memorial Foundation.